CALIFORNIA
VACATION PATHS

A step-by-step guide to
breathtaking sights

California map portrays location of activities listed in guide; directions under each activity. Note: San Francisco, Los Angeles, San Diego, Fresno, and Visalia are shown to give a sense of direction: no activites listed.

Map not to scale.

CALIFORNIA
VACATION PATHS

A step-by-step guide to breathtaking sights

1. Regions of Hwy 395 – Death Valley, Mono Lake…
2. Yosemite National Park
3. Sequoia and Kings Canyon National Parks
4. Santa Barbara
5. Pismo Beach
6. Morro Bay

Pati Anne

River Terrace Books
P.O. Box 302
Woodland Hills, CA 91365-0302
www.CaliforniaVacationPaths.com

Printed and published in the United States of America
ISBN: 978-0-9847536-0-4

Library of Congress Cataloging-in-Publication Data: 2014911551

Anne, Pati
California Vacation Paths, A step-by-step guide to
breathtaking sights 1. Regions of Hwy 395 –
Death Valley, Mono Lake... 2. Yosemite National Park
3. Sequoia and Kings Canyon National Parks
4. Santa Barbara 5. Pismo Beach 6. Morro Bay
/ by Pati Anne – 1st ed.
ISBN: 978-0-9847536-0-4

Editorial assistance by Patricia Fry
Illustrations by Pati Anne
Cover and Interior Design by Teri Rider
Author's photo by Portrait Gallery from Bella Pictures

Go forth into the vast outdoor world and let the sights, scents, and sounds free up your mind and fill you with joy.

See photos of the 6 areas described in this book at:
www.CaliforniaVacationPaths.com

1. Regions of Hwy 395 – Death Valley, Mono Lake…
2. Yosemite National Park
3. Sequoia and Kings Canyon National Parks
4. Santa Barbara
5. Pismo Beach
6. Morro Bay

Contents

California Map. ii
About the Author. xxx
Acknowledgements. xxxi
Foreword. xxxiv
Preface xxxvi
Introduction xxxvii
Warning & Disclaimer xxxviii
Kid Faves – (Listed after each of the six main areas)
Wheelchair Accessible Activities – (Listed at end of
each area's Appendix)

Buddies – poem xlii

BOOK ONE   1

Regions of Hwy 395 – Death Valley, Mono Lake...

Introduction 1
1.1 Regions of Hwy 395, Lone Pine, Death Valley –
What To Do & See. **2**

Lone Pine 2
   Lone Pine Film History Museum 2
   Alabama Hills. 2
   Whitney Portal. 3
   Mt. Whitney Trail 3
   National Recreation Trail 4
   Information (visitor center, ranger station, etc.) . 5
   Eateries. 5
   Lodging (Camping) 6
   Directions – Lone Pine. 7
Death Valley National Park. 7
   Darwin Waterfall 8
   Stovepipe Wells Village 8
   Mosaic Canyon Trail 8
   Mesquite Flat Sand Dunes. 9
   Scotty's Castle. 9
   Salt Creek Boardwalk. 11
   Artist Drive 11
   Natural Bridge 12
   Badwater. 12
   Park Entrance Fees 13
   Information (visitor centers, jeep rentals, etc.) . 13
   Gasoline 15
   Eateries/Lodging (Camping) 15
   Directions – Death Valley. 17

1.2 Independence, Big Pine, Bishop, Rock Creek, Convict Lake – *What To Do & See* **18**
Independence 18
   Historical Homes 18
   Mount Whitney Fish Hatchery 19
   Information (chamber of commerce, etc.). 19
   Eateries/Lodging 19
   Directions - Independence 20

    Wildlife Viewing 20

Big Pine **20**
    Information (chamber of commerce) 20
    Eateries. 20
    Directions – Big Pine 21

Bishop **21**
    Keough's Hot Springs. 21
    Bishop City Park 21
    Laws Museum 22
    Bishop Creek Canyon. 22
    South Lake 22
    Bishop Pass Trail. 23
    Eateries/Lodging – South Lake 23
    North Lake. 24
    Lake Sabrina. 24
    Information (ranger station, chamber of
    commerce, etc.). 25
    Eateries. 26
    Lodging (Camping) 27
    Directions - Bishop 28

Rock Creek **28**
    Rock Creek Lake 29
    Mosquito Flat. 29
    Little Lake Valley Trail. 29
    Information (pack station, etc.) 30
    Eateries/Lodging (Camping) 30
    Directions – Rock Creek 31

Convict Lake **31**
    Eateries/Lodging (Camping), Horseback Rides . 32
    Directions – Convict Lake 33

**1.3 Mammoth Lakes, June Lake Loop, Mono Lake,
Lee Vining** – *What To Do & See* **33**

Mammoth Lakes **33**
   The Lakes of Mammoth 34
   Twin Lakes 34
   Lake Mary 35
   Emerald Lake & Trail 35
   Mammoth Consolidated Gold Mine 36
   Lake George 36
   Crystal Lake & Trail 37
   Barrett & T J Lakes & Trail 37
   Lake Mamie 38
   Twin Falls Overlook 38
   Horseshoe Lake 38
   McLeod Lake & Trail 39
   Inyo National Forest – Reds Meadow Area . . . 39
   Devil's Post Pile Trail 40
   Rainbow Falls Trail 40
   Mammoth Scenic Loop – Inyo Craters 41
   Mammoth Village (Gondola, Shops, Eateries) . 41
   Directions – Mammoth Village 42
Summer Fun **43**
   Swimming 43
   Mammoth Creek Park 43
   Summer Gondola Rides 43
Winter Fun **44**
   Mammoth Mountain (skiing/snowboarding) . . 44
   Cross-country Skiing 45
   Mammoth Ice Rink – Outdoor Ice Skating . . . 45
   Mammoth Dog Teams 45
Mammoth Lakes Information (welcome
station/ranger station, boat rentals, etc.) **45**
   Eateries 47
   Lodging (Camping) 49
   Directions – Mammoth Lakes 52
June Lake Loop **52**
   June Lake 53

June Lake Village 53
Gull Lake 54
June Mountain 54
Silver Lake 54
Grant Lake 55
Information (chamber of commerce, marinas,
dog sled rides, etc.) 55
Eateries 56
Lodging (Camping) 57
Directions – June Lake Loop 58

Mono Lake **59**
South Tufa Nature Trail/Navy Beach 60

Lee Vining at Mono Lake **61**
Lee Vining Creek Trail 61
Mono Lake Trail 61
Mono County Park 61
Information (chamber of commerce, visitor
center, etc.) 62
Eateries 62
Lodging 63
Directions – Mono Lake/Lee Vining 63

**1.4 Day Trips North of Mono Lake – Lundy Lake,
Bodie State Historic Park, Bridgeport, Twin
Lakes** – *What To Do & See* 64

Lundy Lake **64**
Lundy Canyon Falls Trail 64
Market/Lodging (Camping) 65
Directions – Lundy Lake 66

Bodie State Historic Park **66**
Bodie Ghost Town 66

Bridgeport **66**
Information (ranger station & visitor center, etc.) 67
Eateries/Lodging (Camping) 67

Directions - Bridgeport 68

Twin Lakes **68**
Lake Trail & Horsetail Trails 68
Information (ranger station & visitor center, etc.).69
Café/Lodging (Camping). 70
Directions – Twin Lakes. 70

KID FAVES **71**
Independence, Lone Pine, Bishop, Mammoth
Lakes, June Lake Loop, Mono Lake, Bodie
State Historic Park

Appendix **74**
Lone Pine, Death Valley National Park, Eureka
Sand Dunes, Wildlife, Directions, Independence
Wheelchair Accessible Activities 78
Resources/Information 80

Seasons in the Forest – poem 82

BOOK TWO   83
Yosemite National Park

Introduction 83

2.1 Yosemite Southern Park Area
What To Do & See **84**
Wawona – Southern Park Entrance 84
Mariposa Grove of Giant Sequoias 85

Wawona Area **86**
Wawona Golf Course 86
Wawona Meadow Trail. 86
Covered Bridge 87

Pioneer History Village 87
Wawona Stables 87
Swinging Bridge. 88
Lower Chilnualna Waterfall Trail. 88
Texas Flat Picnic Area 89
Information – Wawona (visitor center, grocery
store, gas station, etc.) 89

2.2 Glacier Point Road Area & North of Glacier Point Road Area – *What To Do & See* **90**

Glacier Point Road Area **90**
Badger Pass Ski Area 90
McGurk Meadow. 90
Sentinel Dome 91
Taft Point 91
Washburn Point 92
Glacier Point. 92

North of Glacier Point Road. **93**
Tunnel Viewpoint 93
Bridalveil Fall 93
Swinging Bridge. 94

2.3 Yosemite Village Area – *What To Do & See* . . **94**

Yosemite Village Area **94**
Yosemite Village. 95
Mirror Lake 97
Yosemite Falls 98
El Capitan 99
Happy Isles Nature Center & Trail 99
Mist Trail 100
Half Dome 101

2.4 Yosemite Southern Park Area –
Park Information. **102**

Summer Fun **102**
  Wawona Golf Course, Wawona Stables,
  Swimming, Rafting, LeConte Memorial Lodge
  (library), Bicycle/wheelchair rentals

Winter Fun **103**
  Badger Pass Ski Area, Downhill/cross-country
  skiing, snowboarding, ice-skating 103

Park Information **104**
  Park Entrance Fees 104
  Visitor Centers 104
  Information (medical clinic, gasoline, etc.) . . . 105
  Weather 107
  Tours & Guides 107
  Transportation 108
  Eateries. 109
  Lodging (Camping) 109
  Directions – Wawona Southern Park Entrance . 114

2.5 Towns Outside Southern Entrance –
Oakhurst, Bass Lake, Fish Camp
What To Do & See **115**

Oakhurst **115**
  Oakhurst River Parkway. 115
  Sierra Meadows Country Club. 115
  Information (visitors bureau) 115
  Eateries. 116
  Lodging (Camping) 116
  Directions - Oakhurst. 117

Nelder Grove. **118**

Bass Lake **118**

Information (visitors bureau, chamber of
commerce, etc.). 118
Eateries/Lodging (Camping) 119
Directions – Bass Lake. 120

Fish Camp. **120**
Yosemite Mountain Sugar Pine Train. 120
Yosemite Trails Pack Station. 120
Information (general store). 121
Eateries/Lodging 121
Directions – Fish Camp 121

2.6 Yosemite Northern Park Area
What To Do & See **122**

Northern Park Entrances **122**
Hetch Hetchy – Remote park area 122
Tuolumne River Trail 123
Big Oak Flat – Northwest Park Entrance . . . 124
Merced Grove. 124
Arch Rock – West Park Entrance – Hwy 140 . 125
Tioga Pass – East Park Entrance 125
Outside Tioga Pass Park Entrance **126**
Ellery Lake & Tioga Lake 126
Lodging (Camping) 126
Saddlebag Lake 126
Nunatak Nature Trail 128

**2.7 Northern Park Area – Tioga Pass East
Park Entrance –** *What To Do & See* **129**

Ponds 129
Tuolumne Meadows Area 129
Tuolumne Meadows Information. 130
Lyell Canyon Trail 131
Dog Lake 132

Lembert Dome. 133
Soda Springs/Parsons Lodge Trail 135
Tenaya Lake 135
Olmsted Point 137
May Lake 137
Cones & Needles Trail 138
Siesta Lake 138
Cascade Creek Trail 138
Tuolumne Grove of Giant Sequoias 139

**2.8 Yosemite Northern Park Area –
       Park Information. 140**

Summer Fun 140
Best swimming areas, horse stables. 140
Park Entrance Fees. 141
Visitor Centers 141
Information (medical clinic, gasoline, etc.) . . . 141
Weather 144
Transportation 144
Eateries. 145
Lodging (Camping) 146
Directions (Three Northern Park Entrances/
Lodging Outside the Park) 148
Big Oak Flat Park Entrance 148
Arch Rock Park Entrance. 149
Tioga Pass Park Entrance. 150

KID FAVES **152**
Southern Park Area **152**
Wawona Area, Bridalveil Fall, Yosemite Village,
Yosemite Falls, Curry Village, Mirror Lake,
Winter Fun
Northern Park Area **154**
Tuolomne Meadows Area, Tenaya Lake

Appendix – Yosemite National Park.....155
History, John Muir, Wawona Area, Pioneer
Cemetery, Yosemite Guide, Shuttle & Hikers' Bus,
Half Dome & Wilderness Permits, Southern Park
Wilderness Permits, Northern Park Wilderness
Permits, Internet Access, Post Offices, Altitude
Sickness, Bears, Kennels

Wheelchair Accessible Activities........... 161

Resources/Information, Websites........... 163

Sequoias in the Forest – poem................. 166

BOOK THREE   167

Sequoia and Kings Canyon National Parks

Introduction 167

3.1 Sequoia National Park Near Ash Mountain Entrance – *What To Do & See*...........168

Mineral King – Remote area of Sequoia National
Park – Prior to Ash Mountain Park Area....168

Ash Moutain – Sequoia Park Entrance......169

Indian Head River Trail 169

Marble Falls Trail 170

Hospital Rock – Picnic Area 170

Paradise Creek Trail 171

Crystal Cave 171

3.2 Giant Forest, Crescent Meadow Road *What To Do & See* 172

Giant Forest Area.................... 172

Giant Forest Museum.................. 172

Beetle Rock & Beetle Rock Trail 173

Big Trees Trail. 173

Crescent Meadow Area 174
Crescent Meadow Road 174
Hanging Rock 174
Moro Rock 175
Crescent Meadow. 175
Tharp's Log. 176
General Sherman Tree 176
Congress Trail. 177

3.3   Wolverton & Lodgepole Areas
What To Do & See 178

Wolverton 178
Lodgepole 178
Lodgepole Visitor Center. 178
Tokopah Falls Trail. 179

3.4   Sequoia National Park – Park Information . . 180
Park Entrance Fees 180
Visitor Centers 181
Information (road conditions, weather, etc.) . . 182
Gasoline/Towing 183
Snow Play. 183
Fishing 183
Pets. 184
Transportation 184
Airports 184
Eateries/Lodging (Camping) – Sequoia
National Park Area. 185
Eateries/Lodging – Sequoia National Forest
(Between the two parks). 186
Eateries/Lodging – Outside Sequoia
National Park 187
Directions - Sequoia National Park 190

3.5 Kings Canyon National Park (Adjoins Sequoia National Park) Near Big Stump Entrance

What To Do & See **191**

Big Stump – Kings Canyon National
Park Entrance 192
 Big Stump (Picnic Area) Trail 192
 Hitchcock Meadow Trail 193
 Grant Grove Village...................... 194
 Panoramic Point........................ 194
 Park Ridge Trail 195
 General Grant Loop Trail 195
 North Grove & Dead Giant Loop Trails 196
 Hume Lake............................. 197

3.6 North of Hume Lake Turnoff

What To Do & See **197**

 Boyden Cavern 197
 Grizzly Falls 198
 Cedar Grove Pack Station 198
 Cedar Grove Village 198
 Knapp's Cabin.......................... 199
 Roaring River Falls & River Trail......... 199
 Zumwalt Meadow 200
Road's End 201
 Muir Rock 201
 Road's End Wilderness Permit Station 201
 Mist Falls 201

3.7 Sequoia National Forest – Generals Hwy Area

What To Do & See **203**

 Generals Hwy – Connects the two
 national parks 203
 Redwood Canyon Trail.................. 203

Big Meadows Area 204
  Big Meadows Campground 204
  Weaver Lake Trail. 204

**3.8 Kings Canyon National Park –
Park Information** **205**
  Park Entrance Fees. 205
  Visitor Centers 205
  Information (road conditions, weather, etc.) . . 206
  Airports 207
  Gasoline/Towing 207
  Snow Play. 208
  Fishing 208
  Horseback Riding. 208
  Pets 209
  Eateries/Lodging (Camping) – Kings Canyon
  National Park Area. 209
  Eateries/Lodging – Sequoia National Forest . 211
  Lodging – Outside Kings Canyon National
  Park – Fresno/Sanger 212
  Directions – Kings Canyon National Park . . . 213
  Towns North of Kings Canyon National Park –
  (Leading to Yosemite National Park's Southern
  Entrance) 213

KID FAVES **215**
Sequoia National Park. **215**
  Crescent Meadow, General Sherman's Tree
  & Congress Trail, Family Camp
Kings Canyon National Park **216**
  Big Stump Picnic Area, General Grant Tree,
  Grizzly Falls, Knapp's Cabin, Roaring River Falls,
  Junior Ranger

Appendix – Sequoia and Kings Canyon National Parks **218**
Seasonal Information, History, National Parks
Established, Trees, Kings Canyon, Caves,
Wilderness Permits, Bears, Drowning
Wheelchair Accessible Activities 223
Resources/Information 224

Rekindle by the Sea – poem 228

BOOK FOUR 229
Santa Barbara

Introduction 229
4.1 Santa Barbara – Stearns Wharf, Bicycles, & Arts/Crafts – *What To Do & See* **229**

Stearns Wharf **229**
Eateries, Ty Warner Sea Center, Old Wharf
Trading Company, Coastal Treasures, Deep Sea
Wine Tasting Room, Celebration – 42-passenger
yacht, Water Taxi – The *Little Toot Tugboat*,
Stearns Wharf Bait & Tackle Shop
Directions – Stearns Wharf 232
Bicycles & Arts/Crafts – Near wharf entrance . . 232

4.2 East of Wharf, West of Wharf, West of Santa Barbara Harbor – *What To Do & See.* **233**

East of Stearns Wharf **233**
Chase Palm Park 233
East Beach 233
Santa Barbara Zoo 233
Andree Clark Bird Refuge 234

West of Stearns Wharf **235**
Santa Barbara Harbor, Santa Barbara Maritime
Museum, Outdoors Santa Barbara Visitor Center
Santa Barbara Sailing, Sunset Kidd Sailing, Sea
Landing 235
Eateries – Santa Barbara Harbor 236
Directions - Santa Barbara Harbor. 237
West of Santa Barbara Harbor **237**
Leadbetter Beach Park 237
Shoreline Park 238
Arroyo Burro Beach 238
Waterfront Eateries – East & West of Wharf. . 238

4.3 State Street and North of State Street
What To Do & See **240**

State Street **240**
Eateries, Santa Barbara Museum of Art
Santa Barbara County Courthouse
North of State Street **243**
Alameda Park 243
Alice Keck Garden 244
Old Mission Santa Barbara 244
Rocky Nook Park 245
Museum of Natural History 245
Santa Barbara Botanic Garden 246

4.4 Santa Barbara Area Trails
What To Do & See **247**
Tunnel Trail & Seven Falls Trails 247
Rattlesnake Canyon Trail 248
Cold Springs & West Fork Trails 249
San Ysidro Canyon Trail. 251

4.5   Santa Barbara – Information 253

General Information
Visitor Centers, Parks & Recreation, Ranger Station, Rentals: bike, body board, surfboard, jet ski, and kayak, etc.. 253
Transportation 256
Golf Courses. 257
Wine Tasting 257
Eateries, previously listed under the following areas: Stearns Wharf, East Beach, Santa Barbara Harbor, Leadbetter Beach Park, Arroyo Burro Beach, Waterfront Eateries, State Street. 258
Lodging – Along the waterfront. 258
Lodging – Easy walk to the beach 260
Inexpensive Lodging. 261
Directions – Santa Barbara. 262

4.6   Day Trip South of Santa Barbara
What To Do & See 263

Carpinteria 263
Carpinteria State Beach 263
Carpinteria Bluffs & Seal Sanctuary. 264
Tide Pooling & Harbor Seals. 264
Carpinteria Valley Museum of History. 265
Information (chamber of commerce, visitor kiosk, Amtrak, etc.). 265
Eateries – Carpinteria Ave/Casitas Pass Rd. . 266
Eateries – Linden Ave 267
Lodging (Camping) 268
Directions – Carpinteria 269

4.7   Day Trips North of Santa Barbara
What To Do & See 270

Goleta 270

Goleta Beach 270
Stow House 271
Lake Los Carneros Trail................. 271
South Coast Railroad Museum 272
Coronado Butterfly Preserve, Ellwood Beach .. 273
Goleta Lemon Festival 274
Goleta Golf Courses.................... 274
Information (chamber of commerce, farmer's
market, etc.) 275
Eateries............................... 275
Lodging 276
Directions - Goleta.................... 277

El Capitan & Refugio State Beaches....277

Swimming, Camping, Tide Pooling 277
Information (parking fee, park phone number).. 278
Lodging (Camping) 278
Directions – El Capitan/Refugio State
Beaches............................... 278
Horseback Riding & Cottages 279

Kid Faves – Santa Barbara 280

Stearn's Wharf, Chase Palm Park, Bicycle
Rentals, Santa Barbara Zoo, Andree Clark
Bird Refuge, Leadbetter Beach, Alameda
Park, Alice Keck Garden, Rocky Noon Park

Appendix – Santa Barbara.............282

History, Stearns Wharf, Lodging,
Transportation, Weather
Wheelchair Accessible Activities 285
Resources/Information 287

Beaching – poem 290

BOOK FIVE   291
Pismo Beach

Introduction 291

5.1 Pismo Beach & Shell Beach
What To Do & See **291**

Pismo Beach **291**
  Pomeroy Street 291
  Price Anniversary House 292
  Monarch Butterfly Grove 292

Northern Pismo Beach/Shell Beach **293**
  Dinosaur Caves Park 293
  Margo Dodd Park. 293
  Spyglass Park 294
  Bluffs Coastal Trail 294

5.2 Pismo Beach/Shell Beach – Information. . . . 295
General Information
  Visitor Center, bicycle/surfboard/
  kayak rentals, outlet stores, music, etc. 295
  Wine Tasting 297
  Eateries – Pomeroy Street. 297
  Eateries – Cypress and Price Streets. 298
  Eateries/Lodging Pismo Beach 299
  Inexpensive Lodging (Camping) 300
  Eateries/Lodging on the Bluff 302
  Directions – Pismo Beach/Shell Beach
  (Includes Los Olivos and Arroyo Grande) . . . 305
  Eateries – Los Olivos 306

5.3 Day Trips South of Pismo Beach
What To Do & See **307**

Grover Beach **307**

Pismo State Beach Golf Course 308
Grover Beach Boardwalk 308
Information (beach towing, ATV rentals, etc.). . 308
Eateries/Lodging 309
Directions – Grover Beach 310

Oceano. 310
Oceano Dunes Nature Preserve 310
Guiton Trail 311
Pacific Dunes Ranch (horseback riding on
dunes) 311
Information (park ranger, beach towing,
ATV rentals, etc.) 312
Eateries/Lodging (Camping) 313
Directions – Oceano. 313

Oso Flaco Lake State Park – Boardwalk . . 314
Directions – Oso Flaco Lake 314

Guadalupe 315
Guadalupe Dunes Center 315
Rancho Guadalupe Dunes County Preserve –
Hiking the dunes 315

5.4 Day Trips North of Pismo Beach
What To Do & See .316
Avila Valley Barn 316

Avila – Includes Avila Pier 316
Avila Beach Community Park 317
Avila Beach Resort Golf Course. 317
Eateries/ Shops 317
Harford Pier (Patriot Sportfishing, Olde Port
Fish Market, Olde Port Inn Restaurant) 318
Bob Jones Bicycle/Walking Trail (Woodstone
Market Place 320
Information (fish/farmer's market, mineral
springs, etc.) 321

Lodging 322
Directions - Avila 323
Laguna Lake. 324

San Luis Obispo **324**
Path of History (Mission San Luis Obispo
de Tolosa, History Center of SLO County,
Jack House, and Dallidet Adobe & Gardens . 325
San Luis Obispo Children's Museum. 326
Farmer's Market – Includes arts/crafts 326
Information (chamber of commerce/visitor center,
airport, music, etc.) 326
Eateries. 328
Lodging 329
Inexpensive Lodging. 331
Directions – San Luis Obispo 331

Kid Faves – Pismo Beach **333**
Pismo Beach, Monarch Butterfly Park, Bluffs
Coastal Trail, Arroyo Grande, Oceano, Avila,
Avila Beach, San Luis Obispo

Appendix – Pismo Beach/Shell Beach . . . **335**
Pelicans, Tide Pooling, Lodging, Weather,
Transportation
Wheelchair Accessible Activities 337
Resources/Information 339

Twilight to Dawn – poem 342

BOOK SIX   343
Morro Bay

Introduction 343

6.1 Morro Bay – *What To Do & See* **343**

Morro Rock 343
Sand Spit 344
The Embarcadero (Kayak Horizons, Morro
Bay Aquarium, Sub Sea Tours, Bay Cruises,
Chablis Cruises, and Virg's Sports Fishing. . . 344
Tidelands Park 346
Morro Bay State Park. 346
Morro Bay State Park Golf Course 346
Black Hill Trail. 347
Heron Rookery. 347
Museum of Natural History. 347
Morro Bay State Park Marina 348
Information (visitor center, trolley, music, etc.) . 348
Wine Tasting 350
Eateries. 351
Inexpensive Eateries 352
Lodging 353
Inexpensive Lodging (Camping) 354
Directions – Morro Bay 355

6.2 Day Trips South of Morro Bay
What To Do & See **357**

Montana de Oro State Park **357**

Sand Spit Trail 357
Dune Trail 358
Spooner's Cove 358
Bluff Trail 358
Valencia Peak Trail 359
Coon Creek Trail 359
Point Buchon Trail 360
Information (visitor center, park ranger,
camping, etc.) 361
Directions – Montana de Oro State Park. . . . 361

Los Osos & Baywood Park **362**
    Sweet Springs Nature Preserve 362
    Los Osos Oak State Reserve 362
    Elfin Forest 363
    Baywood Pier 363
    Information (chamber of commerce) 363
    Eateries/Lodging 364
    Directions – Los Osos/Baywood Park 365

6.3 Day Trips North of Morro Bay
What To Do & See **366**

Cayucos **366**
    Information (chamber of commerce,
    kayak/surfboard rentals, etc.) 366
    Wine Tasting 366
    Eateries & Fun 367
    Lodging 367
    Directions - Cayucos 368

Kid Faves – Morro Bay **369**
    Morrow Bay, Aquarium, Museum of Natural
    History, Sub Sea Tours, Tidelands Park

Appendix – Morro Bay **371**
    Morro Rock, Wildlife: Pelicans, Brant Geese,
    Sea Otters, Sea Lions, and Harbor Seals
    (Resources under each wildlife section), Lodging
    Weather, Transportation
    Wheelchair Accessible Activities (Morrow Bay,
    Los Osos & Baywood Park, Cayucos) 376

Acclaim for *California Vacation Paths* 378

About the Author

Pati Anne was born in a small town in upstate New York where she endured freezing winters that turned into long muddy springs and short rainy summers. When she moved to the west coast, she fell in love with sunny California.

Pati has explored hundreds of California paths, in every season, for almost thirty years, enjoying and photographing the amazing natural sights. Her wilderness travels entered her thoughts so often, that she began capturing them in poetry. This led to writing a travel guide, in hopes of making it easier for others to experience the remarkable sights and sounds of California.

The author has personally traveled every path she describes in this guide. She complements her writings with facts obtained through research, conversations with park rangers, specialists, chamber of commerce/visitor center staff, and locals of the area.

She lives in Woodland Hills, California and continues to explore and learn about the many California pathways.

Contact Pati:

e-mail: pati.anne@yahoo.com

www.CaliforniaVacationPaths.com

Acknowledgments

In order to write this book, I traveled many paths throughout California all the while gathering images in my mind. Eventually, the images unfolded into writings. I wanted to extend my writings into a travel guide, thus a great deal of fact finding was required.

People everywhere were helpful and shared their knowledge with me. I would like to thank and acknowledge the following for without their help this book could never have been written:

My parents, Joseph and Flo Cuddy who gave me their love and guidance. They worked hard and long to provide a home for our family.

My children, Michelle and Phillip, and my grandchildren who bring laughter and happiness into my life.

My irreplaceable editor, Patricia L. Fry (freelance writer, author and editorial consultant) who not only changed my style of writing for the better and gave me much encouragement, but offered me insight on how to publish my book through reading her excellent book, recently revised and updated as *Publish Your Book, Proven Strategies and Resources for the Enterprising Author*. Her new book, *Promote Your Book,* is also extremely helpful.

Teri Rider, cover and interior designer, who spent so many hours patiently going over many changes and updates. She molded the book into a wonderful layout and gave me much encouragement.

Cheryl Chipman, National Park Service Management and Program Analyst, who shared with me her knowledge of the wonderful Death Valley National Park.

Tawni Thomson, Executive Director, Bishop Chamber of Commerce, who examined and added valuable information to the Bishop section of my book.

Nancy Upham, Public Affairs Officer, Inyo National Forest, who did a remarkable job of collecting invaluable information from the various Visitor Center managers for the Regions of Hwy 395 chapter of my book.

Laurel Martin, Summer Program Manager/Guest Services Manager, who cheerfully shared wheelchair accessible information for Mammoth Mountain in Mammoth Lakes.

The delightful staff at the Lee Vining Chamber of Commerce & Mono Lake Information Center who happily provided me with much area information.

Kari Cobb, Public Affairs Officer, Office of the Superintendent, Yosemite National Park, who took the time to critique the huge Yosemite National Park section of my book and gave me words of encouragement.

Dana Dierkes, National Park Service, Sequoia and Kings Canyon National Parks, who fit me into her tight schedule and edited my chapter on Sequoia National Park and Kings Canyon National Park.

Marta Stiltz, Interpretive Park Ranger, who helped me with the wheelchair accessible activities of Sequoia National Park and Kings Canyon National Park.

The staff of the Santa Barbara Conference and Visitors Bureau & Film Commission, who took the time to edit my chapter on Santa Barbara.

Kerry Kellogg, Wilderness and Trails Manager, Santa Barbara Ranger District, Los Padres National Forest, who reviewed the lengthy trail section of my Santa Barbara chapter and offered me words of praise.

David Griggs, Director/Curator, Carpinteria Valley Museum of History who audited the Carpinteria section of my book and provided information which was very helpful.

Renee Fortier, Administrative Secretary, City of Pismo Beach who critiqued the Pismo Beach section with enthusiasm and gave me encouragement.

Lindsey Miller, Director of Marketing, San Luis Obispo Chamber of Commerce who cheerfully reviewed the section on San Luis Obispo and offered suggestions.

The staff of the Morro Bay Chamber of Commerce & Visitor Center, who examined the section on Morro Bay, volunteered suggestions, and wished me good luck.

In addition to those listed above, I would like to give special thanks to the many others, such as park rangers and docents, who gave their time to help me better understand their particular special area. I am also thankful for the magnificent land called California. It is a privilege and a blessing to live here.

Foreword

I had the pleasure of working with Pati Anne as she compiled this valuable guide to some of California's most spectacular wilderness areas. I'm impressed by the fact that the author wrote from firsthand experiences and impressions of these six areas. Not only did she travel these areas herself, including the hiking trails, over a period of ten years, she interviewed park rangers, chamber of commerce staff and experts in many fields related to the content of the book.

This could be the most comprehensive, travel-friendly guide available for those who want to explore the great California out of doors. Whether you're an experienced hiker or in a wheelchair, a senior or a parent with small children and pets, you can easily schedule your itinerary in each area, as all activities and excursions are described in great detail. Also hotels, eateries, and shops are listed in each area.

You'll find that this is not just a travel book. It offers a warm look at the surroundings throughout each of these areas, a description of nearby towns and the countryside. While the guide is detailed and organized, the descriptions are crisp and inviting. One peek into this book and you will hunger for the adventures it promises in some of the most beautiful and interesting areas from Death Valley, Yosemite and Sequoia/Kings Canyon National Parks to the beaches of Santa Barbara, Pismo Beach, and Morro Bay. Many memorable sights are revealed like: tall white crystal-like tufa formations at Mono Lake, half mile-deep fissures on a promontory in Yosemite National Park, a rainbow falling through a waterfall at Mammoth Lakes, a cave with a view of the sea in Pismo Beach, the cliff-top path overlooking a frothy turquoise sea in Montana de Oro State Park, and sea otters afloat in Morro Bay.

By Patricia Fry - Author of over 40 books on a variety of topics. She also has a passion for the out of doors and has visited many of these sites over her lifetime, some of them by foot or on horseback.

www.matilijapress.com, www.patriciafry.com

Preface
Author's note to readers

My goal in crafting this guide is to inspire everyone—the young, the old, and the disabled to enjoy better health through outdoor activities.

It has been proven that spending time among nature leads to a less stressful life. The outdoor world is waiting to lift up your spirits. Take some of the day trips described in this book and let the sights, scents, and sounds free up your mind and fill you with joy.

Do you prefer hikes, easy strolls or wheelchair accessible paths? Are you interested in swimming in pristine lakes or streams, walking next to rushing rivers, snowshoeing on fresh snow, taking in an ocean scene, or observing wildlife? Are you looking for activities children will treasure? Do you want to camp, enjoy fine dining, go shopping, or see the local sights? No matter your pleasure, you'll find clear directions and suggestions throughout this useful and complete guidebook.

This easy-to-use guide features six areas of California, and lists Kid Faves, wheelchair activities, and eateries/lodgings for each area. I have placed all activities in successive order so when visiting an unfamiliar area you will find everything easily and not have to ask: "What do I do when I get there?" No planning is needed, just follow along the paths that are already laid out for you in a simple, orderly fashion within the pages of this book.

These are well worn paths for me, but I continue to travel them because I find them invigorating, and believe they promote good health. Hope to see you along the pathway.

Introduction

California, the vacation destination for millions of people, is blessed with some of nature's most awe-inspiring sights. People from all over the world flock here to embrace the nearly perfect weather and to visit the astounding sights which are described in detail within the following six main areas of this book:

1. Regions of Hwy 395 – Death Valley, Mono Lake…
2. Yosemite National Park
3. Sequoia National Park and Kings Canyon National Park
4. Santa Barbara
5. Pismo Beach
6. Morro Bay

This guide lays out a clear path to follow (activities listed in successive order) therefore "no planning" is needed. If an activity along the path isn't appealing, visitors can simply jump ahead to the next activity. Just choose one or more of the six areas listed above; make a camping/hotel reservation from the listings in each area, and enjoy the adventures. There are also listings in each area of activities for children entitled *Kid Faves* and *Wheelchair Accessible Activities*.

This book takes visitors on a journey to the fascinating sights of Death Valley, the picturesque lakes of Mammoth Lakes, the tufa formations of salty Mono Lake, to the river swimming holes and glorious waterfalls of Yosemite National Park, to the raging rivers, waterfalls, and thousand year-old trees in Sequoia and Kings Canyon National Parks. It continues to the wharf and hiking trails of Santa Barbara, to the drive and camp on the beach area near Pismo Beach and to quiet Morro Bay to observe the sea lions, sea otters, and the rare white pelicans.

Warning & Disclaimer

This guide is meant to provide general information only. Listings do not necessarily indicate endorsement by the author. Although every attempt has been made to assure accuracy, mistakes may occur in this guide; all information is subject to change at any time.

The author assumes no liability for accidents, damages, or injuries to readers engaging in activities listed in this guide. Readers participate in these activities at their own risk.

NATIONAL PARKS

Yosemite, Sequoia and Kings Canyon National Parks

Drowning and motor vehicle accidents are the leading causes of death in the parks. Stand back from all swiftly moving water and obey the speed limit. Many bears are killed by motorists exceeding the speed limit. If a bear is encountered in the wild, pick up small children, wave arms, and make loud noises. Don't run; bears can run a football field in six seconds. Don't climb domes when there is any threat of stormy weather.

Death Valley National Park

Heat strokes and dehydration can kill: bring gallons of water and hike only in cooler months (Nov thru March). The leading cause of death isn't from the extreme heat, but car accidents. Please obey the speed limit.

If you do not want to be bound by any of the above, you may return this guide to the author for a full refund. Please feel free to contact the author with any comments, changes, or errors.

e-mail: pati.anne@yahoo.com

www.CaliforniaVacationPaths.com

Buddies

Geese fly in the sky in a special parade.
Wearing upon their gray-brown coat
fine feathers of black and white.
Holding webbed feet behind them, they
search ponds and lakes for one just right.
As their shadows fall upon the water,
landing gears are displayed.
Two webbed feet move forward, like
water skis, skimming the water top.

Pati Anne

Book ONE

Regions of
Hwy 395
Death Valley, Mono Lake...

This highway, like a road on a treasure map, escorts travelers to rare places of raw beauty, and intrigue. It leads to the awesome Lone Pine area with the nearby riches of Mt. Whitney and Death Valley. It then journeys northward through small old-west towns and on to Rock Creek, Mammoth Lakes, and June Lake Loop laden with lakes sparkling like jewels.

Just off the road, absorb awe-inspiring views, bask in the sunshine, swim in the lakes, wade in the streams, climb up the hillsides, fish in the rocky creeks, and snowshoe and ski on winter's snowy blanket. Savor some of nature's outstanding scenery with places to cool down in summer and to warm up in winter. Dogs are allowed in many of the hotels and campgrounds, as well as on most of the trails. At the northern end of this journey, lies Mono Lake–in its stunning glory–a mere 12 miles from Yosemite National Park's summer Tioga Pass East Entrance.

1.1 Lone Pine, Death Valley
What To Do & See

LONE PINE

A tiny town where the old west comes alive especially during the October Film Festival when western movie stars pour into town strutting sparkling attire and cowboy hats. There's a parade, concerts, and an arts/crafts show in the park. Information – Lone Pine Film History Museum (760) 876-9909. (Additional information under Appendix.)

LONE PINE FILM HISTORY MUSEUM

The museum shows off a collection of movie memorabilia including old cars and costumes worn by western movie stars. It tells the story of filming in Lone Pine beginning back in the round-up days. Open Mon-Wed 10am-6pm, Thurs-Sat 10am-7pm, and Sun 10am-4pm. Old-west movies are shown every Sat at 7pm. Movies are included in the $5 admittance fee. (12 and under free.) Museum is wheelchair/stroller accessible. (760) 876-9909. www.lonepinefilmhistorymuseum.com. Located at 701 S. Main Street.

ALABAMA HILLS

Take a fascinating drive, bike, or horseback ride among the amazing rock formations where hundreds of western movie scenes have been shot. Gigantic smooth boulders and jagged rocks scattered endlessly together with scenic snowy mountain peaks in the background, provide a true old west movie setting. Many of the rock formations are named for what they look like: owl, walrus, polar bear, and eagle; with a picture-map it's easy to find them. Free picture-maps of the rock formations are available at the Lone Pine Chamber of Commerce. Mon-Fri 8:30am-4:30pm. (760) 876-4444. 120 S. Main Street (Details under Lone Pine, Alabama Hills in the Appendix.) From Hwy 395, take Whitney Portal Road west (toward the mountains) for 3 miles and turn right on partially-paved Movie Road. After 2 miles, turn around and return back to Whitney Portal Road and turn right. Continue .4 mile, turn left onto Horseshoe Meadow Road, and in two miles turn left on Sunset Drive for .3 mile. Then turn left on narrow-winding Tuttle Creek Road (no trailers). The rock formations along this road are amazing. Tuttle Creek Road loops back to Whitney Portal Road. Turn right to return to Lone Pine.

WHITNEY PORTAL

This area exudes excitement as many of the visitors are busy preparing for the climb up Mt. Whitney. There are stunning views, a fishing pond, streams, a waterfall, store/café, and it's the starting point for the area trails. (Trails listed below.) Store/café open approximately mid-May to mid-Oct. (Depends upon the snow.) From Lone Pine, at the only traffic light, take the winding paved road 13 miles to the end to reach Whitney Portal.

MT. WHITNEY TRAIL

Mt. Whitney's lure, with the highest peak in the contiguous United States (summit 14,497.6 feet), attracts thousands of people from all over the world who are seeking the glory of reaching the top. The strenuous 11-mile path to the summit (wilderness permits required all year for day or overnight trips) begins 50 yards (east) prior to the Whitney Portal Store. Along the way, it passes Lone Pine Lake, a nice day hike. (Moderate 2.8 miles one way to Lone Pine Lake; no wilderness permit needed.) For the less-than-hardy this is a rewarding climb up

3

the Mt. Whitney Trail. Due to snow much of the year, the best trail conditions are found in July, August, and September. **Note:** Trekking up the mountain is especially difficult when not acclimated to the high elevation; many visitors spend the night at nearby Whitney Portal Campground before hiking. The number of hikers allowed on the Mt. Whitney Trail is limited; therefore wilderness reservations are recommended from May 1st to November 1st. Reservations (760) 873-2483. www. recreation.gov. Information at Inter-Agency Visitor Center – Ranger Station (760) 876-6200. (Details under Information.)

NATIONAL RECREATION TRAIL

The trail begins from the day-use parking area found beyond the Whitney Portal Store. The trail sign is posted at the wooden bridge across from the small trout fishing pond. Before reaching the wooden bridge, a tremendous waterfall tumbling down the mountainside comes into view on the right. Cross over the bridge, turn left, and follow the slim path along the roaring Whitney Creek. (Signed *Camp Sites.*) Tall pines tower over aspen trees and green brush along the creek. (Good fishing.) Many unusual rock formations are found just before crossing a wooden bridge leading into the Whitney Portal Campground. For the less-than-hardy, this is the best place to turn around. The trail from here continues 3 miles (from the north side of the creek) and is unshaded and hot in summer. Return on the same trail. Trail Information from the Whitney Portal Store/Café. Store and campground open approximately mid-May to mid-Oct. (Depends upon snow.) Trail: Moderate 1 mile to the Whitney Portal Campground. (Directions above under Whitney Portal.)

INFORMATION

Eastern Sierra Inter-Agency Visitor Center – Information, maps, and wilderness permits for Death Valley and the Lone Pine area including Mt. Whitney. Open 8am-5pm. (Closed Thanksgiving and Christmas.) (760) 876-6222. Located 1.5 miles south of the downtown area of Lone Pine at junction of Hwy 395 and Hwy 136.

Mt. Whitney Ranger Station – (760) 876-6200 press #2 for wilderness permits, #3 camping information, #4 weather/trail conditions. Located in the visitor center mentioned above and open same hours.

Lone Pine Chamber of Commerce – Information, lodging, dining, and activities. Mon-Fri 8:30am-4:30pm. (Various Saturdays in summer.) (760) 876-4444. www.lonepinechamber.org. 120 S. Main Street.

McGee Creek Pack Station – Usually June 1st to Sept 30. (Depends upon weather.) (760) 935-4324, after Sept (760) 878-2207. www.mcgeecreekpackstation.com.

Cottonwood Pack Station – Usually June 1st - Sept 30. (Depends upon weather.) Information – (760) 878-2015. www.lonepinechamber.org. (Click on *Recreation*, then *Horseback riding*.)

EATERIES

Season's Restaurant – Their specialty is steak. Dinner 5-9pm. (Closed on Mon, Nov thru March.) (760) 876-8927. Located at 206 S. Main Street (Hwy 395).

Merry-Go-Round – The specialties are steaks, seafood, and Chinese food. Dinner 4:30-9pm; Lunch Wed-Fri 11am-2pm. Summer only Sat-Sun noon to 9pm. (760) 876-4115. Located at 212 S. Main Street (Hwy 395).

Pizza Factory – Housed in an old bank built in 1917; the original vault is still visible. Kids love the video games found here. Pizza, salad, and sandwiches are served. 11am-9pm, Fri/Sat until 10pm. (760) 876-4707. Located at 301 S. Main Street (Hwy 395).

Bonanza Mexican Restaurant – Homemade Mexican food. 11am-9:00pm, winter 8:30pm. (Closed Tues in winter.) (760) 876-4768. Located at 104 N. Main Street (Hwy 395).

LODGING

Whitney Portal Campground – Close to Mt. Whitney Trail. Leashed dogs okay. Information – (760) 937-6070. Reservations – (877) 444-6777. (8am-9pm). www.recreation. gov (24 hrs.) From Lone Pine, take the winding mountainous Whitney Portal Road 12 miles.

Best Western Plus Frontier Motel – Rooms come with Wi-Fi and a continental breakfast. Heated pool. Dogs okay. (760) 876-5571. (800) 528-1234. www.bestwestern.com. On Hwy 395, just south of town.

Comfort Inn – Rooms have mountain views and Wi-Fi. The hotel provides a swimming pool and continental breakfast. Dogs okay. (760) 876-8700. (800) 800-6468. www. choicehotels.com. On Hwy 395, just south of town.

Mt. Whitney Hostel – All rooms have Wi-Fi and a private bath. Shared rooms, $25 per person. Private room two people $100; rooms for 4, 6, or 8 people available. Call for winter rates. (760) 876-0030. Located at 238 S. Main Street.

Dow Villa Motel and Historical Dow Hotel – This hotel, built in the 1920s, is where many of the old time cowboy stars, including Roy Rogers and Gene Autry, stayed. Dogs okay in motel only. Motel and hotel rooms have Wi-Fi.

Guests may enjoy the pool and spa. (760) 876-5521. www.
dowvillamotel.com. 310 S. Main Street, motel and hotel are
next to each other.

DIRECTIONS – Lone Pine

From Los Angeles, take Hwy 5 north to Hwy 14 east (toward
Palmdale and Lancaster) and continue 68 miles north on Hwy
14 to Mojave. (119 miles from Los Angeles.) Proceed through
Mojave and turn right to continue on Hwy 14. After 48 miles,
and passing Red Rock Canyon State Park, Hwy 14 merges
into Hwy 395. Follow Hwy 395 north for 64.5 miles to Lone
Pine. (15 miles south of Independence.)

DEATH VALLEY NATIONAL PARK

This is a magical land with mysterious sounds and phenomenal
whispers floating through the sand dunes. Out-of-this-world
colors are swirled along canyons and mountain slopes. There
are rock formations in amazing shapes and textures, and
unimaginable critters. Here, extremely hot temperatures are
endured with droughts and occasional flash flooding. It is not
uncommon (spring thru mid-Oct) for daily temperatures to soar
over 100 degrees. Even 120 degrees is not unusual, and there
is almost no shade. Bring lots of water. Winter days are mostly
mild with temperatures between 60 and 70 degrees. Spring is
the best time to visit, when wildflowers brighten the landscape
with many varieties not found anyplace else in the world. Call
the Furnace Creek Visitor Center (mid-March to mid-April) to
determine when and where the best blooms will be located in the
current year. (Additional information on Death Valley, including
wildlife and the Eureka Sand Dunes, under Appendix.)

DARWIN WATERFALL

To find a year round stream and the 20 foot Darwin Waterfall, drive 1 mile west of the Panamint Springs Resort to a graded-dirt road on the left. Continue on this road 2.4 miles to a small parking area, and hike 1 mile out to the falls. The trail may be muddy in places and requires some stream-hopping but, it is fairly easy and flat. Information – (775) 482-7680. (Details for lodging and restaurant under Eateries/Lodging.) When entering the park from Lone Pine at the Lone Pine Inter-Agency Visitor Center & Ranger Station on Hwy 136, Panamint Springs Resort and the nearby Darwin Waterfall are reached in 48 miles.

Note: Hwy 136 begins as a wide, level road and soon climbs and narrows, snaking around the mountain ridges. There are amazing sights from the view points along the way.

STOVEPIPE WELLS VILLAGE

This is a great stopping place; gasoline, ice cream bars, small selection of groceries, water, and gifts are sold at the general store. 7am-9pm. (Details for Stovepipe Wells Village Motel, restaurant, saloon, and RV Park under Eateries/Lodging.) The swimming pool located here may be enjoyed by everyone. Non-guests of motel or RV Park pay $4 per person. **Note:** Mosaic Canyon Trail (described below) is found nearby. When entering the park from Lone Pine at the Lone Pine Inter-Agency Visitor Center & Ranger Station on Hwy 136 (becomes Hwy 190), Stovepipe Wells Village is reached in 80 miles.

MOSAIC CANYON TRAIL

This natural wonder is worth the walk and the bumpy ride on the road getting there. It begins with an expansive opening that quickly narrows with canyon walls as close as four feet apart.

Some parts of the walls are smooth while other parts are full of colorful mosaics (polished marble) which are quite striking. After .5 mile, the cool shade of the passageway is left behind, and hikers walk into a wide sunny wash. For the less-than-hardy, this is the best place to turn around. For those wishing to continue, get complete information at the visitor center. Take this walk in the cooler months (Nov thru March), and never enter the canyon if a storm is predicted. Flash flooding is a real danger. Bring Water! Information – Stovepipe Wells Ranger Station (760) 786-2342 or Furnace Creek Visitor Center (760) 786-3244. Trail: Moderate 2 miles one way. Approximately .25 mile prior to Stovepipe Wells Village (water and gasoline sold) is a gravel road signed *Mosaic Canyon* which leads 2.5 miles to the parking area.

MESQUITE FLAT SAND DUNES

About a mile beyond Stovepipe Wells (off Hwy 190) the phenomenal cream-colored sand dunes appear. Many people walk out on the captivating dunes in the summertime despite the extreme heat. Bring plenty of water. The best time of day to visit, especially for photographers, is at dawn or late afternoon. Winter is the most enjoyable season to walk on the dunes when the sand is cool. (Details for the Eureka Sand Dunes, the tallest sand dunes in California, under Appendix.) Beyond the dunes, Hwy 190 continues 7 miles ahead to a left turn where Scotty's Castle Road leads to the famous Scotty's Castle. (The next left turn travels out of the park and into Nevada.) Continue on Hwy 190 to reach Furnace Creek. (Directions to Las Vegas, Nevada under Appendix.)

SCOTTY'S CASTLE

The castle was originally named Death Valley Ranch. Later it was named for Walter Scott (Scotty), a real wild-west cowboy, who moved to Death Valley in 1902 and began spreading the news of a secret goldmine to attract investors. Millionaire, Albert Johnson of Chicago, invested in Scotty's mine, and although he discovered it was a fraud, he befriended Scotty. In 1922, in Grapevine Canyon, where springs provided plenty of water, Johnson and his wife began construction on a unique Spanish-style winter mansion. Johnson invited Scotty often to the mansion because he loved listening to Scotty's stories of the old west. After Albert Johnson's wife died, in 1943, he ceased going to the property, and gave Scotty the right to live there. Scotty told everyone he bought it with money from his goldmine; and soon it was called Scotty's Castle. There are many variations of the above castle story. (Check websites below.)

This unique castle displays incredible intricate designs and works of art on all of the furnishings and on every wall. Now tour guides show it off; they point out even the doors, hinges, fireplaces, and gates which are all works of art. Visitors will see original furnishings and hear a song played on the original 1,121-pipe organ during the *Living History Tour* (*House Tour*) which is one of 3 different tours presented at this astounding castle. It's guided by park rangers dressed in vintage 1930s clothing. Daily Guided Tours: mid-April thru Oct 10am-4pm, Nov thru mid-April 9am-4pm. Visitor center, museum and bookstore are on the premises. **Note:** Water and prepared sandwiches and snacks are available. Best months to visit are November thru April. House tours Adults $15, Senior (62+) with Senior Park Pass $7.50, kids 6-15 $7.50, 5 and under free. (Subject to change.) Grounds are wheelchair accessible and wheelchair lift is available for house tours. Call for castle information and tour descriptions (760) 786-2392. Reservations (877) 444-6777. Reservations online at: www.recreation.gov. Scotty's Castle information: www.nps.gov/deva/historyculture/scottys-castle.htm

www.desertusa.com/mag98/june/papr/du_dvscotty.html
www.digital-desert.com/scottys-castle/

(View castle photos on last website.) From Stovepipe Wells Village (directions under Stovepipe Wells Village) follow Hwy 190 for 7 miles to a left turn onto Scotty's Castle Road (Hwy 190 continues ahead) and travel 36 miles to the castle. The last few miles are narrow and winding and may be difficult for RVs. 53 miles from Furnace Creek and 43 miles from Stovepipe Wells Village.

Returning from Scotty's Castle, at the intersection of Hwy 190 and Scotty's Castle Road, turn left onto Hwy 190. Continue 3 miles to reach the Salt Creek Boardwalk (details below) or bypass this and, in 17 miles, the Furnace Creek Visitor Center is reached. (Details under Information.)

SALT CREEK BOARDWALK

The (wheelchair/stroller accessible) boardwalk loops along the saltwater creek for .5 mile. Here in March and April, visitors will see the rare Salt Creek Pupfish which are mating during this time. The mating males turn bright blue, and therefore, are easily spotted. Information – Furnace Creek Visitor Center (760) 786-3244. From Stovepipe Wells Village, continue on Hwy 190 for 10 miles to a road signed Salt Creek Boardwalk on the right-hand side. (From the Furnace Creek Visitor Center, it's a left-hand turn in 13.5 miles.) Turn onto a graded gravel road and continue 1 mile to the boardwalk parking area.

ARTIST DRIVE

This is a captivating 9-mile loop drive where shadows and sunrays exaggerate the hues of the canyons. Varying colors from charcoal, mocha, and plum, to shades of radiant yellow, tangerine, and crimson are splattered across the landscape. Best time to visit is in late afternoon. Information at Furnace Creek Visitor Center (760) 786-3244. From the Furnace Creek Visitor Center, travel 2 miles east on Hwy 190 to Badwater Road (Hwy 178). Turn right and drive 8 miles south on Badwater Road to the entrance of this one-way paved loop road. (No vehicles over 25 feet long.)

NATURAL BRIDGE

This very popular stony uphill path leads .25 mile from the parking area into the canyon under a natural stone bridge 50 feet above the wash bed. The reddish rock color is greatly intensified in the sun. From here, the path continues another half mile to a (usually dry) waterfall. Best time to visit is Nov thru March. Information at Furnace Creek Visitor Center (760) 786-3244. Trail: Easy .25 mile to the bridge. From the Furnace Creek Visitor Center, continue east on Hwy 190 for 2 miles to the intersection with Badwater Road (Hwy 178). Turn right onto Hwy 178 and continue 15 miles south to a 1.5 mile dirt road (signed *Natural Bridge*) that leads to a parking area.

BADWATER

Badwater, at 282 feet below sea level, is the lowest elevation point in the United States. Approximately 80 miles west of Badwater is Mt. Whitney with the highest elevation in the contiguous United States–14,497.6 feet. (Details for the trail to Mt. Whitney under the town of Lone Pine.) Badwater's spring-fed pool of water never dries up, but it is salty, has an odd odor and, of course, is undrinkable. Salt crystals mixed with other minerals ooze up between cracks in the mud and form extraordinary designs across the salt flat (200 sq. miles). To observe the white crystals up close, walk out on the flats.

On very rare occasions, with heavy rainfall, a shallow (few inches deep) temporary lake is formed. Best time of day to visit is early morning while there is shade from the nearby Black Mountains. The view is amazing from the (wheelchair/stroller accessible) boardwalk. Information at Furnace Creek Visitor Center (760) 786-3244. www.digital-desert.com/death-valley-geology/badwater/ and www.nps.gov/deva (Type in Badwater and click search, in the top left corner.) From Furnace Creek Visitor Center, continue east on Hwy 190 for 2 miles to the intersection with Badwater Road (Hwy 178). Turn right on Hwy 178 and continue south 17 miles to the parking area.

PARK ENTRANCE FEES – (Subject to change.)

Seven-day Pass: $20 per vehicle; $10 walk-ins, motorcycles.
Annual Pass: $40.
National Park Annual Pass: $80 (Admittance to all national parks.)
Senior Pass: $10 (Age 62+ for lifetime.)
Access Pass: Free for U.S. citizens with permanent disabilities.

Note: Visitors can obtain park passes and pay the entrance fee at the Furnace Creek Visitor Center, Stovepipe Wells Ranger Station, or the Grapevine Ranger Station which is located 5 miles prior to Scotty's Castle. (When they are closed, machines are available to pay park fee.)

INFORMATION
Emergency – Call 911

Inter-Agency Visitor Center & Ranger Station – Information, books, and maps for Death Valley and the Lone Pine area including Mt. Whitney.

(Details under Lone Pine Information.) Summer 8am-6pm. Winter 8am-5pm. (760) 876-6222. Junction of Hwy 395 & Hwy 136, 1.5 miles south of Lone Pine.

Furnace Creek Visitor Center – Maps, books, and information on weather and trails. Call in early March for spring wildflower information. Daily 9am-6pm. (After Oct 1st 8am-5pm.) Ranger programs Nov to mid-April. Rangers and Information (760) 786-3244 or 3200. www.nps.gov/deva or www.nps.gov/deva/planyourvisit/hours.htm. From the Lone Pine Inter-Agency Visitor Center & Ranger Station take Hwy 136 (becomes Hwy 190) 80 miles to Stovepipe Wells and continue 7 miles ahead to the junction with Scotty's Castle Road. Turn right, and travel 17 miles to the Furnace Creek Visitor Center. (24 miles from Stovepipe Wells Village.)

Junior Ranger – Kids can become a Junior Ranger. Pick up a free *Ranger Booklet* at the visitor center. Kids must complete the activities in the booklet for their designated age group. When the booklet is completed, take it to a park ranger to sign, and kids will receive a junior badge.

Pink Jeep Tours – Open mid-Oct to mid-May. Information – (888) 900-4480. www.pinkjeep.com.

Farabee's Jeep Rentals – Open mid-Oct to mid-May. Information – (760) 786-9872. www.deathvalleyjeeprentals. com. Located across from the Furnace Creek Inn. (Directions under Lodging, Furnace Creek Inn and Ranch.)

Stovepipe Wells Ranger Station – (760) 786-2342.

Weather – Current weather forecast www.nps.gov/deva (See Death Valley in Appendix for more information.)

Visitor Guide – View the park guide and maps. www.nps. gov/deva/index.htm.

Wheelchair Accessible Activities – (Details under Appendix.)

Wildlife – (Details under Death Valley Wildlife in Appendix.)

Pets – Okay on park roads, but not on trails or in wilderness areas.

Cell Phones & GPS – Cell phones do not work well in Death Valley and GPS navigation systems may be unreliable. (They can lead to roads no longer in use.) Visitors should stay in their vehicle if it breaks down; rangers patrol major roads for problems.

GASOLINE

Panamint Springs Resort – Gas 24 hrs. with credit card. (775) 482-7680. (Details under Lodging.)

Stovepipe Wells Village – Gas 7am-9pm (Call ahead, may change to 24 hrs. with credit card.) (760) 786-2387. (Details under Lodging.)

Furnace Creek Ranch – Gas 24 hrs. with credit card. (760) 786-2345. (Details under Lodging.)

EATERIES/LODGING

Furnace Creek Campground – Mid-April to mid-Oct. (First-come, first-served.) Open all year. Information – (760) 786-2441.

Stovepipe Wells Campground – Open mid-Oct to mid-April.

Reservations for above campgrounds – (877) 444-6777 (8am-9pm PST). www.recreation.gov (24 hrs.)

Stovepipe RV Park – (760) 786-2387. www.escapetodeathvalley.com.

Panamint Springs Resort RV Campground (tent sites) – (775) 482-7680.

Panamint Springs Resort – The resort includes a motel (Wi-Fi), a restaurant/bar with an outdoor patio (B,L,D), gas station, mini-mart, RV campground, and tent sites. Dogs okay. Open all year. **Note:** It's about 10 to 15 degrees cooler here than the other resort areas in the park. A year round stream and the Darwin Waterfall are nearby. Information is available at the resort (775) 482-7680. (Intermittent phone service.) www.panamintsprings.com. Located 48 miles from Lone Pine's Inter-Agency Visitor Center & Ranger Station (on Hwy 395) via Hwy 136 which becomes Hwy 190.

Stovepipe Wells Village – The village includes a motel (Internet service in the lobby), restaurant (B,D), saloon (lunch served in saloon), swimming pool (non-guest pay $4 per person), gas station, RV Park, and general store with ice cream. (Store and gas station daily 7am-9pm.) Dogs okay. (760) 786-2387. www.escapetodeathvalley.com. Directions under Stovepipe Wells. **Note:** The nearby Stovepipe Wells Campground (not part of the village) is open mid-Oct to mid-April.

Furnace Creek Inn – The inn, with its nice palm tree-strewn garden and afternoon tea, houses the **Inn at Furnace Creek Dining Room**. – B,L,D – Fine dining. Dinner reservations (760) 786-3385. Open mid-Oct to mid-May. (Furnace Creek Inn and Ranch have the same ownership and phone number.)

Furnace Creek Ranch – The ranch offers a general store, gas station, the **Corkscrew Saloon** (cocktails and snacks amid juke box music), the **49er Café** (casual family dining), and the **Wrangler Steakhouse** with buffet breakfast, lunch, and dinner. (Chicken, ribs, and steak are served.) Open all year. **Note:** Both the inn and the ranch have spring-fed swimming pools (84 degrees year round) and all rooms have pay Wi-Fi. Close to the ranch, there is an 18-hole golf course, horseback riding, and an airstrip for private aircraft. Furnace Creek Inn and Furnace Creek Ranch (760) 786-2345 (800) 236-7916. www.furnacecreekresort.com. Follow directions to Stovepipe Wells, and continue on Hwy 190 just past the left turn for Scotty's Castle Road. Stay on Hwy 190 for 17 miles to the Furnace Creek Visitor Center; it's just a mile further to Furnace Creek Ranch (on the right) and, the inn is about .5 mile past it (on the left). (Directions from other areas on their website.)

DIRECTIONS – Death Valley

From Lone Pine, 1.5 miles south of the town, at the junction of Hwy 395 & Hwy 136, is the Inter-Agency Visitor Center & Ranger Station. Hwy 136 runs alongside it and leads into Death Valley. Hwy 136 begins as a flat, wide road (becomes Hwy 190) and turns into a mountainous road which is narrow and twisting in some places. There are many special viewpoints along the way which afford magnificent views. Panamint Springs Resort and the Darwin Waterfall is reached in 48 miles and in an additional 32 miles, Stovepipe Wells Village & Ranger Station is reached. (Directions to Scotty's Castle under Scotty's Castle; directions to Las Vegas under the Appendix.) **Note:** Return to Lone Pine from Death Valley, and continue north along Hwy 395 to reach Independence, Mammoth Lakes, and Mono Lake.

1.2 Independence, Big Pine, Bishop, Rock Creek, Convict Lake
What To Do & See

INDEPENDENCE

This small town boasts historical homes and a church built in 1886. **Note:** Additional information on Independence under the Appendix.

HISTORICAL HOMES

Commander's House – Built in 1872. Located at 303 Edwards Street.

Pioneer Memorial Church – Built in 1886. Corner of Center Street and Washington, one block behind the Winnedumah Hotel.

Edwards House – Built in 1863; the oldest building in the region. Located at 124 Market Street, off Hwy 395.

Mary Austin House – Built in 1903. Author, Mary Austin wrote her first book here, *The Land of Little Rain*. From Hwy 395 turn on Market Street (toward the mountains) and travel to the corner of Market and Webster Streets. **Note:** Austin's books are available at Eastern California Museum. 10am-5pm (760) 878-0258. Located at 155 Grant Street. From Hwy 395, turn on Center Street (in the middle of town) toward the mountains and continue 3 blocks to Grant Street.

MOUNT WHITNEY FISH HATCHERY

The impressive historic building at the hatchery was constructed in the early 1900s of native granite to blend in with the nearby mountains. It's walls are 2 to 3 feet thick to keep it cool. The lobby has displays and a gift shop. Visitors may tour the building 10am-4pm. Donations. (Closed Tues/ Wed.) Wheelchair accessible. There is a large pond in front of the building stocked with trout and a picturesque picnic area. Fish food available for kids to feed fish. Leashed dogs okay. www.mtwhitneyfishhatchery.org/ and www.lonepinechamber. org/sightseeing/fish-hatchery.html. From Hwy 395, turn left about 2 miles north of town onto Fish Hatchery Road.

INFORMATION

Independence Chamber of Commerce – No office. www.independencechamber.org. **Note:** Maps and information on camping and fishing are available at the Eastern California Museum. Daily 10am-5pm. (760) 878-0258. 155 Grant Street, 3 blocks west of Hwy 395.

Sequoia Kings Pack Train – Pack Trips & horseback rides – Memorial Day to mid-Oct. (760) 387-2797. (800) 962-0775. www.sequoiakingspacktrain.com.

EATERIES/LODGING

Jenny's Café – American cuisine. Sat-Tues 7am-2pm. Thurs/ Fri 8pm. (Closed Weds.) (760) 878-2266. 246 Edwards Street, on Hwy 395.

Mt. Williamson Motel – Cabins with hot breakfast. Dogs okay in one cabin. (760) 878-2121. (866) 428-4352. www.mtwilliamsonmotel.com. On Hwy 395.

DIRECTIONS – Independence

Hwy 395, 16 miles north of Lone Pine, 25 miles south of Big Pine.

WILDLIFE VIEWING

Herds of elk are usually seen grazing mornings and again at dusk along Hwy 395, 19.5 miles north of Independence and 5.5 miles south of Big Pine. Driving from Independence, a sign stating *Wildlife Viewing* is on the right side of the road; elk are generally on left side of the road.

BIG PINE

Small town with mighty fine fishing and camping found along the many creeks, streams, and lakes.

INFORMATION

Bishop Area Chamber of Commerce & Visitors Bureau – Maps and information on lodging, dining, and activities; serving Bishop and Big Pine. Mon-Fri 10am-5pm, Sat/Sun 4pm. (Closed Sun in winter.) (760) 873-8405. (888) 395-3952. www.bishopvisitor.com. 690 N. Main Street (Hwy 395).

EATERIES

Country Kitchen – B,L,D – Breakfast items, burgers, sandwiches, fish and chips, pasta, pork chops, and steak. Open 6:30am-8pm. (760) 938-2402. Located at 181S. Main Street.

Copper Top BBQ – Tri-tips, chicken, mac and cheese. 11am-6pm. (Closed Mon-Tues.) (760) 970-5577. www.coppertopbbq.com. Located at 310 N. Main Street.

DIRECTIONS – Big Pine

Hwy 395, 25 miles north of Independence, 16 miles south of Bishop.

BISHOP

The town is complete with shops, restaurants, lodging, golf course, park, and a great railroad museum. Hot springs lie nearby awaiting discovery. Bishop's enchanting mountains are full of streams, creeks, and lakes brimming with fish, creating a fisherman's paradise.

KEOUGH'S HOT SPRINGS

Facility constructed by pioneer Phillip Keough in 1919. Fresh mineral-water pools. Large swimming pool, (86-91 degrees), small pool, (104 degrees), massages, snack bar, gift shop, and camping. Dressing rooms and restrooms are also available. Great place to relax and bring kids for swimming. Water Aerobics classes (one hour) $5. Call ahead for times. June thru Aug, Mon-Thurs 9am-8pm, Fri/Sat 9am-9pm, Sun 9am-7pm. Sept thru May, 11am-7pm, Sat/Sun 9am-8pm. (Closed Tues in autumn, winter, & spring.) (760) 872-4670. www.keoughshotsprings.com. From Hwy 395, follow Keough's Hot Springs Road for 1 mile. It's 8 miles north of Big Pine, 7 miles south of Bishop.

BISHOP CITY PARK

Three bridges cross over the park's stream where, in the springtime, mamma ducks are seen parading their ducklings. The rolling green lawn surrounds huge trees that provide shade for the picnic tables. A path (wheelchair/stroller accessible) leads from the stream to a huge duck pond with a gazebo overlooking it. The park has a swimming pool (open seasonally), playground, skate/bike park, and a brand new dog park. Open 8am-4:30pm Mon-Fri. Information – (760) 873-5863. Located at 690 N. Main Street (Hwy 395), behind the Bishop Area Chamber of Commerce & Visitor Center.

LAWS MUSEUM

An 1800s train, railroad depot, oil and water tanks, ranch house, post office, and fire station with fire equipment and automobiles are sprawled out over 11 acres. 9:30am-4pm, winter 10am-4pm. (Closed some major holidays.) $5 donation. Wheelchair/stroller accessible. No dogs. Information – (760) 873-5950. www.lawsmuseum.org. From the northern end of Bishop turn right on Hwy 6 for 3.8 miles. Then turn right on Silver Canyon Road for .3 mile.

BISHOP CREEK CANYON

This is a wonderful area for viewing autumn's vibrant colors and for fishing, hiking, and camping near the creeks and lakes. Boating allowed on South Lake and Lake Sabrina; horseback riding at North Lake. **Note:** It's 25 to 30 degrees cooler than Bishop. (Directions for South Lake, North Lake, and Lake Sabrina listed below.) Located in the Eastern Sierra Nevada Mountains.

SOUTH LAKE

An amazing vivid blue lake (with great fishing) shows off an island, which is reached by rental boats. The lake is ringed by mountains where remnants of snow cling along the peaks and ridges until late August. For a nice walk, see the Bishop Pass Trail listed below. A snack bar and boat rentals are found at the end of the parking area. Open 7am-7pm. Horseback riding – Rainbow Pack Station

(760) 873-8877. (Details under Bishop Information.) From Hwy 395 take West Line Street (Hwy 168) 15 miles, and turn left at the South Lake turnoff (signed *South Lake*) amid the aspen trees along Bishop Creek. Drive for 7 miles to a small parking area on the left, just prior to the end of the road.

BISHOP PASS TRAIL

At South Lake, the path begins to the left of the parking area (at a trail sign) and goes out to a split in the path. (Right path goes to Treasure Lakes in 2.8 miles.) Follow the left path, and it soon reaches another trail junction. (Left turn goes out to the Chocolate Lakes.) Continue ahead to an overlook, where the view is spectacular, with Long Lake in the foreground followed by Saddlerock Lake and Bishop Lake. The lakes appear in different hues of blue-green-gray with a backdrop of gray granite mountains tipped in snow most of the year. Continue to Long Lake (over half a mile long) which is surrounded by greenery and pine trees. For the less-than-hardy, this is a good turning around point. Bring a camera; the pristine beauty of this area is surreal. The fishing is good; even the great golden trout can be found in these lakes. Wilderness permits required for overnight stays. Dogs okay. Information available at the White Mountain Ranger Station and the Bishop Area Chamber of Commerce & Visitor Center. (Details under Bishop Information.) Trail: Moderate 2 miles one way to Long Lake. (Directions above, under South Lake.)

EATERIES/LODGING – South Lake

Bishop Creek Lodge – The lodge includes housekeeping cabins, a mini-mart, and a restaurant/cocktail bar. Mon/Tues 11am-4pm. Wed-Sun 11am-8pm. From the lodge there is a view of a tall waterfall slipping down the mountainside.

Dogs okay. Open mid-April thru Oct. (760) 873-4484. www. bishopcreekresort.com. From Hwy 395 follow Hwy 168 (West Line Street) 15 miles, and turn left at the turnoff signed *South Lake*. Drive 2 miles to the lodge.

Parcher's Resort – Cabins for rent and hiker showers available. There's a small café on the premises. Breakfast only. Mon-Fri waffle buffet, Sat/Sun full breakfast. Resort open May to mid-Oct. Dogs okay. (760) 873-4177. www.parchersresort. net. Directions above, under Bishop Creek Lodge. Parcher's Resort is 3.8 miles beyond the Bishop Creek Lodge, 1.2 miles from South Lake.

Cardinal Village Resort – Cabins with kitchens sit among the aspens. Cabin descriptions and reservations on website. (2-night minimum, 3 nights holidays.) No pets! Kids love to fish in the nearby trout pond. Cardinal Café – breakfast and great burgers. 8am-3pm. No phone. www.cardinalvillageresort.com. From Hwy 395 follow Hwy 168 (West Line Street) 18 miles to tiny Aspendell and look for sign on right stating *Cardinal Village*.

NORTH LAKE

This area features a small lake, a campground, (first-come, first-served) and horseback riding. (No food.) Bishop Pack Outfitters – (760) 873-4785. (Details under Information.) From Hwy 395 in Bishop, follow West Line Street (Hwy 168) for 15 miles to the South Lake turnoff. Continue beyond this turnoff on Hwy 168 three miles; turn right on the narrow road signed *North Lake*. The lake is reached in 2 miles.

LAKE SABRINA

This aquamarine lake sparkles around islands strewn with pine trees, and is bordered on three sides by mountains. There's a dam across the end of the lake (left of the parking area); and a walk across it reveals a trail that follows the lake, then heads off into the back country to Blue Lake and other mountain lakes. Behind the café and boat rentals, a rocky path winds along the shoreline for about a mile overlooking the boats moored around the tiny picturesque islands. This lake has great fishing. Information – Lake Sabrina Boat Landing/Café (details below) and White Mountain Ranger Station. (Details under Bishop Information.) Best hiking late June to mid-Oct. (Directions below under Lake Sabrina Boat Landing/Café.)

Lake Sabrina Campground – First-come, first-served.

Lake Sabrina Boat Landing/Café – Breakfast and lunch mid-May to mid-Oct. (Exact date depends upon snow.) Fri 7am-5pm, Sat/Sun 8am-4pm. (Closed Mon-Thurs.) Boat launching/rentals: kayaks, canoes, and motor boats. (760) 873-7425. www.lakesabrinaboatlanding.com. Follow the directions to North Lake, except don't take the turnoff for North Lake. Continue ahead .8 mile to the end of the road and Lake Sabrina.

INFORMATION

White Mountain Ranger Station – Trail/weather/fishing information and maps. Summer Mon-Fri 8am-5pm, winter 4:30pm. (Closes for lunch 12 to 1pm.) (760) 873-2500. Located at 798 N. Main Street (Hwy 395).

Bishop Area Chamber of Commerce & Visitors Bureau – Maps and information on lodging, dining, and activities. Mon-Fri 10am-5pm, Sat/Sun 4pm. (Closed Sun in winter.) (760) 873-8405. (888) 395-3952. www.bishopvisitor.com. 690 N. Main Street (Hwy 395).

Bishop Mule Days – Held Memorial Day weekend with

mule racing, BBQs, concerts, parade, and craft fair. (760) 872-4263. www.muledays.org.

Bishop Country Club – Public 18-hole golf course and the **19ᵗʰ Hole Bar and Grill**. 7:30am-3pm. (760) 873-5828. Hwy 395, south end of town.

Mountain Light Gallery – Nature photos. 10am-5pm, Sun 11am-4pm. (760) 873-7700. www.mountainlight.com. Hwy 395, corner of Main Street and Line Street.

Wheelchair Accessible Activities – (Details under Appendix.)

Rainbow Pack Outfitters – Hiking and horseback excursions. (760) 873-8877. www.rainbowpackoutfit.com.

Bishop Pack Outfitters – Horseback riding and hiking/fishing trips. (760) 873-4785. www.bishoppackoutfitters.com.

EATERIES

Note: Bishop Restaurants close an hour earlier in winter.

Jack's – B,L,D – Family style food – turkey, chicken, steak, fish, and burgers. Fresh baked bread. 6am-9pm. (760) 872-7971. www.jackastors.com. Located at 437 N. Main Street.

Erick Schat's Bakkery – This popular place serves sandwiches, soups, and cappuccinos along with bakery items. Bakery 6am-6pm, Fri 8pm. Food 9am-3:30pm, Fri/Sat/Sun 5pm. (760) 873-7156. Located at 763 N. Main Street.

Back Alley Restaurant – Reasonably priced burgers, sandwiches, steaks, and seafood. Open 11:30am-10pm, Fri/Sat 11pm. CD music. (760) 873-5777. Located at 649 N. Main Street, inside the bowling alley. (Behind the La Quinta Inn.)

Upper Crust Pizza Co. – Nice pizza, pasta, sandwiches, salads, and homemade soups. 11am-10pm. (760) 872-8153. Located at 871 N. Main Street.

Petite Pantry – Mexican cuisine and fabulous homemade pies. 7am-8:30pm, Fri/Sat 9:30pm. (760) 873-3789. Hwy 395 on the left side of road, 1.5 miles north of town.

LODGING

Note: Most hotels offer fish cleaning facilities and freezing.

Camping and Cabins/Café – North Lake and Lake Sabrina listed above.

J-Diamond Campground & RV Park – Reservations (760) 872-7341.

Super 8 – Rooms come with Wi-Fi and refrigerators; a laundry room and an outdoor pool are available. Continental breakfast. Dogs okay. (760) 872-1386. (800) 800-8000. www.super8.com. 535 S. Main Street.

Holiday Inn Express – Rooms/suites come with Wi-Fi. The hotel has an indoor pool and spa and there's a full breakfast bar. Dogs okay. (760) 872-2423. (877) 395-2395. www.hiexpress.com/bishopca 636 N. Main Street.

Creek Side Inn – Rooms with Wi-Fi are situated along a creek where a short path leads to the swimming pool and spa. Full hot breakfast. (760) 872-3044. (800) 273-3550. www.bishopcreeksideinn.com. 725 N. Main Street.

Comfort Inn – Rooms include Wi-Fi and the hotel provides an outdoorpool/spa and a breakfast bar. Dogs okay. (760) 873-4284. (800) 4choice. www.choicehotels.com. 805 N. Main Street.

Motel 6 – Rooms come with Wi-Fi and refrigerators; a laundry room and an outdoor pool are available. Dogs stay free. (760) 873-8426. (800) 466-8356. www.motel6.com. 1005 N. Main Street.

Best Western Bishop Lodge – This hotel offers a pool, spa, and a full breakfast. All rooms have Wi-Fi. Dogs okay in some rooms. (760) 873-3543. (800) 528-1234. www. bestwestern.com. 1025 N. Main Street.

Ramada Limited Motel – The rooms have microwaves, refrigerators, and Wi-Fi. The hotel provides a breakfast bar, pool, and spa. Dogs okay. (760) 872-1771. (800) 2ramada. www.ramada.com. 155 E. Elm Street.

DIRECTIONS – Bishop

Hwy 395, 15 miles north of Big Pine, 24 miles south of exit to Rock Creek. 286.5 miles north of Los Angeles.

ROCK CREEK

This is a natural wonderland. In spring and summer, remnants of winter snow are scattered across the mountains like clouds across the sky. Their reflection into blue jay-colored lakes, along with the many green pine trees, is captivating. The air is crisp and clear, the music of the running creek is soothing, the fish are jumping, and the camping is fine. In some places, the creek runs so close to camp sites, campers can fish right from their tents. Hiking trails lead to many wondrous sights with small lakes and quiet places for picnics.

ROCK CREEK LAKE

There is a quiet trail that wraps around the lake; good fishing, boating, horseback riding, and camping are available. Start the trail from the lake's campground parking area. The occasional showers that splash peacefully across the lake seem to disappear into sunshine very suddenly. Information at Rock Creek Lake General Store, across the road from the lake (760) 935-4311. Trail: Easy 1.5 mile loop. Located 9 miles from Hwy 395.

MOSQUITO FLAT

This is the launching point for many trails (including the Little Lake Valley Trail listed below). Catch the trail at the end of the road along the edge of the large parking area. (1.5 miles beyond Rock Creek Lake.) From spring until late July, mosquitoes are prevalent in early morning and at dusk.

LITTLE LAKE VALLEY TRAIL

The sound of swiftly moving Rock Creek, as it flows down the rocky creek bed, can be heard while climbing up the sandy/ rocky terrain. The trail follows alongside the creek where fishermen are usually spotted, and soon leads across small streams where stepping stones are strewn for easy crossing. Small vibrant-blue lakes fringed with tall pine trees and framed by distant snow-clad mountains are found along the path. In .3 mile, at a split in the trail, keep to the left (path to right leads out 2 miles to Ruby Lake). Hike half a mile to Mack Lake. A short distance from there is Marsh Lake. One and half miles further out is Heart Lake. From here, continue to Box Lake (.25 mile) and take the side trail around the lake to find two tiny Hidden Lakes. Return to the main trail, and continue .3 mile to Long Lake. For the less-than-hardy, this is a good turning around point. Dogs okay. The path from Long

Lake continues 1 mile to Chickenfoot Lake, and another half mile to the gorgeous Gem Lakes. Trail information at Rock Creek Lake General Store across the road from Rock Creek Lake (760) 935-4311 or White Mountain Ranger Station in Bishop (760) 873-2500. Trail: Easy 2 miles one way to Long Lake. (Directions under Mosquito Flat listed above.)

INFORMATION

Note: Rock Creek area is 20 to 30 degrees cooler than Bishop.

Rock Creek Lake Resort – Summer information available. (Details under Lodging.) (760) 935-4311.

Rock Creek Lodge – Winter cross-country skiing/ snowshoeing. Rentals available. (Details under Lodging.) (760) 935-4170.

Rock Creek Pack Station – Horseback riding. (760) 935-4493 or (760) 872-8331. www.rockcreekpackstation.com.

EATERIES/LODGING

Camping sites sit among the trees close to the bubbling Rock Creek along nine-mile Rock Creek Road. (Most sites are first-come-first served.) Open mid-May/June to mid-Oct. (Depends upon snow.)

Rock Creek Lake Campground – (877) 444-6777 (8am-9pm PST). www.recreation.gov (24 hrs.)

Sierra Vacation Trailer Rentals – They will set up a rental trailer along Rock Creek. (760) 935-4263. www. sierravacationtrailerrentals.net.

Tom's Place – Rustic cabins with kitchens. Dogs okay in some cabins. There's a market and café/bar (7am-9pm) adjacent to the cabins. (Closed for some holidays.) (760) 935-4239. www.tomsplaceresort.com. On Rock Creek Road just off Hwy 395 at the exit signed *Rock Creek/Tom's Place.*

Rock Creek Lodge – Creek-front cabins offer woodstoves and kitchens. A summer restaurant serves breakfast and dinner. (Lodge closed April 1ˢᵗ to Memorial Day and Oct 31 to mid-Dec.) Winter cross-country skiing and snowshoeing on groomed trails. (Rentals.) Dogs okay in summer. (760) 935-4170. (877) 935-4170. www.rockcreeklodge.com. Located 1 mile prior to Rock Creek Lake, 8 miles from Hwy 395.

Rock Creek Lake Resort – Cottages with kitchens and bathrooms. The nearby general store sells fishing licenses (7am-7pm) and houses a tiny café that serves breakfast and lunch with chili, sandwiches, burgers, and great homemade pies. 7am-3pm. Hiker showers and boat rentals are available. Open late May to Oct. (Depends upon snow.) No Pets. (760) 935-4311. www.rockcreeklake.com. At Rock Creek Lake, 9 miles from Hwy 395.

DIRECTIONS – Rock Creek

Follow Hwy 395 (24 miles north of Bishop) to the exit signed *Rock Creek/Tom's Place.* (10.5 miles south of Convict Lake.) From Hwy 395, it's 9 miles out to Rock Creek Lake.

CONVICT LAKE

This dazzling small lake (with great trout fishing) is bordered by mountains so close they seem to be sliding into the water. Patches of snow may remain on the mountain peaks until August; their reflection upon the lake is captivating. A peaceful trail encircles the lake and is most attractive in autumn when the aspen leaves turn buttercup yellow and shimmer in the breeze. The boardwalk is a splendid place to fish from. Wheelchair/stroller accessible. **Note:** Wheelchair Accessible Activities under Appendix.

Fishing season runs from the last Saturday of April to Nov 15th. Launch your own boat or rent a kayak, canoe, pontoon boat or motorboat. Read the story of how the lake got its name on the website. www.convictlake.com. (Click on *Our Resort*.)

Lake Trail: Easy 2.5 miles around the lake. Follow directions for Convict Lake. At the lake turn right for parking, boat rentals, and the trailhead for the path encircling the lake. (Trailhead is at the end of the parking area.) To reach the boardwalk, turn left at the lake. (150 yards) For the picnic area, continue ahead, and drive to the end of the road (.5 mile) to the parking area. Here another trailhead is found for the loop path around the lake. Begin the trail next to the small trail sign. The picnic area is close to the lake. Information – Mammoth Lakes Welcome Center & Ranger Station (760) 924-5500. Lake open late May to Oct. (Depends upon snow.)

EATERIES/LODGING & HORSEBACK RIDES

Convict Lake Campground – Wheelchair Accessible sites. Reservations – (877) 444-6777 (8am-9pm PST). www.recreation.gov (24 hrs.) **Note:** October, usually on first-come, first-served basis only.

Convict Lake Resort – Snuggled amid the aspens are cabins (some with jetted bathtubs) and houses that sleep up to thirty-two people. They all have fully equipped kitchens, and can be viewed on the website. Dogs okay. The general store offers ice, groceries, bait/tackle, and fishing licenses. Horseback riding – (Memorial Day to mid-Sept.) guided two-hour rides.

Weddings. Lodge open year round. (760) 934-3800. (800) 992-2260. www.convictlake.com.

Restaurant at Convict Lake – Fine dining, dinner all year. Summer 5:30-8:30pm, winter until 8pm. Summer only, lunch 11:30am-2:30pm, Sun brunch from 10am. Happy Hour 3-6pm with snacks and drinks inside or on the outdoor patio. Dinner reservations recommended (760) 934-3803. (Closes for weddings; call ahead.)

DIRECTIONS – Convict Lake

From Hwy 395, travel 10.5 miles north of Rock Creek (4 miles south of the Mammoth Lakes junction). Take the turnoff signed *Convict Lake* and follow the road 2 miles to reach the Convict Lake Resort, restaurant, and horseback riding. Continue .3 mile to the lake.

1.3 Mammoth Lakes, June Lake Loop, Mono Lake, Lee Vining
What To Do & See

MAMMOTH LAKES

Visitors are dazzled by the natural beauty found here, both in summer and winter. Summer fun includes fishing in lakes full of trout and hiking trails that zigzag through forests, across streams, and up mountains. There's exceptional camping around the many lakes. Winters bring snow-adorned trees and mountains creating a white-wonderland backdrop for fabulous dogsled rides, snowshoeing, as well as cross-country and down-hill skiing.

THE LAKES OF MAMMOTH

The Lakes Basin opens approximately late May to late June and closes about mid-Oct (depending upon snowfall). The road to Twin Lakes and Tamarack Lodge (details under Lodging) is open all year. Fishing season runs from the last Saturday in April to November 15, but the lakes are frozen until the end of May or sometime in June.

TWIN LAKES

These two glistening lakes, which can be seen from the road coming in from the town of Mammoth Lakes, are connected by a small wooden bridge. In summer, ducks swim on the lake, and canoes and row boats are lined up along the shore awaiting visitors. Autumn paints a pretty picture when the lemon-yellow leaves of the aspen trees around the lakes sparkle in the sunlight and murmur in the breeze. Many fishermen can be seen casting their lines along the shore. The Tamarack Lodge and Cabins (with boat rentals) is also situated alongside the lakes. (Details under Lodging.) A drive beyond the second lake reveals a bridge that leads to the Twin Lakes Campground. (Details under Lodging.) From the bridge is a view of the huge Twin Lakes Waterfall tumbling down the mountainside into the Upper Twin Lake. The campground is sprawled alongside this lake. From Hwy 395, take the Mammoth Lakes exit (Hwy 203) and continue beyond the Mammoth Lakes Welcome Center (details under Information) to the town where Hwy 203 becomes Main Street. Continue on Main Street for one mile to reach the 3rd stoplight at Minaret Road where Main Street becomes Lake Mary Road. Follow Lake Mary Road ahead for two miles to the Twin Lakes.

LAKE MARY

This picturesque lake with fantastic trout fishing and boating is bordered by the Crystal Crag Lodge Cabins on the southwest side (details under Lodging) and the Pokonobe Resort, with boat rentals and general store, on the northern side. (Details under Information, Boat Rentals.) From the Twin Lakes, follow Lake Mary Road (1.25 miles) and take the first left turn (signed *Lake Mary*). Continue around half of the lake to reach the Crystal Crag Lodge Cabins. To reach the Pokonobe Resort, continue ahead on Lake Mary Road traveling along the length of Lake Mary to the lake's northern edge.

EMERALD LAKE & TRAIL

This jewel of a lake (hidden behind Lake Mary) is reached by a trail that curls around the mountainside. In early summer, the music of the creek is heard from the trail. After .1 mile, there is a wonderful view of the roaring creek where white froth spins around many rocks and boulders. As the trail continues up, look for bear-claw scratch marks on the pine trees; this is bear territory. Soon the dark emerald-green lake emerges. Its beauty is enhanced by reflections of the surrounding mountains that hold patches of snow into mid-summer. Return on the same trail or continue past the lake to a stream and, keeping to the right (west side) of the stream, follow the path to Sky Meadows, which is ablaze with wildflowers in summer. Mosquitoes prevalent spring to late July especially in early morning and at dusk. Leashed or voice-controlled dogs okay. Trail: Moderate 1 mile to Emerald Lake, and 2 miles to Sky Meadows one way. From the Twin Lakes, take the first left turnoff, Lake Mary Road (1.25 miles), signed *Lake Mary*. Follow the road around part of the lake, and turn left at the sign for Coldwater Campground. Parking is at the end of the campground; the trailhead is nearby.

MAMMOTH CONSOLIDATED GOLD MINE

A short path begins after crossing over Coldwater Creek on a wooden bridge and leads out to the remains of a 1920s gold mining town. Just a few years ago, visitors could peer into the windows of the buildings and see the dusty remnants of a time gone by. Now, due to theft, the remaining relics have been removed and the buildings demolished or boarded up. Leashed or voice controlled dogs okay. Information – Mammoth Lakes Welcome Center/Ranger Station (760) 924-5500. Trail: Easy .25 mile to the mining town. Follow the directions above for Emerald Lake, and travel past the parking area for Emerald Lake to the parking area signed *Mammoth Consolidated Gold Mine*. The trailhead is found nearby.

Note: Many lakes can be reached from this general area. Heart Lake – 1 mile, Arrowhead Lake – 1.2 miles, Skelton Lake – 2 miles, and Barney Lake – 2.5 miles. Leashed or voice-controlled dogs okay on the trails. Information – Mammoth Lakes Welcome Center/Ranger Station (760) 924-5500.

LAKE GEORGE

This serene good-fishing lake is situated behind or southwest of Lake Mary. It is edged in tall pine trees and nearly surrounded by mountains where trails climb up high and visitors find amazing views. The Woods Lodge hugs the lake shore. (Details for the Woods Lodge under Lodging.) From the Twin Lakes, take Lake Mary Road and travel to Lake Mary. Follow the edge of the lake north. Just beyond Lake Mary, turn left on Lake George Road. It curves back around the north edge of Lake Mary and continues out to Lake George. The following trails begin at Lake George:

CRYSTAL LAKE & TRAIL

The trail begins left of an information sign found on the right side of the parking entrance. The path is soft between the many rocks and gray granite boulders strewn about the area, and gradually climbs up among the pine trees. The Woods Lodge's cabins (details under Lodging) can be seen from the left side of the trail. Farther up the trail, a view of Lake George emerges below. By September, the nearby mountains reflected into the lake may be patched with snow. As the path ducks into the forest, fragments of snow may be scattered under the pines. Up higher on the path, Lake George comes into view again, radiating in a shade of blue-green; it's in striking contrast to the dark green of Lake Mary, in the distance. The one-mile mark is reached at the trail sign where the trail veers left for Crystal Lake. Now the path levels out and, as it begins to descend, hikers will catch glimpses of the lake as it sparkles between the trees. Crystal Lake is fringed in pine trees and the lake's backdrop is a mountain laden with snow most of the year. By September, jackets are needed as temperatures are usually in the 50s. Great summer fishing. Leashed or voice-controlled dogs okay. Information – (760) 924-5500. Trail: Moderate 1.75 miles one way. Follow the above directions for Lake George. Trailhead is found to the right of the parking entrance.

BARRETT & T J LAKES & TRAIL

The path follows along the edge of Lake George where inviting picnic tables are strewn between the pines, and fishermen line the shore. Continue around the lake to the very end of the path, and cross the tiny bridge among the trees. Beyond the bridge, a sign indicates a right turn to reach Barrett Lake in a quarter mile and T J Lake in half a mile. The trail begins climbing above Lake George, which appears very green due to the many pine trees casting their color onto the lake. The rocky path is steep for about 100 yards, and then become soft under the pines with a moderate climb. Soon a tiny lake appears, mirroring the surrounding pine trees and mountains. By mid-September, snow may be hugging the shoreline. Continue along a sandy path, passing the lake to a junction, and continue to the right (approximately 50 yards) to look down on T J Lake. This larger and more impressive lake is reached from here by a descending path. The mountain directly behind the lake (snow-faced most of the year) spreads its image across the water. In June and July, wildflowers present themselves along the trail. Mosquitoes prevalent spring to late July, especially in early morning and at dusk. Leashed or voice-controlled dogs okay. Information – (760) 924-5500. Trail: Moderate .25 mile to Barrett Lake, and .25 mile further to T J Lake one way. Follow the above directions for Lake George. Trailhead is to the left of the parking entrance.

LAKE MAMIE

This is a photographer's dream come true; a pretty tiny lake surrounded by pine trees and mountains where snow clings usually into June. Summer boat rentals are available at the marina; and there's great trout fishing. Information – (760) 924-5500. The lake is found along Lake Mary Road, .75 miles from Lake Mary.

TWIN FALLS OVERLOOK

At this overlook, water drops 300 feet down the mountainside. Near the bridge on Lake Mary Road, across from Mamie Lake, is a small pull-off area for parking. From here, it's a short walk to the lookout point.

HORSESHOE LAKE

There is a forlorn look here as many of the trees around the lake have died due to the CO_2 emissions seeping up through the soil. Levels are especially high in winter and may be dangerous for pets and small children. Information – Mammoth Lakes Welcome Center (760) 924-5500. The amazing McLeod Lake Trail begins here. (Details below.) Travel to the end of Lake Mary Road to a large parking area, .75 mile from Mamie Lake, and 2.75 miles from Twin Lakes.

McLEOD LAKE & TRAIL

A lovely, clearly marked trail meanders to the lake. Beneath the tall trees, hundreds of tiny new green pine trees are sprouting. Continue along the footpath, beneath the trees, to a trail sign indicating that the lake is to the left. Walk left and take the sandy path which climbs gently up the hillside. In half a mile, turn left at another trail sign. The lustrous, turquoise-blue lake shows itself in approximately fifty yards. Pale gray granite mountains, usually adorned with snow by October, tower above the lake. Bordering the long lake is a gray-beige sandy beach, strewn with logs. A walk along the beach is gratifying. Great fishing. The trailhead signed *Mammoth Pass* is found to the right of the parking area. Trail: Easy .5 mile one way. Follow above directions to Horseshoe Lake.

INYO NATIONAL FOREST – REDS MEADOW AREA

Shuttle buses (fee required) travel the forest road carrying visitors to ten shuttle stops in the Reds Meadow Area. Along the way, the driver explains the highlights of each trail and what time the bus will stop for the return ride.

Note: No cars allowed, except for those belonging to registered campers. Muzzled dogs okay on shuttle. Obtain shuttle tickets and dog muzzles from the Adventure Center at Mammoth Mountain, outside the Mammoth Mountain Inn. (Details for the Inn under Lodging.) (Closed in winter.) Reds Meadow

Trail Rides – summer horseback rides to Rainbow Falls thru September. (760) 934-2345. (Details for Rainbow Falls given below and horseback rides under Information.) From the Mammoth Lakes Welcome Center follow Main Street (Hwy 203) to Minaret Road (stoplight) and turn right. Continue 3 miles to end of the road. Mammoth Mountain is on the left side of the road and the Mammoth Mountain Inn is on the right. Just past the inn is the Adventure Center.

DEVILS POST PILE TRAIL

This is a very popular shuttle stop with little walking required to reach the Devils Post Pile. This site is so named after volcanic lava flows left strange vertical formations in the rocky hillside. Trail: Easy .4 mile one way.

RAINBOW FALLS TRAIL

The trees near the beginning of this trail are blackened from a forest fire. Most visitors get an eerie feeling when passing by them. In early summer, the falls have a tremendous force and can be heard from a long way off. Like a magical illusion, when sunshine escapes from beneath a cloud, (especially in midday) a vivid rainbow appears across the falls. A meandering path follows along the edge of the falls where many viewing areas are found. Eventually the path merges with steep rocky stairs leading down to the base of the falls. **Note:** Continue one shuttle stop beyond the trailhead for Rainbow Falls (#10 located up the hill from the Rainbow Falls Trailhead shuttle stop) called Reds Meadow Resort where there is a market (bottled water), gift shop/café, and restrooms. Information – gift shop/café or shuttle bus driver. Trail: Easy 1.5 miles one way. When starting the trail from shuttle stop #10, look for a small trail sign and walk downhill and cross over the road to reach the trailhead for Rainbow Falls. This is the pick-up stop for the return ride or go up to shuttle stop #10 for pick-up.

MAMMOTH SCENIC LOOP – INYO CRATERS

This soft path is covered with pine needles and shaded by the tall pines of the forest as it climbs slightly uphill. Soon it emerges from the forest into an opening. Continue ahead to a metal railing that circles round most of a large crater. The view from the railing is amazing; the bottom of the huge crater is filled with murky-green stagnant water. Above the water level, the brown sides support pine trees laden with snow usually by October. Follow the path along the right side of the crater to find another crater. **Note:** Trailhead sign is found along the edge of the road just prior to the parking area. The road out to the parking area is usually closed until late June. (Depends upon snow.) Trail: Easy .25 mile one way. From the Mammoth Lakes Welcome Center follow Main Street (Hwy 203) to Minaret Road (stoplight) and turn right. Continue less than a mile to a right turn on Mammoth Scenic Loop Road. Follow this road 2.7 miles and turn left (signed *Inyo Craters*) on a narrow gravel road lined with tall pines. Keep to the right at the three splits in the road. From the third split, proceed 1.2 miles to the parking area. For the return trip, turn right from the parking area and make all left turns at splits in the road. Back at Mammoth Scenic Loop Road, a right turn leads 2.7 miles to Mammoth, and a left turn leads 3.1 miles to Hwy 395.

MAMMOTH VILLAGE

Although the village is open in summer, it's in full swing during winter with clothing/gift/candy shops, eateries, condos, and the ski gondola. (Details for lodging under Mammoth Lakes Lodging.) **Note:** A few businesses close down during Sept/Oct/Nov. Information – (760) 924-5500. www.villageatmammoth.com.

Located in Mammoth Village:

Village Gondola – ski lifts to Canyon Lodge Warming Hut and mountain slopes.

McCoy Sports – Ski/sports clothing and sunglasses. Open all year. 10am-7pm, Fri/Sat/Sun 8pm. (760) 924-7070.

Mountain Center – Ski/snowboard rentals. 8am-5pm. (760) 924-7057.

Bear Creek Pizza Den – Serves pizza, chicken, soup, salads, and sandwiches. Beer/Wine. 11am-10pm. (Closed in Oct.) (760) 924-7700.

Side Door Café – European fare – crepes, fondue, tapas, sandwiches, and salads. Mon-Fri 11am-9pm, Fri/Sat/Sun 9am-9pm. Bar until 1am. Happy Hour daily 5-7:30pm. (Closes for few weeks in autumn.) (760) 934-5200. www.sidedoormammoth.com.

Lakanuki & Tiki Bar – Serves soups, salads, grilled sandwiches, burgers, and tacos. Mon-Thurs 3-10pm, Fri/Sat/Sun noon-10pm. Bar until 1:30am. Happy Hour 3-6pm. DJs Wed/Thurs/Fri/Sat from 10pm. (760) 934-7447. www.lakanuki.net.

Old New York Deli & Bagel Co. – Menu includes, omelets, sandwiches, burgers, soups, homemade bread, pastries, and bagels. 6am-7pm, Fri/Sat 8pm. (760) 934-3354.

DIRECTIONS – Mammoth Village

From the Mammoth Lakes Welcome Center (details under Information), follow Main Street (Hwy 203) to the intersection (stoplight) where a right turn on Minaret Road leads to a parking area across the street from Mammoth Village. To reach Mammoth Mountain (the main ski area) from the village, continue on Minaret Road 3 miles.

SUMMER FUN

SWIMMING

Outdoor six-lane Whitmore Pool (and wading pool) – hot showers and restrooms available. Call for days of closure and hours; subject to change. Open mid-May to early Sept. (760) 935-4222. Located off Hwy 395, 10 miles south of the entrance road to Mammoth Lakes (Hwy 203). Take Benton Crossing Road, and turn left at the green church.

MAMMOTH CREEK PARK

This children's park has a play area, restrooms, and picnic tables. Open in mild weather. Information – Mon-Fri, 8am-12pm and 1-5pm (760) 934-8989 ext. 222. From the Visitor Center drive ahead to the first stoplight, and turn left onto Old Mammoth Road. Proceed through two stoplights, and continue .25 mile. Park is on the right.

SUMMER GONDOLA RIDES

Views from the top of the mountain are spectacular. The **Top of the Sierra Interpretive Center** located here provides the history of Mammoth Lakes and lends the best view of the surrounding mountain peaks. The **Top of the Sierra Food Court** is also found here. Food Court – 10am-3pm. Gondola rides 9am-4:30pm. (Closes for 2 months, mid-Sept to mid-Nov.) Fares change seasonally (2 kids age 7-12 may ride free with an adult.) Admission to Top of the Sierra Interpretive Center is included in the price. **Note:** Take the elevator from Woollywood (kids' ski lesson area in winter) called Adventure

Center in summer, from the lower level to reach upper level and entrance to Gondola rides. Wheelchair accessible rides, details under Appendix. Information (760) 934-2571. Located at Mammoth Mountain ski slopes. From Mammoth Lakes Welcome Center follow Main Street to Minaret Road (stoplight) and turn right. Passing the Mammoth Village, continue 3 miles to the end of the road. Mammoth Mountain is on the left side of the road.

WINTER FUN

MAMMOTH MOUNTAIN – (11,053 feet)

There's great skiing and snowboarding during the nice long season, usually from Oct/Nov to late May or June. 8:30am–4pm. Ski/Snowboard rentals and lessons. Private lessons (760) 934-0684. Visit the McCoy Station Food Court by taking the Broadway Express Chair Lift. 10am-3pm. Top of the Sierra Food Court is located at the top of the mountain via the gondola. Ski lift tickets include gondola rides. (Summer gondola rides, details under Summer Fun.) Shuttle buses run from many lodgings to this area. **Note:** Wheelchair accessible activities, details under Appendix. (760) 934-2571. (800) mammoth. www.mammothmountain.com. Snow Report (760) 934-6166. From the Mammoth Lakes Welcome Center follow Main Street to Minaret Road (stoplight) and turn right. After passing by Mammoth Village, continue 3 miles to the end of the road. Mammoth Mountain is on the left side of the road.

CROSS-COUNTRY SKIING

Groomed trails are located behind the Mammoth Lakes Welcome Center (details under Information) and at the Tamarack Lodge where there are 19 miles of groomed trails. (Details under Lodging, Tamarack Lodge.)

MAMMOTH ICE RINK – outdoor ice skating

Ice skating, lessons, and skate rentals. Daily public hours vary, call ahead. Saturday hours are usually 11:30am-9pm. (Closes for half an hour to clean ice at 2, 5, and 8pm) Extended Holiday hours. Open Dec thru Feb. (Depends upon weather.) Adults $7.50 (16 and older.) Youth $5.50 (Under 16.) Under 4, free. (760) 934-2505. www.mammothicerink.com. From the Mammoth Lakes Welcome Center, continue ahead on Main Street to the stoplight and turn left on Old Mammoth Road. Travel out to the stoplight at Meridian Boulevard and turn left. Turn left on Sierra Park Road; the ice rink is behind the library.

MAMMOTH DOG TEAMS

Dog sledding in winter snow. Day or overnight tours. Call or check website for directions. Reservations (760) 914-1019. www.mammothdogteams.com.

MAMMOTH LAKES INFORMATION

Mammoth Lakes Tourism – Lodging and winter ski lift tickets (888) 466-2666.

Mammoth Lakes Welcome Center & Ranger Station – Maps and information on weather, trails, fall color, winter skiing/ice skating, lodging, restaurants, and festivities like the 4th of July celebration and the Jazz Festival in July. Daily

8am-5pm. (760) 924-5500. www.visitmammoth.com. Located 2.5 miles from Hwy 395, via Hwy 203, just prior to town.

Mammoth Lakes Chamber of Commerce – Mon-Fri 9am-5pm. 2520 Main Street. (760) 934-6717. www. mammothlakeschamber.org.

Cal Trans – Road conditions. (800) 427-ROAD.

Wheelchair Accessible Activities – (Details under Appendix.)

Gondola Rides – (Details under Summer Fun.)

Mammoth Mountain – Winter skiing and snowboarding. Rentals and lessons. (760) 934-2571. (800) Mammoth. (Directions/Information under Winter Fun.)

Mammoth Mountaineering – Rentals, cross-country skis and snowshoes. 8am-8pm. (760) 934-4191. Located at 3189 Main Street.

Mammoth Outdoor Sports – Summer bicycle rentals. Winter downhill skis and snowboards (rentals/sales). 8am-8pm, Fri/Sat 9pm. (760) 934-3239. Corner of 452 Old Mammoth Road and Meridian.

Weddings – www.MammothMountain.com/sales/weddings

Boat Rentals/General Store – The Pokonobe Resort – boat rentals (7:15am-5:30pm) and a general store with fishing licenses and gear. They also offer a scenic place for weddings and family gatherings. (760) 934-2437. www.pokonoberesort. com. Located at the northern end of Lake Mary.

Boat Rentals – Woods Lodge – (760) 934-2261. Found along Lake George's shoreline. (Directions under Lake George.)

Boat Rentals – Summers at Mamie Lake. 8am-5pm. Information – (760) 924-5500.

Sierra Star Golf Course – 18 holes, par 71. **Chip Shot Café** serves salads and sandwiches on a nice outdoor patio. (760) 924-4653. Off Meridian Boulevard.

Snowcreek Golf Course – 9 holes, par 35. (760) 934-6633. www.snowcreekresort.com. Old Mammoth Road.

Snowcreek Athletic Club – Swimming pool, fitness center, Jacuzzis, and spa services. **Bistro East** on the premises Mon-Fri 4:30-9pm, Fri/Sat/Sun 11am-9pm. Club fee per day: $20, under 18 yrs. $13. (760) 934-8511. Old Mammoth Road and Club Drive, beyond the Snowcreek Golf Course.

Mammoth Lakes Pack Outfit – Horseback riding and hiking trips. Summer 8am-4pm. (760) 934-2434. www.mammothpack.com.

Reds Meadow Pack Station – Horseback riding and fishing trips. Summer 7am-7pm. (760) 934-2345. (800) 292-7758. www.redsmeadow.com.

Mammoth-Yosemite Airport – Information – 8am-4:30pm. (760) 934-3825. Horizon Airlines (part of Alaska Airlines) (800) 252-7522. www.alaskaairlines.com. Flights from Los Angeles International Airport to Mammoth Lakes. Flights from mid-Dec to mid-April and one daily flight in summer. **Enterprise Car Rental**, at the airport (760) 924-1094. Airport is located off Hwy 395, 2.7 miles south of the entrance road to Mammoth Lakes (Hwy 203).

EATERIES
Note: Details under Mammoth Village for other eateries.

Chart House – Fine dining offers seafood and steaks.

Dinner 4:30-9:30pm, Fri/Sat 10pm. Happy Hour 4:30-7pm. (Closed Mon in summer.) (760) 934-4526. Located at 106 Old Mammoth Road.

Roberto's Café – Mexican fare 11am-9pm. (760) 934-3667. Located at 271 Old Mammoth Road.

Giovannis – Serves pasta, pizza, and salad. Open11:30am-9pm. Delivery available after 5pm. (760) 934-7563. Located at 437 Old Mammoth Road, in the Vons Shopping Center.

The Stove – Breakfast/Lunch 6:30am-2pm. Dinner 5-9pm. (Spring and fall open Thurs-Sun.) Call ahead hours vary. (760) 934-2821. Located at 644 Old Mammoth Road.

Breakfast Club – Breakfast 6:30am-1pm. (760) 934-6944. Located at 2987 Main Street.

Shea Schat's Bakkery & Café – Serves pastries/breads baked daily. Sandwiches 9am-3pm. Open 6am-6pm, Sat/Sun 7pm. (Closed Christmas.) (760) 934-6055. Located at 3305 Main Street.

Perrys Italian Café – B,L,D – Summer (begins June 15th) 6:30-9pm; rest of the year 11:30am-9pm. (760) 934-6521. Located at 3399 Main Street.

Mountainside Grill – California cuisine and wine with a great view of the mountain. Breakfast 7am-10am. Lunch 11am-3pm. Dinner 5pm-9pm. (760) 934-0601. Found in the Mammoth Mountain Inn. (Directions under Mammoth Mountain.)

The Yodler Restaurant – Nachos, burgers, tacos, and pizza from 11am-5pm, bar until 10pm. (Closed some weeks in May and Oct.) (760) 934-0636. Adjacent to the Mammoth Mountain Inn, across the road from the Mammoth Mountain ski slopes.

Lakefront Restaurant – Fine California/French dining at the Tamarack Lodge. Lunch served Sat/Sun summer to Labor Day 11am-2pm. Dinner 5:30pm-9:30pm. Reservations required. At the full bar (in winter) soups, chili, and snacks are served. Bar 11am-9pm. (Closed few weeks in spring and in autumn.) (760) 934-2442. (Directions under Twin Lakes.)

LODGING

Lodging Information – Mammoth Lakes Welcome Center – (760) 924-5500. www.visitmammoth.com and www.mammothres.com.

Camping reservations – (877) 444-6777 (8am-9pm PST). www.recreation.gov (24 hrs).

Inyo National Forest Camping – Devil's Post Pile & Reds Meadow (877) 444-6777 (8am-9pm). www.recreation.gov

Coldwater, Twin Lakes (wheelchair accessible), & Lake Mary (very popular) Campgrounds – There are a few first-come, first-served sites. Reservations – (877) 444-6777 (8am-9pm). www.recreation.gov

Mammoth Mountain RV Park – Reservations (760) 934-3822. www.mammothrv.com. Located across from the Mammoth Lakes Welcome Center & Ranger Station.

Adventure in Camping – Rental trailers delivered in summer to campsites at Mammoth Lakes. (760) 935-4890. www.adventureincamping.com.

Mammoth Creek Inn – Nice rooms with refrigerators and Wi-Fi; some have kitchens. Outdoor Jacuzzi. Dogs okay in some rooms. Free airport shuttle. (760) 934-6162. (866) 466-7000. www.mammothcreekinn.com. 96 Meadow Lane, off Old Mammoth Road.

Snowcreek Resort – Condos with kitchens. Wi-Fi. Book directly with the resort, and the use of the Snowcreek Athletic Club (swimming pool and fitness center) is included. Resort fee: 5 percent of total room bill, which includes free airport taxi service. Dogs okay in some units. (760) 934-3333. (800) 544-6007. www.snowcreekresort. com. 1254 Old Mammoth Road.

Shilo Inn – Rooms have Wi-Fi and come with continental breakfast. Indoor pool and spa. Dogs okay. (760) 934-4500. (800) 222-2244. www.shiloinns.com. 2963 Main Street, next to McDonalds.

Best Western – Amenities include Wi-Fi, an indoor pool/spa, exercise room, and a full breakfast buffet. On the premises is **Café 203** with American and Indian cuisine. 5-9pm, bar until 11pm. (760) 924-1234. (866) 924-1234. www.bestwestern. com. 3236 Main Street, next to the fire station.

Motel 6 – Affordable rooms with pay Wi-Fi. Summer heated pool. Dogs stay free. (760) 934-6660. (800) 466-8356. www. motel6.com. 3372 Main Street, .25 mile from the Best Western.

Sierra Lodge – All rooms with kitchenettes and Wi-Fi. Continental breakfast. Outdoor Jacuzzi. Dogs okay in some rooms. (760) 934-8881. (800) 356-5711. www.sierralodge. com. 3540 Main Street.

Village Lodge – Condos (studio to three bedrooms) with kitchens, gas fireplaces, and Wi-Fi. Each building has a heated pool, hot tub, and fitness center. Ski/Snowboard rentals. A $20 per night resort fee is charged which gives use of Wi-Fi and the airport shuttle. (760) 934-1982. (800) mammoth. www. mammothmountain.com. Located in Mammoth Village, near the gondola.

Westin Monache Resort – Suites with mountain views, gas fireplaces, and kitchens. Heated outdoor pool, two Jacuzzis, fitness center, and ski rentals. **White Bark Restaurant** – 7am-10pm. Weddings. A $25 per night resort fee is charged which gives use of Wi-Fi and the airport shuttle. Close to Mammoth Village. (760) 934-0400. (888) 627-8154. www.westinmonacheresort.com. 50 Hillside Drive. On Main Street, continue straight ahead at stoplight (intersection with Minaret Road) and turn right on Canyon Blvd, then turn left on Hillside Drive.

Tamarack Lodge Resort – Rooms in the main log-building (some have shared bathrooms) and cabins (kitchens and either gas fireplace or wood-burning stove) along the shore of Twin Lakes. No TVs. A $20 per night resort fee is charged which gives use of Wi-Fi, storage of skis, and includes a continental breakfast and the airport shuttle. Dogs okay in summer cabins. Winter cross-country skiing and snowshoeing from the resort. (Rentals at the Lodge) Guests may use the pool and Jacuzzis at the Mammoth Mountain Inn. **Lakefront Restaurant** on the premises. (Details under Dining.) (760) 934-2442. (800) mammoth. www.tamaracklodge.com. Lake Mary Road at Twin Lakes. (Directions under Lakes of Mammoth, Twin Lakes.)

Crystal Crag Lodge – Summer (mid-May to mid-Oct) rustic cabins – some with views of Lake Mary. Fully-equipped kitchens and fireplaces. Dogs okay. (760) 934-2436. www.crystalcrag.com. Across the road from Lake Mary.

Woods Lodge – Summer (June to Oct) cabins – some with lake views. Cabins come with full kitchens, and a woodstove or fireplace. No credit cards accepted. Dogs okay in some cabins. Boat rentals for trout fishing. (760) 934-2261 www.mammothweb.com. Found along Lake George's shoreline; directions under Lake George.

Wildyrie Lodge – Lakeview summer cabins (June to Oct) with full kitchens, and lodge rooms with continental breakfast. No credit cards accepted. Boat rentals for trout fishing. (760) 934-2444. www.mammothweb.com. Facing Lake Mamie; .75 mile from Lake Mary.

Mammoth Mountain Inn – Rooms, condos, and suites. Amenities: Outdoor heated pool/hot tub, three indoor Jacuzzis, and ski/snowboard rentals. A $20 per night resort fee is charged which gives use of Wi-Fi, the fitness center, and the airport shuttle. **Mountainside Grill** is inside the inn and the **Yodler Restaurant** is adjacent to the inn. (Details under Dining.) (760) 934-2581. (800) 626-6684. www.MammothMountain.com. 1 Minaret Road. (See directions for Mammoth Mountain; the inn lies across the road from the ski slopes.)

DIRECTIONS – Mammoth Lakes

From Hwy 395, follow the Mammoth Lakes exit (Hwy 203). Travel 2.5 miles to the Mammoth Lakes Welcome Center (prior to entering the town); here Hwy 203 becomes Main Street. At the first stoplight, a left turn leads out Old Mammoth Road to restaurants, rental condos, and golf courses. Following Main Street ahead leads to restaurants and hotels, and (at stoplight) a right turn onto Minaret Road leads to the Mammoth Village (parking on right side of road). Continue on Minaret Road to reach Mammoth Mountain (main ski area). Or follow Main Street, past the stoplight at Minaret Road; it becomes Lake Mary Road leading out to the many scenic lakes. 4 miles north of Convict Lake, 14.5 miles south of the June Lake Loop. 325 miles north of Los Angeles.

JUNE LAKE LOOP – (16 miles)

Both ends of the horseshoe-shaped Hwy 158 link to Hwy 395. It's laid out like a necklace, displaying precious deep blue lakes that glisten like jewels. Summer brings the opportunity for swimming, trout fishing, boating, and horseback riding. (Details under Information.) Autumn is the best time for viewing brightly colored leaves, and to hear the whisper of the lemon-yellow aspens. In most winters, snowboarding and skiing on June Mountain, along with nearby snowmobiling, and dog sledding. (Details for dog sledding under June Lake Information. Mammoth Ranger Station (760) 924-5500 www.visitjune.com.

JUNE LAKE

This gorgeous mountain lake is surrounded by trees, campgrounds, boat marinas, and the village of June Lake. Get the best view of the lake from the public swimming beach at the **Oh! Ridge Campground** on the eastern side of the lake. The view from the beach encompasses the entire length of the lake where the nearby mountains (capped in snow most of the year) are mirrored upon the water bearing an awe-inspiring sight. The nice sandy beach is perfect for sun worshipers and the roped off area of the lake separates swimmers from the fishermen's boats. Close to the beach are restrooms and a general store. (Details under Lodging.) The lake is loaded with trout. From the southern junction of Hwy 158 with Hwy 395 take the loop drive .6 mile to a right turn on North Shore Drive, and continue to a left turn signed *Oh Ridge Campground*.

JUNE LAKE VILLAGE

This small charming village has shops, galleries, and restaurants, and is within walking distance to June Lake. To reach the village from Hwy 395, take Hwy 158 (southern end of the Hwy 158 loop) and travel beyond North Shore Drive (.6 mile) where glimpses of June Lake are caught through the aspens before entering the village. (Details for restaurants under Eateries and details for nearby June Lake Marina under Information.)

GULL LAKE

Photographers will love this lake; it's just stunning. Fishing boats, paddle boats, canoes, and kayaks can be rented from the tackle shop. The lake is stocked with trout. (760) 648-7539. www.gulllakemarina.net. Just beyond the June Lake Village make a right-hand turn signed *Gull Lake*. When the road ends, turn left to Gull Lake Park, and then turn left to reach the Gull Lake Marina.

JUNE MOUNTAIN

The mountain has 80 percent beginners or intermediate runs for skiing and snowboarding. There's a cafeteria and a sundeck; ski rentals, lessons, and lockers are available. Slopes open 8am-4pm. Snow Report (760) 934-2224. June Mountain (760) 648-7733 or (888) 586-3686. www.junemountain.com. Located 3.7 miles from Hwy 395.

SILVER LAKE

In autumn, masses of buttery-yellow leaves atop the white-bark aspens glow in the sunshine; their colors stand out against the blue of the sky and lake. (Colors usually peak in early October.) The trees border the road and the lake like a painted picture; their soft jingling is heard with the tiniest breeze. A short narrow path meanders beneath a canopy of yellow leaves to the edge of the lake where a few secluded picnic tables are found; a perfect place for a romantic lunch or a picnic with the kids. From here, the paved path continues, but soon it becomes soft and hugs the glimmering blue lake where small boats cruise around tiny pine tree-covered islands. The path begins from the south end of the parking area. From here looking north across the road, the tremendous Horsetail Fall is visible as it rushes down the mountainside. Silver Lake Resort & RV Park – café, store, cabins, and boat rentals. (Details under Information.) The lake is stocked with trout. Silver Lake is located 2.5 miles, beyond the June Lake Mountain ski area, and 6.2 miles from Hwy 395. (Café and cabins .5 mile north of the lake's parking area.)

GRANT LAKE

Three miles from the Silver Lake Resort, the shallow end of Grant Lake appears. In some years, this end is completely dried up. The long lake usually stretches along the road for nearly two miles. At the deep end of the lake, the Grant Lake Marina is found in a dismal barren landscape. (Details for Grant Lake Marina under Information.) Boat launching and waterskiing (after 10am). The lake is stocked with trout. (760) 648-7964. www.junelakechamber. org. From Grant Lake, it's 6.5 miles to the northern end of the loop road and the junction with Hwy 395.

INFORMATION

June Lake Loop Chamber of Commerce – Currently no phone. **Information** – www.junelakechamber.org. P.O. Box 2, June Lake, CA 93529

Note: The following marinas are open during the fishing season from the last Saturday in April to November 15.

June Lake Marina – Fishing boat rentals, bait/tackle, and boat launching 6am-7pm. It's close to the June Lake swimming beach and windsailing area. (760) 648-7726. www. junelakemarina.net. From the Village of June Lake, turn right on Knoll Street, and in two blocks turn right on Brenner. Continue down to the lake.

Big Rock Resort Marina – Summer boat rentals (including paddle boats and kayaks) and boat launching on June Lake. 7am-7pm. Cabins open all year. Dogs okay in some cabins. (Details under Lodging.) (760) 648-7717. (800) 769-9831. www.bigrockresort.net.

Gull Lake Marina – Fishing boat rentals, pontoon boats, canoes and a tackle shop are available. 6am-7pm. (760) 648-7539. www.gulllakemarina.net. Just beyond the Village of June Lake, a right-hand turn signed *Gull Lake* leads down to the lake.

Silver Lake Resort & RV Park – Boat rentals – motor boats, canoes, kayaks, general store, café and cabins. 7am-7pm. (Details under Lodging.) (760) 648-7525. www.silverlakeresort.net. Directions under Silver Lake.

Grant Lake Marina – Boat launching and rentals. Waterskiing (after 10am). Campgrounds. (No electricity.) (760) 648-7964. www.junelakechamber.org. Directions under Grant Lake.

Mammoth Dog Teams – Dog sledding in winter snow. Day or overnight tours. Call or check website for directions. Reservations (760) 914-1019. www.mammothdogteams.com.

Frontier Pack Station – Equestrian and hiking trips to picturesque spots where wild mustangs roam. (888) 437-mule. www.frontierpackstation.com.

EATERIES

June Lake Junction Shell Gasoline & Food Mart – B,L – Picnic items and fresh baked pastries/breads, ice cream, and sliced meats in the deli. 6am-8pm. Winter 6pm. (760) 648-7509. Southern junction of Hwy 395 and Hwy 158.

The Tiger Bar & Café – B,L,D – Country food – burgers, steaks, and Mexican specialties. CD jukebox. Open 8am-9:30pm. Bar open until midnight. (760) 648-7551. Located in the center of June Lake Village.

Carson Peak Inn – Dinner – steak, seafood, ribs, homemade soups, and beer/wine. 5pm-9pm, Fri/Sat 10pm. (760) 648-7575. Hwy 158, 2.5 miles from June Lake Village.

Eagle's Landing Restaurant – B,L,D Dinner – pasta, chicken, steak, ribs, and seafood. 7:30am-9pm. Bar open until 10pm. (760) 648-7004 ext. 3. Located in Double Eagle Resort. (Details under Lodging.)

LODGING

Oh! Ridge Campground – Close to a nice swimming beach on June Lake.

June Lake Campground – Close to June Lake Village.

Silver Lake Resort & RV Park – Reservations (760) 648-7525. Located at Silver Lake.

Camping reservations – (877) 444-6777 (8am-9pm PST). www.recreation.gov **(24 hrs.)** Located along the June Lake shoreline.

Rainbow Ridge Reservations – Condominiums/cabins with kitchens, fireplaces, hot tubs, and views of the lakes. 9am-5pm. (800) 462-5589. www.rainbowridgereservations.com.

Big Rock Resort Marina – Lakeside cabins with kitchens and Wi-Fi. Summer boat rentals (including paddle boats and kayaks) on June Lake. Cabins open all year. Dogs okay in some cabins. (760) 648-7717. (800) 769-9831. www.bigrockresort.net. From Hwy 158 (prior to entering Village of June Lake), turn into the driveway next to the fire station.

The Haven – Rooms and cottages with kitchens and Wi-Fi. Enclosed spa. Lake views from the outdoor deck. (760) 648-7524. (800) 648-7524. www.junelakehaven.com. In June Lake Village, one block from the June Lake Marina.

Whispering Pines – Cabins with kitchens. WiFi. Indoor spa. (760) 648-7762. (800) 648-7762. www.junelake.com. Hwy 158, 2.5 miles from Village of June Lake.

Double Eagle Resort & Spa – This resort is not on the lake but lies in a wondrous natural setting with cascading streams and towering pine trees. Near the entrance (off in the distance) is a view of Horsetail Falls. The rooms come with spa tubs, fireplaces, and Wi-Fi. The two-bedroom cabins come with Wi-Fi, kitchens, and fireplaces. Dogs okay in some rooms and cabins. The fitness center and spa include a sixty foot indoor pool. Creekside Spa – 7am-9pm. There are three different wedding sites on the premises, and also the Eagle's Landing Restaurant. (Details under Eateries.) (760) 648-7004. Hwy 158, 3 miles from the Village of June Lake, 1.6 miles from the June Lake Mountain ski area. www.doubleeagleresort.com.

Silver Lake Resort & RV Park – Cabins with kitchens among the aspens. (Across the road from Silver Lake) No dogs in cabins. Boat rentals – motor boats, canoes, and kayaks. There's a duck/trout pond, a general store and a café with breakfast and lunch. 7am-2pm. Open last Saturday in April to Oct 15. (760) 648-7525. www.silverlakeresort.net. From Mammoth Lakes, take Hwy 395 north, exit Hwy 158, travel past June Lake and Gull Lake, and continue 3 miles beyond the June Lake Mountain ski area to the end of Silver Lake.

DIRECTIONS – June Lake Loop (two entrances)

The Southern June Lake Loop Entrance, off Hwy 395, is 14.5 miles north of the Mammoth Lakes main entrance.

Here, a left turn onto Hwy 158 leads 2 miles into tiny June Lake Village and the June Mountain ski area. The Northern June Lake Loop Entrance is off Hwy 395, 6 miles beyond the southern loop entrance. The northern loop entrance is 5 miles south of Lee Vining and Mono Lake. (Details for the town under Lee Vining.)

MONO LAKE

The amazing ancient alkali/salty lake presents itself as if in a scene from another world. The immense amount of alkaline and salt in the lake (about 2.5 times more salty than the ocean) spill upon the jagged shoreline like pure-white sand. Mystical tufa formations were all created under water but, as the water level declined, some were left standing along the shore like a forest of crystal-white towers. Some of them are twenty-feet tall, each with a very unique shape. Tufa is formed when the salty water meets underground fresh water springs creating calcium carbonate (limestone). Atop the tufa formations there is an osprey nest.

The lake's many hues of blue and green change according to the seasons. Green shades are prevalent in spring when the lake is full of algae, which the tiny brine shrimp feed on. Millions of migratory birds like yellow warblers, sage thrashers, egrets, herons, snowy plovers, swallows, woodpeckers, and owls come to feed on the shrimp and insects. The ospreys nest here, but travel to the nearby fresh water lakes to capture fish and bring them back to Mono Lake. Small islands loom out in the lake, providing safe nesting grounds for the California gulls, while other birds nest in nearby trees or in the tufa towers. In winter, the islands and tufa are brushed with snow and fog is swirling all around the lake, creating an unforgettable supernatural look. For a close-up look at the tufa, see the South Tufa Nature Trail listed below. Bring a camera. Information – (760) 647-6595 or (760) 647-3044. www.monolake.org.

SOUTH TUFA NATURE TRAIL/NAVY BEACH

The easy lakeside walk among the amazing tufa is one never to be forgotten. The white spindly towers come in all shapes and sizes. At the edge of the lake, many tufas rise up and cast their reflections into the water. A paved path (partially compacted gravel) begins at the kiosk near the parking area and leads to the boardwalk at the lake. Wheelchair/stroller accessible. **Note:** The path among the tufa is not wheelchair accessible. Self-guided tours. Entrance fee – $3 per person, under 16 free. In summer, daily Tufa-guided tours; call for current times. No extra charge after entrance fee is paid. Meet at the entrance kiosk at South Tufa. Information and Sunset Tours – Lee Vining Chamber of Commerce (760) 647-6595.

For a buoyant swimming experience in the salty water, visit nearby Navy Beach. The beach is compacted gravel. Wheelchair/stroller accessible. **Note:** To wash off the salt, showers are available in nearby Lee Vining at the RV parks or bring your own fresh water. Walk the short (15 minute) trail from South Tufa to Navy Beach or park at Navy Beach. (Limited parking at Navy Beach.) Arrange for canoe tours from Navy Beach: summer weekends. $25. (No children under age 4.) Life jackets are provided. (760) 647-6595 or (760) 647-3044. www.monolake.org. From the northern end of the June Lake Loop turn right (south) and in .4 mile turn left on Hwy 120 east. From Lee Vining, take Hwy 395 about 5 miles south, and turn left (east) on Hwy 120. Continue 6 miles on Hwy 120 to a junction; bear to the left to reach South Tufa, and to the right for Navy Beach. Follow the short dirt roads to the lake.

LEE VINING – at Mono Lake

The town overlooks astounding Mono Lake. There's a sprinkling of restaurants and lodgings, as well as gift shops and a market. Half a mile south of town, Hwy 120 (right turn) leads west 12 miles on a winding narrow mountain road to Yosemite National Park's Tioga Pass summer entrance.

LEE VINING CREEK TRAIL

The trail meanders along the roaring creek and climbs up to the visitor center north of town. Trail: Easy 1.5 mile one way. Information – Lee Vining Chamber of Commerce found in the center of town. (760) 647-6595. Trailhead (marked with small trail sign) is found across the road from the Lakeview Lodge.

MONO LAKE TRAIL

The trail runs between the Old Marina at Mono Lake and the Mono Basin National Forest Scenic Area Visitor Center (details under Information). Long ago, when the water level of the lake was higher, boats were launched from the Old Marina. Now there is a (wheelchair/stroller accessible) boardwalk where views of the lake are phenomenal. Trail: Moderately-steep 1.2 mile trail to the visitor center. To reach the Old Marina travel approximately 1 mile north of town; look for a sign (*Old Marina*) and turn right. Then continue to the lake and the parking area.

MONO COUNTY PARK

A fine view of the tufa and Mono Lake is found from the park's small boardwalk. Nearby is a children's grassy play area under tall shade trees. Easy .25 mile to the boardwalk. Wheelchair/stroller accessible. From Hwy 395, 5 miles north of Lee Vining, turn right on Cemetery Road.

INFORMATION

Lee Vining Chamber of Commerce & Mono Lake Information Center – Gifts, books, Ansel Adams art gallery, and information on lodging and Mono Lake. Summer 7am-9pm, after Labor Day Mon-Fri 9am-7pm. (Closed Thanksgiving, Christmas, and New Year's Day.) **Note:** Closes for a couple of days at Christmas time. (760) 647-6629 or (760) 647-6595. www.leevining.com. Corner of Hwy 395 and Third Street.

Mono Lake Committee – Same hours as Chamber of Commerce. (760) 647-6595. www.visitmonolake.org.

Mono Basin National Forest Scenic Area Visitor Center – Fabulous view of Mono Lake (covering over 70 sq. miles) from the back patio. Information, books, maps, displays, restrooms, and road conditions. Opens April – mid-May. (Depends on snow.) 9am-4:30pm. (Closed Tues/Wed.) From mid-May thru mid-Oct open daily 8am-5pm. Mid-Oct thru Nov open 9am-4:30pm. (Closed Tues/Weds.) The visitor center is closed Dec to mid-April or May. (760) 647-3044. www.fs.usda.gov/inyo. Hwy 395, half mile north of Lee Vining.

Wheelchair Accessible Activities – (Details under Appendix.)

EATERIES

Nicely's Restaurant – Country-American food. Summer daily 6am-9pm. Winter 7am-8pm. (Closed Tues/Wed.) (760) 647-6477. Hwy 395, center of town.

Bodie Mike's Barbeque – Summer barbeques. 11:30am-10pm. (Closed last Sun in Sept until late spring.) (760) 647-6432. Hwy 395, center of town.

LODGING

Lakeview Lodge – Motel rooms and cabins with Wi-Fi; some have refrigerator/microwave and others have a full kitchen. Nice grounds with flowers and trees. (760) 647-6543. (800) 990-6614. www.lakeviewlodgeyosemite.com. Hwy 395, southern end of town.

Yosemite Gateway Motel – Perched up above the lake; there's a lake view from every room and Wi-Fi. **Note:** Some rooms have only showers. (760) 647-6467. (800) 282-3929. www.yosemitegatewaymotel.com. Hwy 395, center of town.

Murphey's Motel – Rooms come with Wi-Fi; some have kitchens. Small dogs okay. (760) 647-6316. (800) 334-6316. www.murpheysyosemite.com. Hwy 395, mid-town.

Tioga Lodge – Peaceful cabins overlook Mono Lake. Wi-Fi. No TV or telephones. Hannon Station Restaurant and Saloon on the premises with indoor and outdoor dining. (See menu on website.) Open mid-May to Oct. (760) 647-6423. www.tiogalodgeatmonolake.com. Hwy 395, 2.5 miles north of town.

DIRECTIONS – Mono Lake & Lee Vining

Off Hwy 395, 5 miles north of the Northern June Lake Loop Entrance, 11 miles from the Southern June Lake Loop Entrance, 7 miles south of the Lundy Lake entrance road, 18 miles south of the Bodie State Park entrance road.

Note: One-half mile south of Lee Vining, Hwy 120 leads 12 miles to Yosemite National Park's Tioga Pass East Summer Park Entrance. (Mobile gas station/café near corner of Hwy 120.) Tioga Road (Hwy 120) open late May/June to late Oct (depending upon snow). 350 miles north of Los Angeles.

1.4 DAY TRIPS NORTH OF MONO LAKE
Lundy Lake, Bodie State Historic Park, Bridgeport, Twin Lakes
What To Do & See

LUNDY LAKE

It's a great place for hiking, fishing, boating, and camping.

LUNDY CANYON FALLS TRAIL

In autumn, shimmering aspens put on a vibrant sunny-yellow show and beavers come out at twilight to work on their dams. The 5-mile paved road out to tiny Lundy Resort is lined with pine trees interlaced with aspens. Adding to the photogenic scene, huge snowy clumps are visible adhering to the nearby mountain tops. At 3.7 miles, the dam at the lower end of Lundy Lake comes into view. The scenery along this road is quite a lovely sight, especially where the mountains reflect down into the water. At the end of the lake is Lundy Lake Resort. (Details for lake under Market/Lodging.) Here the road narrows, becomes gravel, and is bordered by aspens twinkling in the breeze. In .4 mile a tiny stream crosses the dirt road, and then a beaver pond comes into view. The beavers have cut down a lot of trees and built two lodges in the pond. In about a mile, there's a marshy picturesque area with tall reeds and grasses. Beyond this is a split in the road. Turn left or right around this loop which forms the end of the road. Half way around the loop road, the signed trailhead, parking area, and picnic tables are found.

A slim path meanders between the tall brush with gentle ups and downs. It then slips among hundreds of aspens. Follow the path to a junction; continue ahead beyond the fallen tree and huge rock (nearly blocking the path). The huge dam, 30 yards farther up the trail, along the south end of the pond, was built by beavers. Return to the trail junction and take the narrow path (now it's to the left) signed *Welcome to Lundy Canyon*. Continue along the side of the pond, and soon the path climbs up a very rocky hillside making some sharp twists and turns. At the top of the hill, the path levels out on a rocky ledge with a splendid view of the Lundy Canyon Falls off in the distance. The falls dwindle by late July, but are still in motion even in September. No shade is found along this area, and the temperature seems much warmer than it is. This is a good place for the less-than-hardy to turn around. The path descends down the rocky hillside to the base of the falls, and continues on to other waterfalls and Lake Helen. Bring lots of water. Dogs okay. Waterfalls are best viewed in June; in late Sept/Oct the aspens come to life with their yellow glow. (Closed in winter.) Information – Mono Basin National Forest Scenic Area Visitor Center (760) 647-3044. (Details under Lee Vining Information.) Trail: Easy .5 mile one way. (Moderately-strenuous climb near end of the half mile.)

MARKET/LODGING

Lundy Lake Resort – The resort consists of an RV park, tent camping, boat rentals, and a general store where pretty light green hops (used in making beer) hang from vines around the front door. June to late September. Information – (626) 309-0415. Leave a message and they will return the call. The resort is 5 miles from Hwy 395.

DIRECTIONS – Lundy Lake

From Hwy 395, 6 miles north of the Mono Basin National Forest Scenic Area Visitor Center (details under Lee Vining Information) take paved Lundy Lake Road (on left side of Hwy 395). Continue 5 miles to the Lundy Lakes General Store. To reach the Lundy Canyon Falls trailhead, proceed 1.5 miles on the unpaved rough road to a split in the road that forms a long loop around the end of the road. Parking and trailhead are 1.5 miles on the loop road.

BODIE STATE HISTORIC PARK
BODIE GHOST TOWN

From 1877 to 1888, millions of dollars in gold and silver were mined here. A walk through the town transports visitors back in time. Walking into the museum or peering into windows of the old houses, the bank, saloons, bordellos, and the general store with everything as it was in the 1880s, lends an eerie feeling. Entrance fee: $5, under 17 $3, under 1 free. Summer 9am-6pm, fall 5pm, winter 10am-3pm. Winter roads may be impassable. Cal-Trans – Road Conditions (800) 427-7623. No food services. Dogs okay. (760) 647-6445. www.bodie.com. From Hwy 395, 18 miles north of Lee Vining turn right on Hwy 270, continue 13 miles. The last 3 miles are unpaved and closed in winter, but the hardy can ski those last 3 miles. Bodie is 6.6 miles south of Bridgeport.

BRIDGEPORT

A small town with a general store, food market, small museum, lodging, and restaurants. It serves as the gateway to the **Twin Lakes**. (Details for lakes under Twin Lakes.)

INFORMATION

Bridgeport Ranger Station & Visitor Center – End of June to Sept 15 open 8am-4:30pm. (After Sept 15, closed Sat/Sun and holidays.) (760) 932-7070. www.fs.usda.gov/htnf Hwy 395, .5 mile south of Bridgeport.

Bridgeport Chamber of Commerce – The office is open in summer and is located next to the Bridgeport Museum (listed below). No regular hours, call for information. (760) 932-7500. www.bridgeportcalifornia.com.

Bridgeport Museum – It's housed in an 1880 schoolhouse and displays artifacts of the native Paiute and the mining days. Memorial Day to end of Sept. Open Tues-Sat, 9am-4pm. Adults $2, seniors $1.50, 6-12 years $1, under 6 free. (760) 932-5281. www.monocomuseum.org. A half block north of the huge white courthouse in the center of town, turn right and proceed to the end of the street to a church. Turn left to 129 Emigrant Street. (Museum is on the left.)

EATERIES/LODGING

Virginia Creek Settlement – Log-cabin motel rooms, suites, and cabins with kitchenettes come with Wi-Fi and refrigerators. Campground, tent cabins, or sleep in a camp wagon. (See rooms on the website.) Fish cleaning and freezing. The restaurant on the premises serves Italian/American food. Kids love the pizza. 6:30am-9pm. (Closed July 4th.) Menu on website. Rooms/cabins open most of the year. (760) 932-7780. www.virginiacreeksettlement.com. Located 1 mile north of the turnoff for the Bodie Ghost Town State Park on Hwy 395 and 5 miles south of the downtown area of Bridgeport.

Bridgeport Inn – The hotel (built as a stagecoach stop in 1877) has a lovely large front porch that is the perfect place to linger and sip a drink. The hotel/motel rooms and cabins come with Wi-Fi. (Stagecoach economy rooms do not have private bathrooms.) Dogs okay in motel rooms. There's a computer and TV in the inn's parlor. Guests will receive meal coupons for use in the dining room. Dining room/bar – B,L,D – (Kids' menu.) 8am-8pm. (Closed Wed.) Hotel open mid-March to mid-Nov. (760) 932-7380. www.thebridgeportinn.com. On Hwy 395, the main street of Bridgeport.

DIRECTIONS – Bridgeport

On Hwy 395, 6.6 miles north of Bodie Ghost Town and .4 mile south of Twin Lakes Road (Hwy 420). 375 miles north of Los Angeles.

TWIN LAKES

Two enchanting lakes (with fabulous brown trout fishing) follow each other end to end. A general store is conveniently located alongside the first lake. Deer may be spotted hiding among the aspens that hug the lakes. Just beyond the second lake lies a campground and tiny **Mono Village**. (Details under Café/Lodging.) The village has boat rentals and a small café.

LAKE TRAIL & HORSETAIL TRAILS

Lake Trail offers a pleasant walk. However, it crosses a few creeks that overflow in spring and early summer; some may find it difficult to ford them. The first creek comes up quickly toward the beginning of the trail. It is narrow enough for an easy crossing over the stones. Across the creek, glimpses of the sparkling lake become visible between the tall pines. Soon hikers will encounter a short wooden post (a trail sign in summer, no sign on the post in autumn and winter). Here, the path climbs uphill to the right. Ahead, the path narrows among the aspens, and reaches a split. Follow the main path as it descends (a pipe crosses over the path) and leads to two rocky creeks side by side (in spring they may appear as one). These creeks require some difficult rock hopping to cross. Then in a short time, the wider Cattle Creek is reached and, although there is a small bridge for crossing, this is a good turning around point for the less-than-hardy. The path continues its course along the lake. Trail: Easy (except fording the creeks) 1.5 miles one way.

Horsetail Trail leads uphill and follows switchbacks higher and higher to reach the first waterfall in approximately ten minutes, and the second waterfall in another twenty-five minutes, and the third in twenty more minutes. Although it is all uphill to reach the falls, the scenery is worth the climb. Trail: Moderate (uphill climb) 2 miles one way. The trail parking area is beyond the Mono Village Café. To locate the trailheads, walk from the parking area into the Mono Village Campground and immediately turn left. Pass under a metal cable hanging across the path. Stroll down to the creek and travel over the wooden bridge; then take the path straight ahead through the brush. Continue along the path, following the small trail sign to the left among the pines. Soon the path crosses a tiny creek on a bridge of thin logs, and continues to the left uphill for about 100 feet. From here, the path veers to the left for the Lake Trail which follows the lakeshore to Cattle Creek. Look uphill to the right (beyond an old tall frame for a long gone wilderness sign) to locate the trailhead for Horsetail Trail which climbs up to three waterfalls.

INFORMATION

Bridgeport Ranger Station & Visitor Center – (760) 932-7070. (Details under Bridgeport Information.)

Twin Lakes General Store – Information, gifts, groceries, and ice cream. Alongside the first of the Twin Lakes. (760) 932-7751.

Mono Village – (760) 932-7071. www.monovillage.com. (Details under Café/Lodging.)

CAFE/LODGING

Mono Village – Café/Bar – B,L,D – Fishing boat rentals, fishing licenses, gift shop, and market are available. Wi-Fi (first ten minutes free). There's swimming, and on some Saturday nights there are concerts which are held at the beachfront. (Check website for dates.) Waterskiing (10am-3pm). Housekeeping cabins (reservations Saturday to Saturday only) and a motel. Mono Village Campground – first-come, first-served basis. Open last Saturday in April to October 31. (760) 932-7071. www.monovillage.com. Located at the end of the second lake.

DIRECTIONS – Twin Lakes

From Bridgeport travel .4 mile north, and turn left on paved Twin Lakes Road (Hwy 420). The road is surrounded by pastureland teeming with grazing cattle. The nearby mountains are capped with snow by mid-October creating a picturesque landscape. In 10 miles, the first lake is visible, and alongside it is the Twin Lakes General Store. Just beyond the second lake (13.5 miles) is Mono Village. Twin Lakes Road (Hwy 420) is located 7 miles north of Bodie State Historic Park, 51 miles north of Mammoth Lakes.

See photos of the 6 areas listed in this book at: www. CaliforniaVacationPaths.com.

Attraction prices and times listed in this guide are subject to change; call ahead. Information missing or incorrect? Contact author: Pati.Anne@yahoo.com.

KID FAVES

REGIONS OF HWY 395

Note: Details for the following activities are found under main section of Regions of Hwy 395. (See Table of Contents for page numbers.)

INDEPENDENCE

Mt. Whitney Fish Hatchery – Kids love to run around on the grass and feed the fish in the trout pond.

LONE PINE

Alabama Hills – Many western movies were filmed among the gigantic boulders. Pick up a picture-map (at the Lone Pine History Museum) of the rock formations named owl, walrus, polar bear, etc. Modern movies filmed here include Iron Man and Tremors. **Note:** Kids will also like the old-west movies shown at Lone Pine Film History Museum.

BISHOP

Keough's Hot Springs – Adults and kids love swimming in these fabulous warm enclosed mineral pools.

Bishop City Park – Kids enjoy the swimming pool and playground. There are many ducks in the nearby pond; large trees shade several picnic tables. Paths are wheelchair/stroller accessible.

Laws Museum – The young-and-old love the 1800s train, railroad depot, fire station, and the old automobiles. Wheelchair/stroller accessible.

MAMMOTH LAKES

Whitmore Pool – Toddlers and kids of all ages adore this outdoor swimming pool and wading pool.

Mammoth Creek Park – Children's play area and picnic tables.

Inyo Craters – Short trail travels through the forest and emerges at an opening with fascinating craters. (Mammoth Scenic Loop.)

Mammoth Mountain – Winter skiing and snowboarding. (Rentals/lessons.) Summer gondola rides.

JUNE LAKE LOOP

Oh Ridge Campground – There is a lovely (public) sandy swimming beach on the eastern side of June Lake.

MONO LAKE

South Tufa Nature Trail – A walk among the amazing

white tufa (limestone) towers (up to twenty feet tall) at the edge of Mono Lake is an unbelievable sight. Kids will also like the canoe trips on the lake.

BODIE STATE HISTORIC PARK

Bodie Ghost Town – This gold-mining town (built in the 1800s) lets visitors peek in windows to see things as they were long ago.

APPENDIX

REGIONS OF HWY 395

Death Valley, Mammoth Lakes, Mono Lake...

LONE PINE

Alabama Hills – Many movies and TV shows have been filmed here since the early 1920s; *Hopalong Cassidy*, *The Lone Ranger*, *Gunga Din*, *How The West Was Won*, and the *Gene Autry Show* are among them. Information available from the Lone Pine Chamber of Commerce. Mon-Fri 8:30am-4pm. (760) 876-4444. 120 S. Main Street.

DEATH VALLEY NATIONAL PARK
(3.4 million acres)

In the summer of 1913, Death Valley had the highest recorded temperature in the western hemisphere at 134 degrees Fahrenheit or 56.7 Celsius. In winter, there are freezing temperatures; the lowest recorded was 15 degrees Fahrenheit or -9 Celsius. Furnace Creek in Death Valley is the driest place in the United States. The park has little rain, and because the soil is so dry, rain water is absorbed slowly. Flash floods may occur suddenly (usually in August) like the severe one in 2004, which killed two people, destroyed buildings, and closed the park down. **Warning:** When stormy weather is predicted, do not take trails leading into the canyons (like Mosaic Canyon) where flash flooding may occur.

WARNING

Heat strokes and dehydration can kill; bring gallons of water and hike only in cooler months (Nov thru March). Although Death Valley is considered one of the world's hottest places, the leading cause of death here is not from extreme heat, but car accidents. Please obey the speed limit. Beware of poisonous rattlesnakes, scorpions, and black widow spiders that seek shade especially in rocky areas. (See flash flood warning above.)

EUREKA SAND DUNES

In an area only 3 miles long and 1 mile wide, these amazing dunes rise up 680 feet and are the tallest in California. Sometimes, when the sand is very dry, there is an unforgettable soft eerie sound present as wind blows through the shifting sand. This phenomenon is known as "singing sand." These large dunes are more difficult to reach than the smaller dune area near Stovepipe Wells, as they are farther away from paved roads. Exploring the top of the Eureka Dunes requires strenuous hiking through the dry sand, and takes about 3 hours round trip. The Eureka Dunes are located at the base of the Last Chance Mountain Range. No drinking water available. Recommended visiting time is November thru March. From Scotty's Castle it's 43 miles via dirt roads. Directions are available at Furnace Creek Visitor Center in Death Valley and Inter-Agency Visitor Center in Lone Pine on Hwy 395. (Details for Inter-Agency Visitor Center under Lone Pine.) The best route leads 50 miles from Big Pine off Hwy 395. The paved road turns to gravel 8 miles before the turnoff to the sand dunes. The turnoff road is 10 miles of rough road.

WILDLIFE

A wide variety of wildlife is found in the different sections of Death Valley, and it is illegal to feed them. The following are a few of the common ones:

COYOTES

They are found along the roads actually begging for human food because they have been fed by previous visitors. They are excellent hunters (run up to 40mph) and eat almost anything from snakes, lizards, and rabbits to nuts and grass. At night their eerie howling is heard across the desert.

CHUCKWALLA LIZARDS

These lizards look like sinister pre-historic creatures, but they are actually quite harmless. They are usually found among rock outcroppings on slopes. Males are beige or a tan tone and they can reach up to 18 inches long. Females are not quite as large as the males and are a brownish color with dark brown and red spots.

HORNED LIZARDS

These lizards are bumpy and creepy looking; they have pointed scales sticking out everywhere. They change color to match their background when threatened. This lizard may also shoot a stream of blood from its eyes up to 4 feet long.

SCORPIONS

Scorpions are feared for their venomous sting, but they are not deadly. They are nocturnal and are usually found in rocky areas.

BLACK-TAILED JACKRABBITS

These rabbits have long black-tipped ears and black tails with a white underside. They burrow in the ground during the daytime, but can be seen at night especially with a full moon.

Note: Information and photos of the above and other wildlife can be found on the following websites: www.digital-desert.com/deathvalley/wildlife and www.nps.gov/deva/planyourvisit/hours.htm.

DIRECTIONS – From Death Valley to Las Vegas

Death Valley is sometimes used as a mere path for those answering the lure of glitzy Las Vegas. To reach Las Vegas (via Death Valley) from Hwy 395 in Lone Pine turn on Hwy 136 alongside the Inter-Agency Visitor Center just south of the downtown area of Lone Pine. Hwy 136 becomes Hwy 190 just past the town of Keeler and reaches Stovepipe Wells in 80 miles. Travel ahead 7 miles, passing the Scotty's Castle Road, and continue 17 miles on Hwy 190 southeast to the Furnace Creek Visitor Center. From the Visitor Center continue beyond the Furnace Creek Inn (reached in 1 mile). Continue ahead for 29 miles to the intersection with Hwy 127 (Death Valley Junction). Travel about 100 yards, and turn left in front of the Amargosa Opera House onto State Line Road and continue until it meets Hwy 160 in Pahrump. Turn right on Hwy 160 and drive through the town of Pahrump. Travel southeast on Hwy 160 for 53 miles to meet Hwy 15 leading north (in 10 miles) into Las Vegas. **Note:** For other directions and maps, see the website www.nps.gov/deva.

DEATH VALLEY WEBSITES
www.nps.gov and www.nps.gov/deva

www.nps.gov/deva/planyourvisit
www.nps.gov/deva/planyourvisit/eureka-dunes.htm
www.nps.gov/deva/planyourvisit/lodging.htm

SCOTTY'S CASTLE
www.nps.gov/deva/historyculture/scottys-castle.htm

INDEPENDENCE

Established as a US Army Camp in 1862 for protection of the settlers against Indian hostilities, it was closed and re-established as Fort Independence in 1865. Abandoned in 1877, it became a reservation for Native Americans.

WHEELCHAIR ACCESSIBLE ACTIVITIES

Note: See Table of Contents for page numbers of activities.

Following are some of the wheelchair accessible activities found in Regions of Hwy 395.

Lone Pine:

Lone Pine Film History Museum – See old west movies.

Death Valley:

Scotty's Castle – Beautiful grounds and house tour.

Salt Creek Boardwalk – See rare tiny pupfish.

Artist Drive – Amazing colors are displayed across the landscape.

Badwater Boardwalk – The special salt crystals lend a unique sight.

Independence:

Mount Whitney Fish Hatchery – Tour the building and grounds.

Bishop:

Bishop City Park – Paved walkway and bridges along creek.

Convict Lake:

Fishing Boardwalk – Fishing season last Sat of April to Nov 15.

Mammoth Lakes:

Mammoth Mountain – Gondola Rides, seek gondola crew assistance. Top of the Sierra Interpretive Center – At the top of the mountain (via the gondola) use the elevator to get down to the exhibit/café level. Disabled Sports Eastern Sierra Program offers year-round adaptive recreation opportunities. Summer activities include: cycling, boating, hiking, horseback riding, etc. Winter activities include: downhill ski and snowboard lessons. Fee required, but they do not turn anyone away due to financial disability. Information – (760) 934-0791. www.disabledsportseasternsierra. org. **Note:** Buddy passes available. The disabled person pays full price for gondola or ski lift and their assistant rides free.

Mono Lake:

South Tufa Nature Trail – Take trail to boardwalk at Mono Lake.

Navy Beach – Buoyant salty swimming in Mono Lake.

Mono Lake Trail – Trail runs between Old Marina at Mono Lake and the visitor center.

Mono County Park – Path leads to short boardwalk.

RESOURCES/INFORMATION

Bishop Area Chamber of Commerce & Visitor Center – (760) 873-8405. www.bishopvisitor.com.

Bishop – White Mountain Ranger Station – (760) 873-2500.

Bridgeport Ranger Station & Visitor Center – (760) 932-7070. www.fs.usda.gov/htnf.

Death Valley Natural History Assoc. – (800) 478-8564. www.dvnha.org.

Death Valley – Furnace Creek Visitor Center – (760) 786-3244. www.nps.gov/deva **Note:** Additional Death Valley websites listed under Directions for Death Valley.

June Lake – www.junelakechamber.org.

Lee Vining Chamber of Commerce – (760) 647-6595. www.leevining.com.

Eastern Sierra Inter-Agency Visitor Center/Ranger Station – (760) 876-6200. www.fs.usda.gov/inyo.

Mammoth Lakes Welcome Center & Ranger Station – (760) 924-5500. www.visitmammoth.com.

Mono Lake – Mono Basin National Forest Scenic Area Visitor Center – (760) 647-3044. www.fs.usda.gov/inyo.

Seasons in the Forest

Summer's sunbeams change dull to brilliant, adding
sparkle to lakes and rivers in a showy array.
Summer's breath is jubilant, warm, and comforting
setting the stage for lazy carefree days.
By day songbirds croon melodies, by night crickets
chirp songs, while fireflies light up to simply amaze.
Spotted fawns frolic in golden meadows, while
cuddly bear cubs tumble and play.
Summer's journey ends, as breezes send a chill
through the air signaling in the new season.

Pati Anne

Book TWO

Yosemite National Park

The wonder of it all! This is where Mother Nature worked especially hard to provide the very best for all to enjoy, and where precious wildlife like bears, deer, badgers, squirrels, beaver, fox, and birds may often be observed. This serene park displays the four seasons in earnest.

In springtime, colorful wildflowers lie amid the green hues of the meadows, while the sound of streams and waterfalls, bursting with winter's melted snow, is heard from nearly every pathway. The summer sun, with its golden gilt, makes the streams and lakes sparkle and the pine trees seem greener and the sky bluer. Hiking paths lead up mountains, along rivers, creeks, and lakes, and pass by giant boulders and treasured gigantic Sequoia trees. Evenings bring out starry skies and campfire stories. Autumn's lower temperature is perfect for bike-riding and hiking. In winter, white cotton-candy snow, spun around the trees and mountains, creates awe-inspiring views and a playground for skiing, ice-skating, and snow-shoeing.

Visit each season to discover all the layers of the park. Experience the rush of skiing down a hill or the feel of the river in old swimming holes. Discover the peacefulness of riding a bicycle along rivers and over bridges where no cars travel, or hiking around the lakes, up the domes, and across the meadows. The park offers intense comfort and memorable experiences.

2.1 Yosemite Southern Park Area
What To Do & See

While temperatures soar and visitors gather in Yosemite Village, the temperatures lower and the crowds thin when climbing the nearby trails. Many of the park's attractions can be seen with minimal walking and there are hotels, restaurants, and campgrounds available. The rugged and pristine Northern Park Area is less crowded and the temperatures are cooler, but the lodging and restaurants are very limited. (Details under Northern Park Area.)

WAWONA – Southern Park Entrance

Hwy 41 becomes Wawona Road in the park and leads north past the Bridalveil Fall to Yosemite Village. (35 miles to Yosemite Village.) The park entrance lies 15 miles from Oakhurst. (Details for Oakhurst under Towns Outside Southern Entrance.) This is the closest entrance from the Los Angeles area. **Note:** Free park guide/map at all entrances. (Details for other park entrances under Northern Park Entrances.)

The following attractions are listed in sequential order beginning at the Wawona South Park Entrance and traveling to Yosemite Village and the surrounding Southern Park Areas:

MARIPOSA GROVE OF GIANT SEQUOIAS

An ancient grove of giant sequoias offer shade from summer's hot sun. These trees with rich, reddish-brown bark are the largest trees in the world in volume. (The redwoods are the tallest.) The trail amid the trees begins from the end of the parking lot (maps at trailhead) and climbs uphill beyond the Fallen Monarch Tree to the gnarled Grizzly Giant Tree (2,700 years old), and continues 50 yards further to the California Tunnel Tree. Visitors may walk through this tree, which was cut in 1895 to allow stagecoaches to pass through. From here, a road climbs .5 mile to the Faithful Couple (two trees joined together) and .25 mile further along is the Clothespin Tree. (Trees are described on the trail map.) This is the 2 mile point and, for the less-than-hardy, this may be a good place to turn around. Trail: Moderate 2 miles one way.

Beyond the Clothespin Tree, there is a descending road which forms a 2-mile loop. Along the loop lie the Mariposa Grove Museum (cabin built in 1930), Galen Clark Tree, Fallen Wawona Tunnel Tree (fell in 1969) and the Telescope Tree.

Guided accessible tram tours leave from the gift shop; cars with a handicapped placard may follow along and listen to tour narration. Tram tours. 9am-5pm. $26.50, seniors $25, kids 5-12 $19. Under 5 free. Gift shop 9am-6pm; after Labor Day 5pm. Open last 2 weekends in April and daily May thru Oct, weather permitting. (209) 375-1621. From the Wawona South Park Entrance, a right turn leads 2 miles to the Mariposa Grove parking area. When this road is closed to cars, there is a free accessible shuttle bus running (9am-4pm) from the gas station/market parking area just past the Wawona Hotel on Wawona Road (Hwy 41) 4.7 miles from the park's entrance.

WAWONA AREA

WAWONA GOLF COURSE

Challenging 9-hole course (play eighteen holes) where mule deer graze while tolerating the golfers. (Cart and club rentals.) The pro-shop and snack bar are located in front of the Wawona Hotel in the building closest to the road. (Details for hotel under Lodging.) April-Nov, weather permitting. (209) 375-6572. Located 4.5 miles from the park's South Entrance and across the road from the Wawona Hotel.

WAWONA MEADOW TRAIL

A dirt path meanders along an old fire road. It's covered with fallen leaves and long pine needles, and is bordered by forest and meadows. Many boggy side-paths lead into the meadows where, in late spring and early summer, a profusion of wildflowers bloom. June brings the beautiful azaleas into bloom, and autumn's cool air turns leaves to yellow, orange, and red creating a lovely contrast against the green forest. The path loops around a golden meadow and soon reaches Wawona Road. Carefully cross the road and follow the trail to the Wawona Hotel. (Details for hotel under Lodging.) From the hotel, walk along the hotel's entrance driveway to Wawona Road (Hwy 41). After crossing Wawona Road, follow the old narrow fire road across the golf course to the trailhead and small parking area. Trail maps are available at the Wawona Hotel or at the adjacent Visitor Center. Leashed dogs okay. Trail: Easy 3.5 mile loop. From the Wawona South Park Entrance follow Wawona Road (Hwy 41) 4.5 miles; turn left on the narrow old fire road directly across from the Wawona Hotel which crosses the golf course; the trailhead is on the left, and a small parking area is on the right. Guests of the hotel may park in the hotel's parking area and walk across Hwy 41 and the old fire road to the trailhead.

COVERED BRIDGE

The bridge, originally built in the 1800s, spans the Merced River. Guests of the hotel may walk down the path behind the Wawona Hotel to reach the bridge. Other visitors should drive north of the hotel .2 mile, and turn right alongside the gas station into the parking area. Continue ahead beyond the market to the far end of the parking area. Visitors may walk across the bridge (wheelchair/stroller accessible) and visit the Pioneer History Village. (Details below.)

PIONEER HISTORY VILLAGE

Historical pioneer cabins and a working blacksmith shop make up this tiny village. Kids love to ride the stagecoach that runs along the dusty pathways in the summer. Tickets in the village. From Memorial Day, weekends only, noon to 4pm. From mid-June Wed-Sun 10am-2pm. (Dates and hours subject to change.) Information – (209) 375- 9531. From the Wawona Hotel, travel .2 mile north of the Wawona Hotel and (just beyond the gas station) take the stone bridge across the Merced River. Immediately turn right on Chilnualna Falls Road and proceed .25 mile.

WAWONA STABLES

Horseback riding – June to mid-Sept. 8:30am-3pm. (209) 375-6502. The stables are adjacent to the Pioneer History Village. Travel .2 mile north of the Wawona Hotel, and (just beyond the gas station) take the stone bridge across the Merced River. Immediately turn right on Chilnualna Falls Road and proceed .25 mile.

SWINGING BRIDGE

A narrow wooden walking bridge sways gently over the Merced River. To reach the bridge, take the wonderful drive down a 2-mile narrow forest road which ends at the Seventh Day Adventist Camp. Take the dirt path to the right amid the pine trees. It follows along the river to the bridge. In spring and early summer, the river is raging with white frothy spindrifts. But by the end of summer, the boulder-strewn bottom is quite visible. No Swimming. Trail: Easy .25 mile. The drive to the bridge begins from the end of the parking area beyond the gas station and market, just beyond the horse barn. Drive 1.7 miles and, at the fork in the road, turn left. Continue to the end of the road. The trailhead is to the right and the parking area is to the left.

LOWER CHILNUALNA WATERFALL TRAIL

From the trailhead sign, follow the sunny path to the right as it climbs up among huge boulders and becomes shaded under pine trees. The path is rocky and narrow along steep ridges; therefore it's not a good path for young children. Monstrous boulders hugging the edge of the trail can be used as a viewpoint for the tumbling waterfall as it gushes through a narrow passage in late spring and early summer. The waterfall is almost dry by August. For the less-than-hardy this may be a good turning around point. To reach the Upper Chilnualna Waterfall, climb up the steep rocky stairs left of the Lower Chilnualna Waterfall. (Slippery and dangerous, especially in spring.) Watch for a small trail sign. Beyond the sign, the trail begins a strenuous 4-mile climb. The falls are best in late spring and early summer. Obtain trail maps at the Wawona Hotel or the visitor center adjacent to the hotel. Trail: Easy .25 mile one way to the lower waterfall, 4 strenuous miles to the upper waterfall. To reach the trailhead from the Wawona Hotel, drive past the gas station, cross the Merced River bridge, turn right on Chilnualna Falls Road, and (passing the Wawona Horse Camp) continue 1.7 miles to the signed parking area on the right. Cross the road and walk up .1 mile to the signed trailhead, and bear right climbing up the hill.

TEXAS FLAT PICNIC AREA

Picnic tables, strewn along the river's edge, provide a place to sit and watch the lovely Merced River running by. On a hot day when the river is low (usually by mid-July), it's mighty refreshing to sit upon the river rocks (close to the shore) while dipping one's feet into the cool water. Warning: Stand back from the river when it's rushing and full. From the intersection of Wawona Road (Hwy 41) and Chilnualna Falls Road; continue north .5 mile (just prior to the Wawona Campground).

INFORMATION

Wawona Area – (Details under Appendix.)

Wawona Visitor Center at Hill Studio – Mid-May to mid-Oct 8:30am-5pm. Mid-Oct to Thanksgiving Fri/Sat/Sun until 4pm. (Details under Visitor Centers.) (209) 375-9531. Located in the building left (north) of the Wawona Hotel. It is 4.5 miles from the Wawona South Park Entrance.

Wawona Grocery Store & Gas Station – Gas 24 hrs. with a credit card. Store 8am-8pm; after Labor Day 7pm. Open all year. Store – (209) 375-6574. Gas station – (209) 375-6567. A free shuttle bus transports visitors to the Mariposa Grove (9am-7pm) from the gas station/market parking area. Located .2 mile from the Wawona Hotel, 4.7 miles from the park's entrance on Wawona Road (Hwy 41).

2.2 Glacier Point Road Area, Bridalveil Fall, Swinging Bridge
What To Do & See

GLACIER POINT ROAD AREA

The awe-inspiring area adjacent Glacier Point Road is one not to be missed. The road leads to trailheads and the phenomenal views at Glacier Point. It also lends winter access to the Badger Pass Ski Area. On Wawona Road (Hwy 41), 11.3 miles north of the Texas Flat picnic area (directions above), travelers should look for the sign of *Yosemite West* (condo/house rentals). Continue beyond this sign .5 mile to a tiny sign indicating *Chinquapin 6,000 ft. elevation.* Just beyond this sign, turn right (east) onto Glacier Point Road.

Note: Glacier Point Road is closed late fall to late spring (depends upon snow) beyond the turnoff road to the Badger Pass Ski area. Trails and Glacier Point details listed below:

BADGER PASS SKI AREA

From Wawona Road (Hwy 41), travel 5 miles on Glacier Point Road to reach the turnoff road to ski area. (Details under Winter Fun.)

McGURK MEADOW

From the trailhead, a path runs through a conifer forest decorated with vibrant wildflowers in late June and July. The trail descends, levels out, and reveals the McGurk 1800s cabin. From the cabin, the path crosses a small wooden bridge over a meandering brook which may be hidden by tall grass. The path continues along the edge of the meadow and leads back into the forest. The trail ends as it reaches a junction with other trails. Return on the same path. Wildlife is often visible in early morning and at dusk. Open late May thru Oct. (Depends upon snow.) Trail: Easy 1.8 miles one way. Take Glacier Point Road 7.5 miles to the trailhead (signed *McGurk Meadow*) on the left side of the road, just before the Bridalveil Creek Campground.

SENTINEL DOME

A footpath meanders amid the pines and gradually climbs up rocky terrain to the base of the towering dome. From here, the ascent up the dome is steep and un-shaded. Along the climb, there are a few windswept bushes and many large boulders. From atop the dome are inspirational views of the valley, Half Dome, and Yosemite Falls. This hike is a poor choice in hot weather due to the lack of shade while climbing up the dome. Warning: Never climb any dome when rain or thunder/ lightening are predicted. Late May thru Oct. (Depends upon snow.) Bring plenty of water. Trail: Moderately/Strenuous 1.1 miles one way. Trailhead is found off Glacier Point Road, at the Sentinel Dome parking area, 13.5 miles from Wawona Road. (2.4 miles from Glacier Point located at the end of the road.) The trail begins to the right of the trailhead sign.

TAFT POINT

This mostly flat trail passes through the forest where huge boulders lie beneath pine trees with patches of snow, which may linger even into June. The path leads to a stream where some tricky rock jumping is required for crossing. Soon the forest opens up to a huge rocky clearing where the path zigzags downhill. The trail ends on the top of a huge promontory hanging over the valley. Here many chasms, one as large as 25-feet across and 40-feet long, cut back into the promontory. Straight down the sheer cliffs of the chasms are awe-inspiring sights. This is a dangerous area (especially for children) as there are no guard rails around the fissures. Up on a ridge, left of the fissures, is Taft Point, where a small railing is perched on the edge of an overhang. From here, hikers can look down more than half a mile to the valley below, and are presented with a fabulous view of Yosemite Falls. Late May thru Oct. (Depends upon snow.) Trail: Easy/Moderate 1.1 miles one way. The Taft Point Trail begins at the Sentinel Dome parking area just left of the trailhead sign. (Directions to the parking area above.) It's 13.5 miles from Wawona Road (Hwy 41) and 2.4 miles from Glacier Point located at the end of Glacier Point Road.

WASHBURN POINT

A fabulous lookout point – 15.4 miles from Wawona Road, .6 mile prior to the end of Glacier Point Road.

GLACIER POINT

One of the park's finest lookout points is found here. The imagery, one of grandeur, viewed from a ledge at the end of the road dwarfs visitors against the tall backdrop of the granite sun-gilded mountains. The sight is astonishing, as if a gigantic surreal landscape painting has been hung at the road's end. From here, Vernal Fall, Nevada Fall, Yosemite Falls and Half Dome can all be viewed together. Just beyond the viewing area, a short trail (wheelchair/stroller accessible) guides the way to a small outdoor amphitheater. Here (an hour prior to sunset) park rangers give nightly talks. Gift shop/snack bar 9am-5pm. Late May thru Oct. (Depends upon snow.) Located 16 miles from Wawona Road (Hwy 41) at the end of Glacier Point Road.

NORTH OF GLACIER POINT ROAD

TUNNEL VIEWPOINT

Photographers flock to this viewpoint, especially as sunset draws near. This is the place to capture some of the colors of Yosemite in its glory. From this vantage point, visitors will be in awe as the sunset transforms the gray granite of El Capitan, Half Dome, and the Sentinel Dome into glowing gold and red. (Details under each of these attractions.) The viewpoint is found via a pullout along Wawona Road (Hwy 41). The pullout is just beyond the northern end of the Wawona Tunnel. It's 8 miles north of Glacier Point Road and just south of the entrance road to the Bridalveil Waterfall.

BRIDALVEIL FALL

The Ahwahneechee Native Americans called it "Pohono" which means Spirit of the Puffing Wind. The tumbling water (620 foot drop) is lifted by the wind and swirled in the air creating a veil of mist, which can be felt even along the pathways in spring and early summer. In late afternoon, luminous rays, filtering through the mist, create a rainbow of colors. The waterfall is visible from the parking area but, for an up close look, follow the paved pathway signed *Vista Point* which reaches the base of the waterfall in a quarter mile. By late summer, the waterfall is greatly diminished. From Wawona Road, it's 1.3 miles north of the Wawona Tunnel, and 9.3 miles north of Glacier Point Road.

Note: 1.3 miles north of the Bridalveil Fall, Wawona Road (Hwy 41) ends. From here, Southside Drive (one-way road) leads into Yosemite Village. Visitors may, instead, choose to cross the bridge over the Merced River and turn left to reach Hwy 120 and Hwy 140 in the Northern Park Area.

SWINGING BRIDGE

Prior to entering Yosemite Village, visitors will see a sign for the Swinging Bridge (on the left side of the road). Follow the short path to the wooden bridge. It doesn't swing any more, but a walk across it leads to the Yosemite Lodge where bicycles/wheelchairs can be rented for the pathway. A shaded picnic area is found to the left of the bridge. It's 3.5 miles north of the Bridalveil Waterfall along Southside Drive.

Note: To reach Yosemite Village, from the Swinging Bridge, continue along Southside Drive to a left turn crossing a traffic-bridge over the Merced River. (Photos taken from the right side of the bridge at sunset will capture Half Dome in its glory and photos from the left side will capture Yosemite Falls beautifully illuminated.) After crossing the bridge, turn left to reach the Yosemite Lodge and Yosemite Falls. Turn right to enter Yosemite Village and reach the Ahwahnee Hotel. Travelers that do not cross over the bridge, but continue ahead on Southside Drive will come to the Housekeeping Camp and Curry Village. (Details under Lodging.)

2.3 Yosemite Village Area
What To Do & See

YOSEMITE VILLAGE AREA

This area is the most populated part of the park. It embraces restaurants, hotels, a visitor center, wondrous trails, swimming holes in the Merced River, and magical sights like Yosemite Falls and Mirror Lake. One of the busiest places is Yosemite Village especially the Village Market. Follow the path in front of the market to reach Degnans Café, Deli, and Loft just a short stroll away. The post office and Wilderness Center are next along the path followed by the Ansel Adams Gallery, Yosemite Valley Visitor Center & Bookstore and the Yosemite Museum. Nearby is the Pioneer Cemetery (details under Appendix). From here, the path (wheelchair/stroller accessible) leaves the village and travels out to Yosemite Falls and Yosemite Lodge. Free shuttle buses leave from the front of the Village Market and the Visitor Center. The buses travel through the village to Yosemite Falls, Curry Village, and Happy Isles Nature Center and hiking trailheads. (Details under Transportation Shuttle Buses.)

YOSEMITE VILLAGE

Village Market – Gifts, groceries, film, hats, and an ATM. Summer 8am-10pm, winter 8am-8pm.

Village Grill – Hamburgers, fries, chicken strips. Summer only. (Next to the front door of the Village Market.)

Degnans Café – Pastries, ice cream, smoothies. 11am-5pm. Mid-April to Sept.

Degnans Deli – Sandwiches, salads, espresso. 7am-6pm, all year. (209) 372-8454.

Degnans Loft – Pizza, salad, soups. 5-9pm, spring to fall. (Above the deli.)

Wilderness Center – Wilderness permits and bear resistant canisters. 8am-5pm. (209) 372-0745.

Village Sport Shop – Film, camping/fishing gear and licenses. 9am-5pm, all year.

Ansel Adams Gallery – Landscape photographs, posters,

gifts, camera rentals, film, postcards. 9am-6pm, winter 10am-5pm. (209) 372-4413. www.anseladams.com.

Yosemite Valley Visitor Center & Bookstore – Information, books and maps. Mid-May to Labor Day 9am-7pm, after Labor Day 9am-5pm. (209) 372-0298.

Yosemite Theatre – Movie on Yosemite Park, every half hour from 9:30am-4:30pm; most summer evenings live shows at 7pm. Information – (209) 372-0304. Adjacent to the visitor center.

Yosemite Museum – Indian artifacts and demonstrations. Behind the visitor center, via a short loop trail, lies a reconstructed Ahwahnee Village. Quite often visitors will see deer, which wander in to feed here. 9am-5pm, all year. (209) 372-0304.

Village Garage – 24-hour towing. Auto repairs 8am-5pm. (Closes sometimes from noon to 1pm.) Open all year. (209) 372-8320. Across the parking area, behind the Village Market.

Parking for Yosemite Village

To reach Yosemite Village after crossing the Merced River bridge turn right (toward Yosemite Village), take the first left turn and park behind the Village Market for short term parking. (Handicapped parking close to the Village Market and Yosemite Museum.) For all-day parking, take the first right turn into the huge day-use parking area. Walk from the day-use parking entrance across the road to the parking area behind the Village Market. From the parking area, walk through the back door of the Village Market and out the front door to reach the walkway that leads through the entire village. **Note:** The parking areas are not lit at night; visitors should bring flashlights if going to Yosemite Village and returning to the parking area after dark. The shuttle bus stops in front of the market.

To find the Yosemite Medical Clinic (details under Information), the Ahwahnee Hotel and a golden meadow where sweet deer are likely to be found feeding at dawn and dusk, travel north across the Yosemite Village parking area and turn right on Ahwahnee Drive. The meadow is on the immediate right side of the road and, on the left side, is the Yosemite Medical Clinic. (Details under Information.) Follow this road a short distance to the end to reach the huge parking area for the Ahwahnee Hotel. Be sure to visit the hotel and stop in the gift shop or have a snack or drink on their outdoor patio. A lovely path meanders from the back patio down along the Royal Arch Creek. (Details for the path and the hotel under Lodging, Ahwahnee Hotel.)

MIRROR LAKE

Catch the shuttle bus in Yosemite Village in front of the Village Market or the Yosemite Visitor Center; the shuttle stops at the trailhead to Mirror Lake. From the bus stop, walk ahead to the junction; a paved path goes to the left and a dirt path to the right. Stay to the left on the paved walkway (wheelchair/stroller accessible), and follow the turquoise Tenaya Creek which is raging wild in spring and early summer. At the small shallow lake (April to mid-July) is a sandy swimming/wading beach. Young children love it here. Usually by mid-July the lake begins to dwindle, and by August there may be just small pools of water. (Depends upon the past winter snowfall.)

Beyond the swimming beach, the path continues along the lakeshore where mirror images of Half Dome (details under Half Dome) appear in the lake. (Viewing is best late in the day.) This is a good place for the less-than-hardy to turn around. Visitors may continue on the path for about a mile, but can no longer cross the Tenaya Bridge and return on the other side of the lake due to rock slides. Follow the path downstream back to the shuttle stop. Leashed dogs okay on paved trail only. Trail: Easy 1 mile to Mirror Lake. Only vehicles displaying a placard (temporary placards obtained at park entrances or visitor centers) may drive on road to reach lake. (Those driving on this road should drive at 15 mph and use emergency flashers. Follow signs to "Pines Campground" and proceed beyond the "No Entry" sign and look for signs to Mirror Lake.) All visitors may take the free accessible shuttle bus from Yosemite Village, the hotels, and camping areas (details for shuttle under Transportation), or ride a bicycle from the rentals at Curry Village. Bicycles can be ridden on the paved path to the bike stand just prior to the lake, but are not allowed beyond that point. (Details for bicycle rentals under Summer Fun.) Information - Mon-Fri 9am-noon, 1-4:30pm. (209) 372-0826.

YOSEMITE FALLS

One of world's tallest waterfalls (2,425 feet) is actually comprised of three falls sitting atop one another. There is the Upper Fall, Mid-Cascades, and the tremendous Lower Waterfall which makes the earth shake at its force in spring and early summer. (Falls may dwindle to a trickle or disappear by late summer.) A viewing bridge, at the base of the Lower Waterfall, brings visitors up close to feel the misty spray and to witness rainbows that drift in and out. The (wheelchair/stroller accessible) path continues over the bridge and, bearing to the right, meanders over some small bridges as the trail loops back to the starting point. (Great views of the falls along the way.) In winter, the frozen falls are silent until some frozen mist crashes down upon the icy base with a thunderous sound reverberating across the valley. Falls are best mid-May thru June. Trail Information – Mon-Fri 9am-noon, 1-4:30pm. (209) 372-0826 (press 3 and then 5). Falls Information – www.nps.gov/yose. Trail: Lower

Falls Loop (shuttle stop #6), easy 1 mile. Upper Yosemite Falls Trail (shuttle stop #7), strenuous 3.6 miles one way. (Trailhead for the Upper Fall is just beyond Yosemite Lodge in Camp 4, the Sunnyside Campground.) **Note:** Same trail is used to reach El Capitan. Take the shuttle bus from Yosemite Village, the hotels, camping areas, or walk across the street from the Yosemite Lodge parking area.

EL CAPITAN

Reported to be the largest granite monolith in the world, El Capitan rises up 3,600 feet from the valley floor; and many climbers come to scale it. When the sun sits low on the horizon, it turns the massive rock first honey gold and then scarlet red. Capture it on film from Tunnel View Point. (Details under Tunnel View Point.) Trail Information – Mon-Fri 9am-noon, 1-4:30pm. (209) 372-0826. Trail: Strenuous 8 miles to summit one-way. The trail to the summit begins just beyond Yosemite Lodge in Camp 4, the Sunnyside Campground.

HAPPY ISLES NATURE CENTER & TRAIL

This was named for the small islands found in the Merced River near the center. From the Happy Isles Nature Center, take the paths (wheelchair/stroller accessible) and cross the small bridges to the islands. In springtime and early summer, visitors may watch and listen to the river jumping up over huge boulders. Open 9am-5pm. (Closes for lunch; times vary.) Open mid-May to mid-Sept. (209) 372-0631. **Note:** Nearby is the trailhead for the popular Mist Trail, which leads to the top of Vernal Fall, continues to Nevada Fall, and connects to the John Muir Trail which leads to Half Dome. (Details for trail below.) The road to Happy Isles is located east of Yosemite Village, but no cars are allowed on the road (except those with disability stickers which can be obtained at park entrances and visitor centers); take the free shuttle bus from the hotels or the Yosemite Valley Visitor Center to stop #16. (Details for shuttle under Transportation.) Near the shuttle stop is a food cart with drinks, snacks, and ice cream. The short pathway straight ahead leads to the nature center and restrooms. To find the trailhead for Mist Trail, turn left from the shuttle stop and cross over the small bridge.

MIST TRAIL

The trail to the fabulous Vernal Fall (317-foot drop) begins with a climb along the Merced River. The air temperature along this part of the trail is usually quite warm, but it cools down after climbing up .8 mile to the bridge crossing the river. The Vernal Fall can be viewed at a distance from the bridge. Across the bridge is a resting spot with a drinking fountain and restrooms. For the less-than-hardy this is a good turning around point. From here, the climb is more strenuous. When nearing the waterfall, visitors are cooled down by the billowing mist surrounding it. A thin rain jacket would be welcomed when climbing up the hundreds of huge wet and slippery rock steps close to the roaring falls. The temperature drops dramatically, and many rainbows appear in the dancing cool mist.

The view from the top, when gazing down over the waterfall is thrilling. The nearby green-water Emerald Pool looks inviting, but no swimming is allowed due to the very strong currents. This is a picturesque place to rest before the descent back down the trail or before climbing the 1.5 miles to the top of the Nevada Fall with a 594-foot drop. Mid-May to mid-Oct. Trailhead – details above under Happy Isles. Information: Mon-Fri 9am-noon, 1-4:30pm. (209) 372-0826. Trail: Moderate to moderately-strenuous near the waterfall, 1.5 miles to top of Vernal Fall.

HALF DOME

This smooth granite dome (east of Yosemite Village) reaches up nearly 5,000 feet from the valley floor and offers awesome views of the park. It is believed that it was shaped by glaciers millions of years ago. The shortest trail to the summit begins by taking Mist Trail to the top of Vernal Fall (details under Mist Trail above) and then following the John Muir Trail. To assist with the strenuous last 400 feet up the dome, cables are strung from late-May to mid-Oct. (Exact dates vary from year to year.)

Half Dome is visible from many viewpoints in the park; it's especially nice from Glacier Point. A Native American legend tells of an Indian girl named Tissaack, who was turned into granite and became Half Dome. Look for her tears (dark streaks) running down her face. The legend says that her tears formed Mirror Lake. (See images of Half Dome displayed in Mirror Lake.) Currently an advanced permit must be obtained by those wishing to climb the dome. (Details under the Appendix.) Warning: Always check the weather before climbing. Do not climb the dome if there is a chance of rain or lightning. Allow at least twelve hours for this climb. Trail Information – Mon-Fri 9am-noon, 1-4:30pm. (209) 372-0826. Trail: Strenuous approximately 8 miles one way.

2.4 Yosemite Southern Park Area PARK INFORMATION

SUMMER FUN

Wawona Golf Course – 9-holes (play 18 holes). April thru Oct (weather permitting). Carts and clubs for rent. (Details under the Wawona Area.) (209) 375-6572. Located across the road from the Wawona Hotel.

Wawona Stables – Open first week in June thru Sept. 7am-5pm. Reservations (209) 375-6502. (Details under Wawona Area.)

Yosemite Valley Stables – Two-hour rides to Mirror Lake. Open May thru Sept 7am-5pm. Call for reservations (209) 372-8348. In Curry Village. (Details for Curry Village under Lodging.)

Swimming – Inner tube floating (inner tube rentals at Curry Village $25) and swimming in the Merced River at Cathedral and Sentinel Beaches (near Curry Village), and the swimming pools at Curry Village, Yosemite Lodge, and Wawona Hotel. (Non-guests pay a nominal fee at the swimming pools.) To reach Sentinel Beach, drive to Curry Village and ask directions at the recreation building (where inner tubes and raft rentals are available), or take the free shuttle from the Yosemite Valley Visitor Center or the Village Market to stop #11 and walk .25 mile to the river. To reach Cathedral Beach, take the special free El Capitan shuttle (runs from Memorial weekend to second weekend of Oct) from Yosemite Valley Visitor Center or Camp 4 (campground) near Yosemite Lodge. (Ask the driver to stop on Southside Drive near Cathedral Beach.) It's a 5 to 10 minute walk to the river.

Rafting – Three-mile floats in the Merced River include shuttle ride back to starting point. Must weigh at least fifty pounds. May/June to July/Aug (depending upon melted snow level in river). Raft rentals in the recreation building in Curry Village. (209) 372-8341. (Take the shuttle or drive to Curry Village.)

LeConte Memorial Lodge – Library with a kids' corner. Open May thru Sept, Wed-Sun 10am-4pm. Evening programs, Fri/Sat/Sun at 8pm. (209) 372-4542. Southside Drive, Shuttle Stop #12.

Bicycle/Wheelchair Rentals – (Includes tandem bicycles) **Yosemite Lodge** – Rentals, summer 8am-7pm, spring/fall 9am-6pm. Open mid-April to Nov (weather permitting). Bicycle trail maps available. A nice path leads from the rental area across the meadow and crosses bridge over the river. Information and wheelchair reservations. (209) 372-1208. Located near hotel lobby, in the parking area.
Curry Village – Rentals, summer 8am-8pm, spring and autumn 9am-6pm. Open mid-April to mid-Oct (weather permitting). Bicycle trail maps available. Information and wheelchair reservations – (209) 372-8319. Located at the recreation center.

WINTER FUN

Badger Pass Ski Area – Downhill (state of the art chair lifts) and cross-country skiing, snowboarding, tubing, and snowshoeing. (Eighty-five percent of slopes are beginner and intermediate.) Rentals, lessons, food service, sport shop with ski/snowboard clothing, sunglasses, film. Seniors 62+ ski free mid-week/non-holidays. Handicapped sit-ski lessons; reservations required. (209) 372-8430. Snowshoeing – Hike through forests from the Badger Pass Ski Area with rangers;

full moon walks in January, February, and March. Snowshoe rentals available. **Note:** Free shuttle in winter from Curry Village, Yosemite Lodge, Wawona Hotel, and Ahwahnee Hotel. Badger Pass open 9am-4:30pm, mid-Dec to April. (Depends upon snow.) Information – (209) 372-8430 or (209) 372-1000. (Press 0 for questions, press 2 for road conditions, and press 5 for Badger Pass.) www.yosemitepark. com Badger Pass is located off Glacier Point Road, 5 miles from Wawona Road (Hwy 41). (Full directions under Glacier Point Road.)

Ice-Skating – Outdoor rink with views of Half Dome includes a warming hut, fire pit, and ice skate rentals. Nov to early March. (Depends upon weather.) Hours vary, call ahead (209) 372-8319 or call Curry Village (209) 372-8333. Located in Curry Village.

PARK INFORMATION

PARK ENTRANCE FEES – (Subject to change.)

Seven-day Pass: $20 per vehicle; $10 walk-ins, motorcycles.
Annual Pass: $40.
National Park Annual Pass: $80. (Admittance to all national parks.)
Senior Pass: $10. (Age 62+ for lifetime.)
Access Pass: Free for U.S. citizens with permanent disabilities.
Note: Passes available at park entrances.

VISITOR CENTERS

Wawona Visitor Center at Hill Studio – (Historical building.) Books, maps, wilderness permits. Mid-May to mid-Oct 8:30am-5pm. Mid-Oct to Thanksgiving Thurs-Sun until 4pm. (209) 375-9531. Adjacent to the Wawona Hotel, in the building left (north) of the hotel. It is 4.5 miles from the Wawona South Park Entrance.

Yosemite Valley Visitor Center & Bookstore – Information, books, and maps. Mid-May to Labor Day, 9am-7pm. After Labor Day, 9am-5pm. (209) 372-0298. The shuttle bus stops here. (Details for shuttle under Transportation.) Visitor center is located in Yosemite Village. (Details under Yosemite Village.)

INFORMATION

Emergency – 911 – Fire, Police, Medical.

Yosemite Medical Clinic – 24-hour emergency care. Appointments 8am-5pm Mon-Fri. (Wheelchair rentals) (209) 372-4637. Located northeast end of Yosemite Village parking area on Ahwahnee Drive.

Altitude Sickness – (Details under Appendix.)

Visitor Centers – (Details above.)

Park Information/Weddings/Road Conditions – (209) 372-1000 or (209) 372-0200 or (209) 372-0356. www.nps.gov/yose (up-to-date trail info) and www.yosemitepark.com.

Lodging Reservations/Park Directions – Includes tours, weather, and winter ski pkgs. (801) 559-5000. (Details under Lodging.)

Park Tours & Guides – (Details below under Tours & Guides.) www.yosemitepark.com/activities.aspx.

Yosemite Park Guide – (Details under Appendix.) See website to download a copy. www.nps.gov/yose/planyourvisit/guide.htm.

Gasoline – Gas station on Hwy 41, near the Wawona Hotel, 4.7 miles from the park's South Entrance. 24-hrs. with credit card. No gas is available in the Yosemite Village area. (Gasoline also available in the Northern Park Area.)

Village Garage – Emergency Road Service – 24-hour towing. Garage is open 8am-5pm. (Sometimes closes noon-1pm.) Yosemite Village, behind the Village Market. (209) 372-8320.

Internet Access – (Details under Appendix.)

Post Offices – (Details under Appendix.)

Yosemite National Park History – (Details under Appendix.)

Accessibility Guide – www.yosemitepark.com/accessibility. aspx.

Accessibility Information – Mon-Fri 7am-4:30pm. (209) 379-1035. (Details under Appendix.)

Wheelchair Accessible Activities – (Details under Appendix.)

Trail & Wilderness Information – Mon-Fri 9am-noon, 1-4:30pm. (209) 372-0826.

Trail and Wilderness (Half Dome permits) – Wawona Visitor Center at Hill Studio & Yosemite Village Wilderness Center. (Details under Appendix, Wilderness.) Advance Permits – (209) 372-0740.

Rentals (bicycles/wheelchairs) and Riding Stables – (Details under Summer Fun.)

Swimming, Rafting, Golf, Fishing – (Details under Summer Fun.)

Skiing, Snowshoeing, Ice Skating – (Details under Winter Fun.)

Bears – (Details under Appendix.)

Pets – Leashed dogs okay on paved bike paths, paved roads, paved trails, and in some campgrounds. They are also allowed on the Wawona Meadow Trail. (Details under the Wawona area.)

Kennels – Call Yosemite Valley Stables. (209) 372-8348. (Details under Appendix.)

Lost & Found – (209) 372-0200 (press 2 then 4).

WEATHER

Caltrans – California Road Conditions – (800) 427-7623.

Weather – Trail Conditions – Park Information – (209) 372-0200. www.nps.gov/yose. **Note:** Chains required in winter.

Average Temperatures – Yosemite Village Area (4200 ft.) Jan-April high 47-60, low 25-35; May/June high 73-82, low 45-51; July/Aug/Sept high 85-89, low 51-57; October high 71, low 42; November high 56 low 33; December high 47 low 28.

TOURS & GUIDES

Yosemite Sightseeing – (209) 372-1000 ext. 3. www.yosemitepark.com.

Tours/Buses – Tram tours from Yosemite Lodge. June/July to Sept or Oct (depends upon weather). Reservations – (209) 372-4FUN (4386).

Guided Hikes – From the hotels. Information – (209) 372-8344.

Tours and Kids' Programs – Listed in the Yosemite Guide, available at all park entrances. www.yosemitepark.com/activities.aspx.

TRANSPORTATION

Shuttle Buses – Many roads around Yosemite Village are closed to cars. Free shuttles run from the Village Market and the visitor center in Yosemite Village to Yosemite Falls, Curry Village (ice rink/bike and raft rentals), Happy Isles Nature Center and Trailheads, Ahwahnee Hotel, Mirror Lake, Yosemite Stables, and, in winter, to the Badger Pass Ski Area from the Yosemite hotels. Shuttle buses (wheelchair/stroller accessible) run year round from 7am to 10pm. Summer every 10 minutes, early morning and evenings every 20 minutes. (Winter every twenty minutes.) A shuttle map and information is found in the *Yosemite Guide*; free at all park entrances and the Yosemite Valley Visitor Center. Information – (209) 372-8441. (Details under Transportation in the Appendix.)

Yosemite Hiker's Bus – Buses leave from Yosemite Lodge and Curry Village in the Southern Park Area and travel to Tuolumne Meadows in the Northern Park Area. June/July to Labor Day. (Depends upon snow.) Fare $14.50, RT same day, return on a different day $23. (209) 372-1240 or 8441.

Fresno/Yosemite International Airport – Daily flights from Los Angeles. Information – (559) 621-4500. The airport is located 64 miles from Yosemite Park's South Entrance via Hwy 41. There are many car rentals available like: Avis (800) 331-1212, Hertz (800) 654-3131. **Note:** Car rentals close between 10 and 11pm. Call ahead for late flights.

Gold Country Tours – Tours from Fresno to Yosemite National Park. (559) 641-6789. www.yosemiteandbeyond.com.

YARTS – Buses from Merced to Yosemite Village. Office Mon-Fri 8am-5pm. (209) 384-1315. (877) 989-2787. www.yarts.com.

EATERIES

Ahwahnee Hotel – Dining room and Ahwahnee Bar. (Details under Ahwahnee Hotel.)

Curry Village – Lunch: pizza, and Mexican cuisine. (Details under Curry Village.)

Curry Pavilion – Breakfast and dinner buffet. (Details under Curry Village.)

Yosemite Lodge – Mountain Room and Food Court. (Details under Yosemite Lodge.)

Yosemite Village – Degnans Café/Loft. (Details under Yosemite Village.)

Wawona Hotel – Dining room. (Details under Wawona Hotel.)

Note: Call hotels direct for current hours and dates open. Restaurant open/close dates and times are subject to change as the park's weather is unpredictable. Park Dining Information – (209) 372-1000. www.yosemitepark.com.

LODGING

Lodging Reservations – Reservations inside the park, up to 366 days in advance. (801) 559-5000. www.yosemitepark.com.

Camping – Thirteen sites inside park – some open all year. Reservations – (877) 444-6777 (8am-9pm PST). www.recreation.gov. (24 hrs.)

Wawona Campground – Open all year. Some sites first come-first served basis, and there are 2 wheelchair accessible sites. Horse sites open approximately April thru Sept by reservation only. Information www.nps.gov/yose/planyourvisit/campground.htm.

Yosemite West – Condos, homes, and B & Bs (view them on website) found inside the park. Some have hot tubs TVs, fully equipped kitchens, and marvelous views. No dogs. Office open Mon-Fri 9am-5pm. (559) 642-2211. www.yosemitewest.com. Located 16 miles from the Wawona South Park Entrance (just prior to the turnoff for Glacier Point Road). Travelers should look for a tiny sign (on the right) stating *Yosemite West* and *turn left here*. (15 miles south of Yosemite Village.)

Wawona (Big Trees) Hotel – In a yesteryear setting, the white wooden buildings (built in the 1800s) sit so sweetly upon the long, soft-green lawn with a heated summer swimming pool amid tall pine trees. White wicker rocking chairs line the verandas surrounding the hotel on two floors. Tennis courts and a golf course are provided along with quiet evening (pianist/singer) entertainment. (Tues-Sat.) Cocktails served on the front veranda. Rooms have verandas, antiques, and some private baths with claw-foot tubs. No A/C, TVs or telephones. Low autumn, winter and spring rates.

The dining room looks out over the green front lawn, which is scattered with pine trees. Rooms come with a complimentary continental breakfast. Lunch 11:30am-2pm, Fri/Sat/Sun 3pm. (After Labor Day 11:30am-1:30pm). Dressy-casual evening dining 5:30-9pm. (209) 375-1425. Mother's Day, Easter, and New Years, brunch is served. Summer Saturdays there are lawn barbeques. (Ribs/steaks/hamburgers) 5-7pm. $24.95 and kids, 7-11 $13.95, 4-6, $5.75. Weddings and receptions outdoors or in the sun room. (Details for the golf course, gas station, covered bridge, riding stables, and hiking trails under the Wawona Area.) Hotel open April-to New Years. Front desk (209) 375-6556. Reservations (801) 559-5000. www.yosemitepark.com. Hwy 41, 4.5 miles from the park's Southern Entrance, 30 miles south of Yosemite Village.

Ahwahnee Hotel – (Built in 1927.) The granite exterior blends soothingly into the landscape with an interior of American Indian décor. Room rates above average. (Summer rooms $470, suites $1000 and up.) Elegant hotel rooms with private baths, come with TVs, air-conditioning and Wi-Fi. (Cottages have ceiling fans.) Outdoor heated swimming pool and tennis courts are available to guests. The indoor/outdoor **Ahwahnee Bar**, overlooks the swimming pool, and connects to an outdoor terrace (with tables and chairs) that stretches along the edge of the beautiful lawn at the back of the hotel. Morning coffee, pastries, and fruit are available at the bar 7am to 10:30am. Light menu 11:30am to 11pm. (209) 372-1289. The path from the terrace meanders past the hotel's cabins where a right turn leads down to the Royal Arch Creek. Along the path, which follows the creek, many silver-gray fluffy-tailed squirrels play among the fallen trees, brush, and boulders. Stone bridges span the creek casting their reflections in the shallow water. A bicycle path, journeying from the bicycle rentals at Curry Village and Yosemite Lodge, traverses the bridges.

The **Great Lounge** plays host for guest teas with piano entertainment while sunbeams dance through floor-to-ceiling windows and easy chairs invite relaxation. (4pm-5pm) Beyond the Great Lounge are three small quiet rooms with French doors showing off views of the lovely grounds. In the Ahwahnee dining room, with ceiling-to-floor windows fringed with stained glass, guests are served breakfast, lunch, dinner, and Sunday brunch (7am-3pm) on lovely china. Open

7am-3pm and 5:30-9pm. Dinner (dressy-casual dress code.) & brunch reservations (801) 559-5000.

The famous Bracebridge Dinners are named for a character in Washington Irving's *Sketch Book*. This special Christmas celebration held on eight evenings during the Christmas holidays includes seven-course dinners with seventeenth century pageants and music. Reservations – (801) 559-4935. January features famous chefs lending great culinary experiences. Sweet Shop – candy, wines, gourmet snacks, film, cards, and sun hats. Nature Shop – native jewelry, apparel, and music. Gift shop – gifts, china, and photographs. Weddings. Concierge – activities and trail maps. Shuttle service year round to park activities. Open all year. Front desk (209) 372-1406. Reservations (801) 559-5000. www.yosemitepark.com. Located at First Ahwahnee Drive (end of the road) .5 mile east of Yosemite Village.

Housekeeping Camp – Snuggled along the Merced River, with sandy beaches and swimming holes, rustic concrete rooms with canvas roofs have outdoor fire-pits, grills, and picnic tables. There are common restrooms with showers, soap, and towels. Camp store/laundromat – camping supplies and groceries. Open spring to fall. (209) 372-8339. Reservations (801) 559-5000. www.yosemitepark.com. Located on Southside Drive, .25 mile west of Curry Village, shuttle stop #12.

Curry Village – It lazes in the cool shadow of Glacier Point and includes a few standard motel rooms and cabins with electric lights, heat and some private baths. There are also tent cabins with heat and central baths. No cooking is allowed. The village has an outdoor swimming pool, bicycle rentals, river raft rentals, horse stables, and, in winter, there is outdoor ice-skating. (Details for horse stables, bicycle and raft rentals under Summer Fun; ice-skating under Winter Fun.) **Curry Village**

Mountain Shop – sportswear, camping, hiking/backpacking gear. **Meadow Grill** – hamburgers, hotdogs, fries. **Curry Village Pavilion** – breakfast and dinner. (Cafeteria style.) April to Oct. **Pizza Patio/Bar** – noon-10pm. Spring to fall. **General Store** – groceries, film, and apparel. All year. 8am-10pm, winter 9am-7pm. Lounge – game room with Wi-Fi. Amphitheater – summer evening ranger programs. Village open March/April to New Years, then weekends and holidays. **Note:** The grounds are not lit up at night so that visitors may see the stars clearly; bring a flashlight. Front desk (209) 372-8333. Reservations (801) 559-5000. www.yosemitepark.com. Located on Southside Drive, 2 miles southeast of Yosemite Village. (Do not cross over the bridge leading into Yosemite Village, but continue ahead on Southside Drive.) From Yosemite Village Market or the visitor center, take the free shuttle.

Yosemite Lodge at the Falls – The hotel is nestled in the natural wooded setting with views of Yosemite Falls. Standard motel rooms; some larger rooms have a patio and view of falls. All rooms have TVs and Wi-Fi. Request one with ceiling fans. Outdoor heated pool open Memorial Day to Labor Day. (Non-guests pay Wi-Fi in lobby $5.95 per day.) Gift shop – newspapers, gifts, sundries. Tour desk – information on horseback riding, hiking, guided tours, and the free shuttle buses and sight-seeing-tour buses which stop at the lodge. Ranger Programs – summer programs in the outdoor amphitheater; in colder weather, programs are held indoors. Bicycle & wheelchair rentals – near the hotel's lobby, in the parking area. Reservations for wheelchairs – (209) 372-1208 May to Oct. (Depends upon weather.) A bicycle/wheelchair path begins across the road from the rentals, crosses the meadow, and the bridge over the Merced River. (The hardy may want to continue to Curry Village.) Lodge open all year. Front desk (209) 372-1274. Reservations (801) 559-5000.

www.yosemitepark.com. Located on Northside Drive, west of Yosemite Village, across the road from Yosemite Falls.

The following eateries are located in the courtyard adjacent Yosemite Lodge: Food Court – pizza, pasta, chicken, fish, and box lunches. 6:30am-2pm and 5-8:30pm, winter 7:30pm. **Mountain Room Lounge** – tall glass windows line three sides of bar; sports TVs and sandwiches and cocktails. Indoor and outdoor seating. 4:30-11pm, Sat/Sun 12:30-11pm. (209) 372-1035. **Mountain Room Restaurant** – fine dining. Dinner from 5:30pm. The back glass wall affords views of Yosemite Falls. (209) 372-1281.

Note: Leaving Yosemite Village, all traffic is one-way. At the Bridalveil Fall intersection, left-turn lane is for Hwy 41 (Wawona Road) and Bridalveil Fall; the right lane travels northwest to Hwys 120 & 140. (Crane Flat General Store/ Gas Station is 12.5 miles north via Hwy 120.)

DIRECTIONS – Wawona South Park Entrance

From Los Angeles, travel north on the Golden State Fwy (5). Just south of Bakersfield, take Hwy 99 north to Tulare. Continue 45 miles north to Fresno. Take Hwy 41 north 48 miles to Oakhurst, and continue 15 miles north to the park entrance. Los Angeles to the Wawona South Park Entrance is 270 miles. In winter, it is best to enter the park at the Arch Rock Park Entrance. (Details under the Northern Park Directions.) **Note:** Directions from Kings Canyon National Park to Yosemite National Park are located under Kings Canyon National Park. Directions from San Francisco and other areas may be found on the park's website. www.yosemitepark.com. To reach Morro Bay from Yosemite National Park take Hwy 41 west from Fresno 135 miles.

2.5 TOWNS OUTSIDE SOUTHERN ENTRANCE – Oakhurst, Bass Lake, Fish Camp
What To Do & See

OAKHURST

Lodging, restaurants, gas stations, Starbucks, and a variety of shops are found here; nearby is a golf course, the Nelder Grove, and Bass Lake. This is a great stopping-off place before the final 15 miles to Yosemite's South Park Entrance.

OAKHURST RIVER PARKWAY

From the parking area, cross the Fresno River Bridge to the lush green lawn strewn with picnic tables or walk the mile path along the river and adjoining creeks, where ducks and beavers play. Leashed dogs okay. From Hwy 41, traveling north, turn right on Road 426, and turn right at the first stoplight. Trailhead is reached by following the small signs to Oakhurst Community Park. Parking is beyond the library, behind the fire station.

SIERRA MEADOWS COUNTRY CLUB

An 18-hole golf course, non-members okay. Open all year, weather permitting. (559) 642-1343. From Oakhurst, take Hwy 49 for 2.5 miles; turn right on Harmony Lane.

INFORMATION

Yosemite Sierra Visitors Bureau – Lodging and area information. Mon–Sat 8:30am–5pm. Sun 9am-1pm. Winter

9am-4:30pm. (Closed Sun from Nov 1st.) (559) 683-4636. www.yosemitethisyear.com. 41969 Hwy 41, northern end of Oakhurst, 15 miles from the Southern Yosemite Park Entrance.

EATERIES

Pizza Factory – Pizza, pasta, salads. Mon-Thurs 11am-11pm, Fri/Sat midnight, Sun noon-11pm. In summer; Dixieland jazz band Thurs 6:30-9pm. (559) 683-2700. Hwy 41, next to McDonalds.

Time For Tea – Charming decor. Teas, lunch, and gifts. Menu and pictures of tea rooms on website. Weds-Sat 11:00 am-4pm. Reservations (559) 683-4535. www.timeforteaoakhurst.com.

Crab Cake – Seafood, chicken, and pasta. 11am–9pm. (559) 641-7667. Hwy 41.

South Gate Brewing Co. – American pub fare. In-house brewed beer and pizza, fish tacos, hamburgers, soups/salads. Mon-Thurs 11am-10pm, Fri/Sat 11pm, Sun 9pm. (Winter closed Mon.) 40233 Enterprise Drive, on Hwy 49. (559) 692-BREW. www.southgatebrewco.com.

Todd's Barbeque East – Family restaurant – pulled-pork sandwiches, fries, steaks, burgers, shrimp, and bread pudding. Summer 11am-9:00pm. Winter 8:30 pm. 40713 Hwy 41, #5. (559) 642-4900.

Sweet Water Steak House – B,L,D – Steak, pasta, seafood, and salads. Summer 8am-10pm. Winter 8am-8pm (559) 658-5252. Hwy 41, northern end of Oakhurst.

LODGING

KOA Campground – (Closed in winter.) (559) 683-7855.

www.koa.com. Located in nearby Coarsegold, 23 miles from Yosemite Park.

Best Western Plus Yosemite Gateway Inn – Situated among tall oak trees. Rooms have Wi-Fi and some kitchens. Indoor and outdoor pools/hot tub. Dogs okay. (559) 683-2378. (800) 545-5462. www.bestwestern.com. 40530 Hwy 41, 15 miles from the park.

Yosemite Southgate Inn – All rooms have Wi-Fi and refrigerators and come with continental breakfast. Outdoor heated pool, spa, and fitness center. (559) 683-3555. (800) 222-2244. www.shiloinns.com. 40644 Hwy 41.

Hound's Tooth Inn B/B – Victorian-style with a garden patio, lovely grounds and rooms, some fireplaces and spas. Wi-Fi. Buffet breakfast and evening wine. (559) 642-6600. (888) 642-6610. www.houndstoothinn.com. 42071 N. Hwy 41, 3 miles north of Oakhurst.

Pine Rose Inn – Nice rooms with fireplaces or wood stoves, and some in-room Jacuzzis. Wi-Fi. Full breakfast served. (559) 642-2800. www.pineroseinn.com. Road 222, north of town. (Turnoff road to Bass Lake.)

Sierra Sky Ranch – The ranch lies amid meadows, oak trees, and trout streams. Wi-Fi. Swimming pool. Weddings. Steak House – summer dinners 5-10pm. Dogs okay in some rooms. (559) 683-8040. www.sierraskyranch.com. 50552 Road 632, north of town.

DIRECTIONS – Oakhurst

From Sequoia National Park, take Hwy 198 (40.5 miles) to Hwy 99 north to Fresno, and exit onto Hwy 41 north (signed *Yosemite National Park*). Continue 47 miles.

From Kings Canyon National Park, take winding Hwy 180 west, 53 miles, (toward Fresno) to Hwy 41 north (signed *Yosemite National Park*) and continue 47 miles. Oakhurst – 15 miles from Yosemite's South Park Entrance.

NELDER GROVE

In the Giant Sequoia Preservation Area, take the *Shadow of the Giants Trail*. The trail lies among mammoth sequoia, pine, and cedar trees; it's quite shaded. The path is mostly soft as it's covered in pine needles, but there are some rocky sections. In the springtime, wildflowers display themselves among the white dogwood's magnificent exhibition. Information – Yosemite Sierra Visitor Center (559) 683-4636. Trail: Easy one mile loop. Travel on Hwy 41, five miles north of Oakhurst, then turn right on Sky Ranch Road (Road 632) and continue 9 miles (if you reach an unpaved road, you've gone too far) to a left turn signed *Nelder Grove*. (Tiny sign.) Follow it for 2 miles to the parking area; it's signed *Shadow of the Giants*. Follow the rutted driveway to the parking area.

BASS LAKE

A picturesque setting is provided for swimming, boating, hiking, fishing, and camping. Bordering the lake–on the north shore–are several lodgings and tiny Pines Village with apparel, gifts, antiques, a market, a bakery/ice cream store, and a sandy swimming beach. Beasore Road, near the village, gives access to winter snow fun including snowmobiling and cross-country skiing.

INFORMATION

Yosemite Sierra Visitors Bureau – Lodging and area information. Mon-Sat 8:30am-5pm, Sun 9am-1pm. Winter

9am-4:30pm. (Closed Sun from Nov 1st.) (559) 683-4636. www.yosemitethisyear.com. Located at 41969 Hwy 41, northern end of Oakhurst.

Bass Lake Chamber of Commerce – Information on jazz festivals, craft shows, 4th of July fireworks, and nearby trails. (No office; leave message and get call back within hours.) (559) 642-3676. www.basslakechamber.com.

Bass Lake – Boat Rentals-Water Sports – Summer jet skis and fishing boats 8am-8pm. (559) 642-3200. (800) 585-9283. Adjacent to the Pines Resort.

EATERIES/LODGING

Camping along Bass Lake – Reservations (877) 444-6777 (8am-9pm). www.recreation.gov. (24 hrs.)

Pines Resort – Cottages/suites are nestled along the north shore of the lake. Spa/massages, heated swimming pool, two Jacuzzis, boat rentals, jet skis, and tennis courts are available. **Ducey's Bar & Grill** – Casual outdoor patio dining with lake views. 11am-9pm, Fri/Sat 10pm. Music and Dancing. Fri/Sat from 9pm. **Ducey's on the Lake** – B,L,D – Steak is their dinner specialty. 7am-noon, and 4-9pm, Fri/Sat 4-10pm. Weddings. Resort – (559) 642-3121. Reservations both restaurants – (559) 642-3131. www.basslake.com. Located at 54432 Road 432, North Shore.

Miller's Landing – Rustic-to-luxurious cabins are nestled amid the pines, some with fireplaces and kitchens. Boat rentals and general store with groceries, ice cream fountain, and a grill. Water skiing, fishing, boating, and swimming. (Rustic cabins & store closed Oct-March.) Dogs okay. (559) 642-3633. www.millerslanding.com. 37976 Road 222, South Shore.

Fork's Resort – Nice one/two bedroom cabins with kitchens and views of the lake. (No in-room phones.) Fork's Restaurant – B,L,D – Family dining. See menu on website. General store, swimming, boat rentals, and fishing. Dogs okay in some rooms. (Closed Oct–March.) 39150 Road 222, South Shore. (559) 642-3737. www.theforksresort.com.

DIRECTIONS – Bass Lake

From Hwy 41, in the north end of Oakhurst, turn right on Road 222, signed *Bass Lake*. Located in the Sierra National Forest.

FISH CAMP

This tiny town sits among tall trees and bubbling streams. It's the last chance for lodging and dining before entering the park. (2.5 miles from Yosemite Park's South Entrance.) Dine at one of Tenaya Lodge's restaurants for breakfast, lunch, or dinner before entering the park. (Details under Eateries/Lodging below.)

YOSEMITE MOUNTAIN SUGAR PINE TRAIN

Train follows old logging routes. Daily, April thru Sept. (Closed Easter Sunday.) After Labor Day, days vary. Times vary and are subject to change; check website or call ahead. Adults $21, kids 3-12 $10.50. Moonlight Special – dinner/music. May thru Oct. Weather Permitting. Adults $55, kids 3-12 $27.50. Information/Reservations (559) 683-7273. www.ymsprr.com. 56001 Hwy 41, 4 miles south of Yosemite's South Entrance.

YOSEMITE TRAILS PACK STATION

One and two-hour horseback rides, wagon rides with a BBQ dinner. 8am-5pm June to Nov. Winter sleigh rides on Sat/

Sun from the Tenaya Lodge. Mid-Dec – Jan 4th. (559) 683-7611 or call the Tenaya Lodge (559) 683-6555. (Ask for the concierge.) www.yosemitetrails.com. Jackson Road, 2 miles from Yosemite's South Entrance.

INFORMATION

Fish Camp General Store – Information – 8am-6pm. (559) 683-7962. Located 2.5 miles from Yosemite National Park.

EATERIES/LODGING

Tenaya Lodge & Cottages – Nice rooms surrounded by trees on thirty-five acres. Cottages have fireplaces. Free Wi-Fi. (High-speed connection $9.95 per 24 hrs.) Spa/fitness center, swimming pool, and four spa tubs. Summer golf and horseback riding nearby. Winter brings cross-country skiing, sleigh rides and ice skating. (Ski/snowshoe/skate rentals.) Weddings. Dogs okay in some rooms. Restaurants: **Embers** – Fine dining and wine 6-9pm. Reservations (888) 514-2167 ext. 3. (Closes for some winter months.) **Sierra Restaurant** – Breakfast 6:30-11am, winter 7am-11am. Dinner 5:30-10pm, winter 5-9pm. (Kids' menu.) **Jackalopes** – B,L,D – Casual dining indoor or outdoor patio . (Kids' menu.) 11am-11pm. **Parkside Deli** – Baked goods and picnic foods. Lodge and cottages open all year. Front Desk (559) 683-6555. Reservations (800) 635-5807. www.tenayalodge.com. 1122 Hwy 41, 2.5 miles from Yosemite.

DIRECTIONS – Fish Camp

On Hwy 41, 12.5 miles north of Oakhurst (via Hwy 41); 2.5 miles from Yosemite National Park's South Entrance.

2.6 YOSEMITE NORTHERN PARK AREA
What To Do & See

The Northern Park Area is pristine and serene–a hiker's dream come true–away from all the crowds, hotels, and restaurants of the Southern Park. The Northern Park holds secluded cabins (few with private baths) and tent camps with common baths and dining areas. (Details under Lodging.) No air conditioning is needed, the air is always crisp. Temperatures (except at Hetch Hetchy) are about twenty degrees cooler than Yosemite Village. The park has its own rhythm, and when the sun shuts out its rays, the park shuts down except for amazing stargazing, campfire stories, and moonlit walks.

NORTHERN PARK ENTRANCES

Big Oak Flat (northwest), Arch Rock (west), and Tioga Pass (east). In addition to the park's three main entrances, is the Hetch Hetchy Park Entrance. It leads to the park's remote area and is located 1 mile prior to the Big Oak Flat Park Entrance. (Details listed below.) **Note:** Park guide/map free at all park entrances.

HETCH HETCHY – Remote Park Area

In Hetch Hetchy, from the bridge crossing O'Shaughnessy Dam, the thunderous rage of the Tuolumne River is heard as it runs through the gorge below. (Walk close to the railing on the left side of the bridge to feel the cool mist of the river.) The path over the dam leads through a dark, cool granite tunnel. Beyond the tunnel, hiking trails are found. The trail to Tueeulala Falls (1.5 miles one way) is reached along the way to Wapama Falls (2.5 miles one way from the dam). The waterfalls are usually dry by mid-summer, but when they are flowing, they can be seen from the parking area near the dam. When hiking to the falls, follow the trail signs, stay on the path closest to the reservoir, and watch out for bears and rattlesnakes. **Note:** In some years, the early spring falls are so full that they create flooding making the trails impassable. For an up-close look at the river, take the **Tuolumne River Trail**. (Details for trail below.) Best hiking in spring and autumn. This is the only Northern Park Area where temperatures soar from early June to October. (Details for nearby lodging under Lodging Outside the Park Entrances.) In winter, the park is open when the road is plowed. Information – Hetch Hetchy Park Entrance (209) 379-1922, Big Oak Flat Information Station (209) 379-1899. From Hwy 120, 1 mile prior to the Big Oak Flat Northwest Park Entrance, take Evergreen Road for 9 miles to a split in the road, and turn right on Hetch Hetchy Road. After passing through the Hetch Hetchy Park Entrance, (open from first light until 9pm) continue 8 miles to the road's end and a large parking area. (No vehicles over 25 feet.)

TUOLUMNE RIVER TRAIL

Just prior to the O'Shaughnessy Dam, which crosses the Tuolumne River, turn left on the old paved road and pass under the metal gate. Soon the pavement ends and a dirt path zigzags downhill to a split; bear right, and head upstream along the edge of the river toward the base of the dam for .25 mile. The sound of the river up close is amazing. Then go back to the split in the path, turn right, and continue .25 mile to a bridge crossing over the Tuolumne River, marking the 1-mile turning around point. Reservoir (no swimming) provides drinking water for San Francisco. Trail: Moderate 1 mile one way. To find the trailhead, walk to the bottom of the parking area; turn left just prior to the dam onto an old paved road.

BIG OAK FLAT – Northwest Park Entrance

Big Oak Flat Information Station – Lies just inside the park entrance. (Details under Northern Park, Visitor Centers.)

Inside the park, West Hwy 120 becomes Big Oak Flat Road and travels 7.8 miles to Crane Flat (gas station and mini-mart). Here a left turn takes visitors to Tioga Road which travels across the Northern Park Area to the Tioga Pass East Park Entrance. Tioga Road (Hwy 120) open late-May/June to mid/late-Oct. (Depends upon snow.) **Note:** To reach Yosemite Village (details under Yosemite Village) in the Southern Park Area, follow Big Oak Flat Road from Crane Flat (gas station) south 9.5 miles, turn left at the junction with Hwy 140 and follow the signs to Yosemite Village. Southern Park attractions, including Yosemite Village, are listed in sequential order from the Wawona South Park Entrance.

All Northern Park activities are listed in sequential order beginning from the Tioga Pass East Park Entrance except for the Merced Grove which is located near the Big Oak Flat Park Entrance. When entering the park from the northwest area at the Big Oak Flat Entrance, follow the activity listing under the Tioga Pass East Park Entrance in reverse order.

MERCED GROVE

Follow the wide, old dirt road downhill to approximately twenty large sequoia trees near an old cabin. The cabin was built in 1934 as a summer retreat for park superintendents. It's a lovely walk along the road bordered by pine trees, but the return uphill trip is a tough climb. (Cross-country skiing and snowshoeing take place here in winter.) Trail: Moderate 1.5 miles one way. Located 4.5 miles from the Big Oak Flat Park Entrance.

ARCH ROCK – West Park Entrance – Hwy 140

This is the best winter entrance to the park (usually no chains are required); it's the easiest road for RVs. The park entrance lies 12 miles from El Portal and 38 miles from Mariposa on Hwy 140. Upon entering the park, Hwy 140 becomes El Portal Road and follows the Merced River. The river, strewn with gigantic boulders, is very turbulent especially in May and June and roars as it smashes against the boulders. In spring and early summer, the Wildcat and Cascades Waterfalls are visible from Hwy 140, at the picnic area (viewing pullout, just beyond the picnic area) 2.8 miles from the park entrance. To reach the Northern Park Area, continue 1.7 miles on Hwy 140 and turn left at the junction with Big Oak Flat Road (Hwy 120). Continue 9.5 miles to Crane Flat (gas station/market) and turn right onto Tioga Road (Hwy 120). Tioga Road is open late-May/June to mid/late-Oct. (Depends upon snow.) To reach Yosemite Village, in the Southern Park Area, continue straight ahead beyond the junction with Big Oak Flat Road and follow the signs. (20-minute drive.)

Note: Northern Park activities are listed in sequential order **beginning from the Tioga Pass East Park Entrance**. When entering the park from the Arch Rock Entrance, follow listings in reverse.

TIOGA PASS – East Park Entrance

This is the closest park entrance from Mammoth Lakes. From Hwy 395, (25.5 miles north of Mammoth Lakes and .5 mile south of the town of Lee Vining which has gasoline) take a left turn onto East Hwy 120, a winding 12-mile mountainous road which leads to the park. At the park entrance, it becomes Tioga Road, traveling across the Northern Park Area to Crane Flat, which is 7.8 miles from the Big Oak Flat (northwest)

Park Entrance. Tioga Road open late-May/June to mid/late-October. (Depends upon snow.)

OUTSIDE TIOGA PASS PARK ENTRANCE

ELLERY LAKE & TIOGA LAKE

Here the sparkling clean air lends a hand in the remarkable sharp images of a dramatically blue sky hung with big white puffy clouds, green pine trees, and silver-gray mountains laden with huge clumps of snow even in early summer. All images are reflected into the two lakes of emerald-green which are studded with patches of sapphire-blue creating a lovely photogenic landscape.

LODGING

Ellery Lake/Campground – Great fishing. Located 3 miles outside park's East Entrance.

Tioga Lake and Campground – Great fishing. Located .2 miles outside park entrance.

Note: No reservations taken at Ellery Lake or Tioga Lake Campgrounds.

Tioga Pass Resort – Cabins, café and gasoline. On Hwy 120, 1.9 miles outside the Tioga Pass Park Entrance. (Details under Lodging Outside The Park, Tioga Pass Park Entrance.)

SADDLEBAG LAKE

Travel down the partially paved and gravel road which follows alongside a stream. At 2.3 miles, the lake appears. Continue ahead to the parking area and take the stairs down to a small café (breakfast and lunch) and the fishing boat rentals. (Great trout fishing is found here.) A marvelous loop trail showing off extraordinary beauty, while displaying many lakes, lies at the northern end of Saddlebag Lake (elevation 10,050 feet). It can be reached by trails which travel along Saddlebag's lakeshore from the café. The trail beginning from the right side of the café (2.1 miles from the café parking area), is slightly longer than the left side, but it's an easier trail to connect to the loop trail. But the best way to reach the amazing loop trail is to take the taxi boat ride across Saddlebag Lake from the café, and begin the loop trail from the north shore of the lake.

From the boat dock (on the north shore), take the rocky trail uphill. Stay to the right; the path soon levels out and becomes dirt. At the junction, take the trail to the left to begin the five-mile loop. Greenstone Lake is reached in .25 mile. Continue on the trail along the right side of Greenstone Lake as it travels down close to the lake and then meanders up to a small pond. From here, the path goes uphill and then descends to reach Wascoe Lake. The walk here in the high elevation among the mountain tops and clouds makes it seem as if heaven is just a step away. For the less-than-hardy, this may be a good place to turn around. The path then follows a series of ponds before reaching the long Steelhead Lake, closely followed by Excelsior Lake and Shamrock Lake. Further along the loop, other lakes emerge. This is a moderate walk because the paths meander gradually up and down.

Here in the high elevation, winter brings between 30 and 50 feet of snow and huge chunks of snow cling to the mountains framing the lakes, even through summer and autumn. In July, August, and September, when the temperatures are soaring in Yosemite Valley, the temperatures here are usually in the low 50s. Rain storms (snow storms possible by September) blow in quite suddenly. Saddlebag Lake is 70 feet deep in parts. Dogs are allowed on the taxi boat and on the trails. Trail maps, fishing licenses, boat taxi, and fishing boat information are available at the café. Hourly roundtrip taxi boat – adults $11, seniors $10, age 3-12 $6, dogs $5. Fishing boat rentals (fourteen feet) half day $60, ten hours $90, boat launching $5. Café open for breakfast and lunch July to late Sept. Summer 7am-7pm, autumn 8am-5pm. www. saddlebaglakeresort.com. (No telephone.) Bring a wind-breaker jacket, sunscreen, bug repellant, and water. Visitors should get acclimated to the high elevation prior to hiking the loop trail. (Details for Ellery Lake Campground, Tioga Lake Campground, and Tioga Pass Resort under Lodging Outside The Park, Tioga Pass Park Entrance.) Trail: Moderate 5 mile loop. **Note:** Walking just a small portion of this trail is very rewarding. From Hwy 120 (.2 mile prior to Tioga Pass Resort) 2.1 miles prior to the East Park Entrance, turn right on Saddlebag Road and travel 2.5 miles to the end of the road into the parking area.

NUNATAK NATURE TRAIL

From the trailhead, follow the paved path straight ahead (instead of turning right and taking the loop around the first pond). The trail soon becomes soft dirt. It leads to a second pond (on the left) where a few picnic tables are surrounded by pine trees. Signs along this loop trail tell about this area from glacier days to the present time. The trail continues among the pines then skirts a third pond. The trees, mountains, and clouds above are reflected down into the ponds creating a lovely sight. The trail splits as it returns to the first pond (near Tioga Road). Take either path around the pond to return to the parking area. Trail: Easy one-mile loop trail. Trailhead is found 1.7 miles prior to the park entrance, at the brown and yellow Inyo National Forest sign. Then continue 1.7 miles on Hwy 120 to the Tioga Pass East Park Entrance.

2.7 NORTHERN PARK AREA – Tioga Pass East Park Entrance
What To Do & See

Listings are in sequential order from this entrance. From all other Northern Park entrances, follow the listings in reverse order.

PONDS

Picturesque ponds lie along Tioga Road, just inside the park gate. The first one, Dana Meadows Pond, appears deep green; its color is intensified by the reflection of surrounding pine trees. Faint paths meander around the pond. Near the pond is a large parking area found just .1 mile from the park's entrance, on the left side of the road. (Traveling east, it is 6.5 miles from the Tuolumne Meadows Lodge turnoff.) Beyond Dana Meadows Pond is a large meadow strewn with many small boulders, and further along is a tiny pond where tall reeds hug the shore. In early summer, the pond displays amazing reflections of the tall pine trees and mountains with patches of snow still clinging. The narrow trail, leading along the right side of the pond, becomes boggy in the spring. The parking pullout is located 1.8 miles from the park entrance on the left side of the road. (Traveling east, it is 4.8 miles from the Tuolumne Meadows Lodge turnoff.)

TUOLUMNE MEADOWS AREA

Here, freedom rules; wade the creeks, scramble across the boulders, hike across the streams and bridges, observe honey-wheat colored meadows, and, in July, the wildflowers in tangerine, violet, pink, and sunny yellow. The air is scented with the perfume of pine trees, and filled with the sound of birds calling to each other. Visitors, who open themselves up to adventure, will discover a world of true serenity and extravagant beauty. The color of gold slipping through the trees at dawn lends itself to sunny summer days, and cool evenings with cranberry sunsets closing the day. Many trails are found threading their way into the dazzling back-country.

TUOLOMNE MEADOWS INFORMATION

Tuolumne Meadows Lodge – The starting point for memorable hiking trails. (Trail details are given below.) Non-guests may join guests for dinner. Dinner reservations required; call (209) 372-8413. This is especially nice for the campers at the nearby Tuolumne Meadows Campground. (Details for the lodge and campground under Lodging, Northern Park Area.) From the Tioga Pass Park Entrance, travel 6.6 miles to the turnoff for Tuolumne Meadows Lodge and continue down the road beyond the Dog Lake parking area to the lodge.

Wilderness Center – Trail information, wilderness permits, maps, bear-resistant canisters. 8am-5pm. Mid-June to mid-Oct. (209) 372-0309. Travel 6.6 miles from the Tioga Pass Park Entrance, turn left at the Tuolumne Meadows Lodge turnoff.

Tuolumne Meadows Horse Stables – Horseback riding. 7am-5pm. July to mid-Sept. (209) 372-8427. Travel .4 mile beyond the turnoff for the Tuolumne Meadows Lodge. Turn right; it's signed *Soda Springs/Dog Lake* and *Horse Stable*. (7 miles from the Tioga Pass Park Entrance.)

Tuolumne Meadows Store – Gifts, film, sunscreen, camping and fishing supplies. 9am-5pm. Summer until mid-

Sept. (209) 372-8428. Located .1 mile from the turnoff signed *Soda Springs/Dog Lake*.

Tuolumne Meadows Grill – Breakfast and sandwiches, hamburgers, hot dogs, and fries. 9am-5pm. Mid-June until mid-Sept. The grill is adjacent to the Tuolumne Meadows Store.

Tuolumne Meadows Gas Station – Gas 24 hrs. with credit card. (Next gas station is 39 miles in Crane Flat.) Open 8:30am-6pm. Mid-June until mid-Sept. (209) 372-8436. 24-hr towing (209) 372-8320. Located .2 mile from the turnoff signed *Soda Springs/Dog Lake* and .4 mile from the turnoff for Tuolumne Meadows Lodge.

Tuolumne Meadows Visitor Center – Books, maps, and information about the free shuttle bus. (Details under Northern Park Area, Visitor Centers.) (209) 372-0263. Located .8 mile from the gas station and 8 miles from the Tioga Pass Park Entrance.

LYELL CANYON TRAIL

From the trailhead, the path travels downhill to the riverbank, and turns left (upstream). Be sure to pause along this very clear river to take in its beauty and watch the small swirling pools as they spill over huge granite slabs. Follow the path to the small wooden bridge crossing the river. After crossing, head left (upstream) on the meandering path alongside the river. The trail meets a left turn (to Gaylord Lakes) keep to the right, and follow the path amid the pine trees. Soon it passes a marshy area and continues ahead to twin wooden bridges over the Lyell Fork of the Tuolumne River. This is a wondrous place to rest and absorb the beauty, and it's a great place to bring children to swim and go wading. The shallow pale-turquoise river swirls and cascades, forming tiny white spindrifts that spill over the rocks. Adding to the river's beauty, gigantic boulders and pine trees cling to the shore. For the less-than-hardy, this may be a good place to turn around. Trail: Easy .7 mile to the twin bridges.

To continue on to Lyell Canyon, cross over the twin bridges and walk ahead passing an open meadow to a split in the trail. Turn left on the John Muir Trail and follow it among the pine trees. The path passes by a meadow strewn with many boulders and soon reaches the wooden John Muir Bridge which crosses the shallow Rafferty Creek. This is a great place to cool off on a summer's day. Trail: Easy .7 mile to the creek from the twin bridges. (The path continues ahead along the Lyell Fork for many miles; return on same trail.) Expect to see mosquitoes in early morning and at dusk in spring and early summer. Trail information – Tuolumne Meadows Visitor Center. (Details under Visitor Centers.) From the Tioga Pass Park Entrance, travel 6.6 miles and turn left at the Tuolumne Meadows Lodge turnoff. Continue to the large Dog Lake hikers' parking area (.4 miles on left). To find the trailhead, walk downhill from the middle of the parking area and cross over the entrance road. It's signed *John Muir Trail*. Continue down to the river and turn left upstream. (Traveling east, it is 1.4 miles from the Tuolumne Meadows Visitor Center to the Tuolumne Meadows Lodge turnoff.)

DOG LAKE

Two separate paths lead up to Dog Lake, and the first one starts from the Dog Lake parking area just prior to the Tuolumne Meadows Lodge. (The parking area is also used for the above detailed Lyell Canyon Trail.) To find the trailhead, walk uphill from the parking area and carefully cross over Tioga Road. The trail begins with a steep climb and ascends up through the forest, passing a side trail which leads out to Lembert Dome. It continues ahead, levels out, and soon reaches a tiny lake with the back side of Lembert Dome as its backdrop. At 1.2 miles, the trail splits and continues to the right. (Left turn goes to the Lembert Dome parking area.) The path climbs up .3 mile to Dog Lake. The shallow lake, fringed with tall reeds, boulders, and tall pine trees, is warm enough for swimming in summer. A narrow path follows the south shoreline. The east and north shores are fragile and boggy especially in spring and early summer. The lake sits at 9,240 feet, and it is advisable to become acclimated to the high elevation prior to hiking up to the lake. Trail: Moderately-strenuous 1.5 miles one way. From the Tioga Pass Park Entrance, travel 6.5 miles and turn left at the Tuolumne Meadows Lodge turnoff. Proceed to the large Dog Lake parking area (.4 miles on left). The trailhead is found uphill of the parking area, at the opposite end of the parking area from the Lyell Fork Trail. **Note:** The second trail up to Dog Lake (the easiest one) begins at the Lembert Dome parking area. (Details under Lembert Dome.)

LEMBERT DOME

The gray face of the granite dome (the steepest part) is quite close to the parking area. To observe the dome up close, and for the less-than-hardy not wishing to climb the dome (also climbers scaling the face of the dome), take the short trail close to the entrance road of the Lembert Dome parking area. To hike to the top of the dome, climbers have a choice of two trails. The first one is from the above mentioned Dog Lake parking area beginning at the trail signed *Dog Lake*. (Details are given above.)

The second choice is from the Lembert Dome parking area. The trail begins climbing up into the forest; look for a short side trail to the left signed *Lembert Dome*. This leads up to the back side of the dome. Once on the dome, the trail becomes quite obscure and the climbing is steep with no level spots.

From the summit are wonderful views of the Tuolumne River and the surrounding meadow, as well as distant peaks. Sunrises and sunsets are quite memorable from here. It is advisable to become acclimated to the area's high elevation prior to climbing up the dome. The elevation is 9,450 feet at the dome's highest point. Warning: Never climb any dome when rain or thunder/lightening are predicted. Trail information – Tuolumne Meadows Visitor Center. (Details under Visitor Centers.) Trail: Moderate to the dome (strenuous climbing up the dome), 1.4 miles one way.

To reach Dog Lake, from the Lambert Dome parking area, take the path meandering among the pine trees which passes over huge rock slabs and continues up to a signed split in the trail. At this first junction turn left; continue on, passing by two horse trails that come in from the stables. Keep to the right. The trail crosses a small creek and then the climbing becomes easier. Further up (one mile from the trailhead) another junction is reached; stay to the left (right turn leads back to the starting point at the Dog Lake parking area). Continue to the final trail junction and, keeping to the right, take the uphill .3 mile path to the lake. This is a nice place for a picnic; the water is warm enough in summer for wading and swimming. Trail information – Tuolumne Meadows Visitor Center. (Details under Visitor Centers.) It is advisable to become acclimated to the high elevation prior to hiking up to the lake. Trail: Moderate 1.6 miles one way. To observe the front of the dome up close, travel .4 mile from the Tuolumne Lodge turnoff to the turnoff signed *Soda Springs/Dog Lake*. Then turn right, and park in the first parking area for Lembert Dome. This is also the best parking area to reach Dog Lake. (Driving east from the Tuolumne Meadows Visitor Center, travel on Tioga Road beyond the gas station. The road soon crosses a bridge. Just beyond the bridge, turn left at the signed *Soda Springs/Dog Lake* turnoff, and park in the first parking area.)

SODA SPRINGS/PARSONS LODGE TRAIL

From one starting point, the path meanders through a quiet corner of the Tuolumne Meadow where badgers sun themselves. A second path leads across the middle of the meadow which is woven with wildflowers in early summer. Both paths are pleasant short walks and meet at a fine swimming area near the bridge over the Tuolumne River. From the bridge, the path travels uphill to the site of the old Parsons Lodge (oldest stone building in a national park) and the remains of the McCauley's Cabin built in the late 1800s. Nearby is Soda Springs where the marmots play among the rocks and clean carbonated water bubbles up from the ground. Early in the day and at dusk, mule deer come to lick the salt found at the springs. Trail information – Tuolumne Meadows Visitor Center. (Details under Visitor Centers.) Trail: Easy first trail .5 mile one way. Easy second trail .6 mile one way. To find the first trailhead, travel on Tioga Road .4 mile from the Tuolumne Lodge turnoff, and turn right; it's signed *Soda Springs/ Dog Lake*. (Traveling east, coming from the Tuolumne Grill, proceed .3 mile and turn left at sign.) **Note:** Go past the first parking area on the right to a locked gate on the left and park along the road and walk around the gate. The second signed trailhead is found just east of the Tuolumne Meadows Visitor Center on Tioga Road.

TENAYA LAKE

On a sunny day, the lake sparkles as if sprinkled with diamonds. The transparent water, in shades of mint and emerald green, mixes with the brilliant blue like the Steller's jays that are found all around the lake. The jays are especially busy around the picnic tables. The vision of the lake surrounded by tall green pine trees, cream-colored sand and boulders, and glacier-polished granite domes (reflecting into the lake), is remarkable as the crisp, clear air makes the images so sharp. Windy days fill the lake with thousands of tiny ripples that send gentle waves splashing on rocky and sandy shorelines. The soft lapping sound at the lake's edge entices visitors to linger especially at the eastern sandy beach. Swimming is allowed, but the water is very cold. Follow the path around the lake where its tremendous beauty is revealed. In the early morning or at dusk, deer are sometimes seen drinking on the lake's south shore.

Tioga Road (Hwy 120) runs along the northern edge of the lake and the turnouts along the northwest side (toward Olmsted Point) provide parking for picnickers. These are also good places to begin a lakeside-loop walk. Follow the path west, beyond the picnic tables and the pine trees at the water's edge and walk past a lone picnic table sitting out in the sun. The path zigzags across a narrow shallow creek where rocks have been strewn for crossing. The level path hugs the lake and soon joins a dirt trail coming in from Olmsted Point. Continue along the lakeshore where the mostly-flat path meanders past huge boulders and pine trees. Captivating views of the lake are flaunted through the pines where Steller's jays chirp and play. Hug the edge of the lake around the eastern shore to the left (trail straight ahead beyond the lake, travels to Tuolumne Meadow). Soon a nice sandy beach is reached where picnic tables sit out on the sand. From here, follow along the lake's shore, beyond the restroom and telephone area, until the path becomes too rocky and close to the lake's edge. Then continue along the edge of Tioga Road, to the starting point. **Note:** For a short walk, follow the edge of the lake from the sandy eastern beach/picnic area and walk along the lake clockwise;

return any time. A wheelchair/stroller accessible boardwalk leads from the parking area to the sandy east beach. Trail: Easy 3-mile loop around lake or take short walk. For parking, turn left at the signs for the picnic area (just prior to lake) or continue ahead .25 mile to another parking area on the left (with more picnic tables) or continue to the roadside pullouts with a few isolated picnic tables. Tenaya Lake is 6.5 miles west of the Tuolumne Meadows Visitor Center. (Traveling east, it's 1.5 miles east of Olmsted Point and 31 miles east of the Crane Flat Market/Gas Station.)

OLMSTED POINT

Artists, with their easels, are sometimes scattered along the nearby hillside, painting the picturesque landscape set against jade-green pine trees, distant gray granite peaks (including Half Dome) and a very blue sky. The most impressive view is found a short walk from the parking area. Take the trail to the left. It descends and then climbs up to a rocky lookout with fabulous views. Lots of squirrels and marmots play in this area. Return on the same trail. From the east end of the parking area, off in the distance, is a striking view of the blue-green Tenaya Lake. Trail: Easy .3 mile one way. Located 9 miles from the Tuolumne Meadows Visitor Center and 1.5 miles west of Tenaya Lake. (Traveling east it's 29.5 miles from the Crane Flat Market/Gas Station.)

MAY LAKE

From Tioga Road, take the 2-mile narrow winding entrance road to the parking area near a small pond. A sandy trail begins to the left of the pond among the pines and many gigantic boulders. The hillside along the first part of the steep trail is covered with granite slabs. The trail ambles up under the pine trees and soon climbs more steeply and leads across granite slabs with lovely mountain views in the distance. Near the end of the trail, especially due to the high altitude and rocky path, it's a moderately-strenuous climb. May Lake is a peaceful lake in a pretty setting where a white-granite mountain provides a backdrop for the deep blue water, while tall green pines straddle the shoreline. Close to the lake is the High Sierra May Lake Camp. (Details under Lodging.) Returning on the same trail, visitors will find the descent slippery due to crushed loose granite being swept across the rocky path. Mosquitoes are prevalent in early morning and at dusk in spring and early summer. Trail: Moderate 1.2 miles one way. It is 11.2 miles from the Tuolumne Meadows Visitor Center and 2.4 miles from Olmsted Point to the turnoff road for May Lake. (Traveling east, it's 27.2 miles from the Crane Flat Market/Gas Station.)

CONES & NEEDLES TRAIL

Along this short educational walk, the trees, such as California red fir, white fir, and western white pine, are identified by markers. Look for an unmarked turnout (on the left) 5 miles west of Olmsted Point. (Traveling east, it's on the right 24.5 miles east of the Crane Flat Market/Gas Station.)

SIESTA LAKE

This charming miniature lake provides a perfect photo spot. It is visible from Tioga Road (on the left) 15.7 miles from Olmsted Point (Traveling east, it's on the right 13.7 miles east of the Crane Flat Market/Gas Station.)

CASCADE CREEK TRAIL

From the campground, follow the secluded path beyond the locked gate as it rambles uphill on an old road covered with fallen pine needles from the surrounding trees. In less than half a mile, the path turns downhill and comes to a creek (dry by August). The shady path, surrounded by lots of pine trees and ferns, crosses another stream (also dry by August) and continues uphill and then descends. The path becomes partially rutted in places, and leads to an overgrown creek bed where rock-hopping is needed for crossing. Continue another .25 mile to some trail signs and go straight ahead to reach the rippling creek, where cascades turn it frothy white. A footbridge crosses the creek, marking the 2.5 miles point. (The creek is greatly diminished by mid-July.) Many small pools are found, but the best swimming hole is .25 mile upstream. Trail: Easy 2.5 miles one way. Travel 24.7 miles from Olmsted Point (10 miles west of Siesta Lake) to the turnoff signed *Tamarack Campground*, on the left. Large RVs are not advised. (Traveling east, from the Crane Flat Market/ Gas Station, take Tioga Road (Hwy 120) east 3.7 miles to the turnoff signed *Tamarack Campground* on the right.) Continue 3 miles to the end of the gravel road (watch for deer), and travel straight ahead through the campground to a locked gate and the trailhead signed *Yosemite Valley*. (It's not signed for Cascade Creek.) This road closes in mid-September. **Note:** A wilderness permit is needed when the campground road is closed and visitors must walk the three miles from Hwy 120 to the trailhead.

TUOLUMNE GROVE OF GIANT SEQUOIAS

To stand among the twenty five giant sequoias and the Dead Giant tree (tunneled in 1878 for horse-drawn wagons), follow the old road downhill through the forest. A variety of pines hug the road and, in springtime, lovely white dogwoods bloom between them. The dogwoods are also a marvelous sight in autumn when they turn a bright yellow-orange. At the trail junction, where many sequoia trees grow, take the path to the right to reach the old Tunnel Tree. After walking through the tree, take the narrow path to the right, and continue to the huge fallen tree. From here, take either the left or the right trail; soon the paths meet and cross over a stream on a wooden bridge close to the picnic area. Return to the parking area on the furthest trail to the left. Trail: Easy 1.2 miles downhill; the return trip is a moderate uphill climb. From the turnoff signed *Tamarack Campground*, travel 3.2 miles to a parking area on the right signed *Tuolumne Grove*. From the Big Oak Flat Park Entrance, travel east 7.8 miles to the Crane Flat Market/Gas Station and continue east on Tioga Road (Hwy 120) .5 mile to a parking area on the left signed *Tuolumne Grove*.

From the Arch Rock Park Entrance, proceed on Hwy 140 for 4.5 miles and turn left (north) onto Big Oak Flat Road. Continue 9.5 miles (near the Crane Flat Market/Gas Station) and turn right (east) on Tioga Road (Hwy 120). Travel .5 mile to a parking area on the left signed *Tuolumne Grove*.

2.8 Yosemite Northern Park Area PARK INFORMATION

SUMMER FUN

Best Swimming Areas

Lyell Fork of Tuolumne River – at the twin wooden bridges. (Details under Lyell Canyon Trail.)
Tenaya Lake Beach – (Details under Tenaya Lake.)
Cascade Creek – (Details under Cascade Creek Trail.)

Tuolumne Meadows Horse Stables – (209) 372-8427. (Details under Tuolumne Meadows Area.)

PARK ENTRANCE FEES – (Subject to change.)

Seven-day Pass: $20 per vehicle; $10 walk-ins, motorcycles.
Annual Pass: $40.
National Park Annual Pass: $80 (Admittance to all national parks.)
Senior Pass: $10 (Age 62+ for lifetime.)
Access Pass: Free for U.S. citizens with permanent disabilities.

Note: Passes available at park entrances.

VISITOR CENTERS

Tuolumne Meadows Visitor Center – Information, books, maps, trail maps, and shuttle information. Mid-June 9am-5pm. July 1st thru Sept 9am-6pm. (209) 372-0263. Located 8 miles from the Tioga Pass Park Entrance.

Big Oak Flat Information Station – Wilderness permits, maps, day-hike handouts. Book/gift store 9am-5pm. Information – 8am-5pm. May to Oct/Nov. (Depends upon snow.) (209) 379-1899. Just inside the Big Oak Flat Park Entrance on west Hwy 120.

INFORMATION

Emergency – 911 – Fire, Police, Medical.

Yosemite Medical Clinic – 24-hour emergency care. Appointments Mon-Fri 8am-5pm. (Wheelchair rentals) (209) 372-4637. Located in Yosemite Village, Southern Park Area.

Altitude Sickness – (Details under Appendix.)

Visitor Centers – (Details above.)

Park Information/Weddings/Road Conditions – (209) 372-1000 or (209) 372-0200 or (209) 372-0356. www. nps.gov/yose (up-to-date trail info) and www.yosemitepark.com.

Lodging Reservations/Park Directions – Includes tours, weather, and winter ski pkgs. (801) 559-5000. (Details under Lodging.)

Tours and Kids' Programs – Listed in the Yosemite Guide, available at all park entrances. Information – 7:30am-7pm. (209) 372-1240. www.yosemitepark.com/activities.aspx.

Tours – From San Francisco – (888) 307-6194. www.yosemitetours.us.

Yosemite Park Guide - (Details under Appendix.) See website to download a copy. www.nps.gov/yose/planyourvisit/guide.htm.

Gasoline – Crane Flat gas station/store – 9am-6pm, winter 5pm. Gas 24-hrs. with credit card. Open all year. (209) 379-2742. Located at the junction of Hwy 120 and Big Oak Flat Road.

Tuolumne Meadows Gas Station – 9am-5pm. Gas 24-hrs. with credit card. Open summer only. Located 7 miles from the Tioga Pass Park Entrance. (Gas available at the Tioga Pass Resort, 1.9 miles outside the Tioga Pass Park Entrance, and also in the Southern Park Area.)

Village Garage – Emergency road service – 24-hour towing. Garage is open 8am-5pm. (Sometimes closes noon-1pm.) Southern Park area in Yosemite Village, behind the Village Market. (209) 372-8320.

Internet Access – (Details under Appendix.)

Post Offices – (Details under Appendix.)

Yosemite National Park History – (Details under Appendix.)

Accessibility Guide – www.yosemitepark.com/accessibility. aspx.

Note: National Park Ranger service is available to provide American Sign Language interpretation for Ranger programs. Information – Tuolumne Meadows Visitor Center or Big Oak Flat Information Station.

Accessibility Information – Mon-Fri 7am-4:30pm. (209) 379-1035. (Details under Appendix.)

Wheelchair Accessible Activities – (Details under Appendix.)

Tuolumne Wilderness Center – Ranger information and wilderness permits. (Details under Tuolumne Meadows Area.) Information – (209) 372-0309.

Wilderness Permits – Information – (209) 372-0740 (Details under Appendix, Wilderness Permits.)

Swimming – (Details above under Summer Fun.)

Tuolumne Meadows Horse Stables – Information – (209) 372-8427. (Details under Tuolumne Meadows Area.)

Bears – (Details under Appendix.)

Pets – Leashed dogs okay on paved bike paths, paved roads, paved trails, and in some campgrounds.

Kennels – (Details under Appendix.)

Lost & Found — (209) 372-0200. (Press 2 then 4.)

WEATHER

Caltrans – California Road Conditions – (800) 427-7623.

Weather – Trail Conditions/Park Information – (209) 372-0200. www.nps.gov/yose. **Note:** Average park temperatures under Southern Park Area Information, Weather.

TRANSPORTATION

Tuolumne Shuttle Bus – Free throughout the Tuolumne area. Information – Tuolumne Meadows Visitor Center. (Details under Visitor Centers.)

Yosemite Lodge Hikers' Bus – From Tuolumne Meadows Visitor Center (Northern Park Area) to Yosemite Lodge or Curry Village in the Southern Park Area. June/July to Labor Day. (Depends upon snow.) (209) 372-1240.

Note: Additional information under Appendix-Shuttle & Hikers' Bus.

San Francisco Int'l Airport – It's a five hour drive to the Big Oak Flat Park Entrance.

Amtrak Train – San Francisco – Train from Fisherman's Wharf (Pier 39) to Merced (75 miles from Yosemite) with connecting YARTS Bus. Information – (800) 872-7245. www.amtrak.com.

YARTS – Buses from Mammoth to the Northern Park Area. Office, Mon-Fri 8am-6pm. Information – (209) 384-1315. (877) 989-2787. www.yarts.com.

Mammoth Airport – Information – 8am-4:30pm. (760) 934-3825. Horizon Airlines (part of Alaska Airlines). (800)

252-7522. www.AlaskaAirlines.com. One daily flight in summer (thru Sept) from Los Angeles International Airport. (Yosemite's Tioga Pass Park Entrance open late May/June to late Sept. (Depends upon snow.) Enterprise car rental, at the airport. (760) 924-1094. The airport is off Hwy 395, 2.7 miles south of the turnoff for the town of Mammoth Lakes. To reach Yosemite Park from the Mammoth Lakes turnoff, travel 25.5 miles north to Hwy 120 and turn left. (.5 mile south of Lee Vining.) Continue traveling west 12 miles.

EATERIES

Dining Information – Dinner reservations are needed at the Lodges and Camps. Information – (209) 372-1000.

Tuolumne Meadows Lodge – Non-guests may join the guests for dinner. Dinner reservations required; call (209) 372-8413. This is especially nice for the campers at the nearby Tuolumne Meadows Campground. From the Tioga Pass Park Entrance, travel 6.6 miles to the turnoff for Tuolumne Meadows Lodge and continue beyond the Dog Lake parking area to the lodge. (Traveling east, it is 1.4 miles from the Tuolumne Meadows Visitor Center to the Tuolumne Meadows Lodge turnoff.)

Tuolumne Meadows Grill – Hamburgers, fries, chili, drinks, and ice cream. June–mid-Sept. Located 8 miles from Tioga Pass Park Entrance; next to the market.

The following is outside the Tioga Pass Park Entrance:

Tioga Pass Café – B,L,D with great homemade pies. Open 7am-9pm. It is just 1.5 miles outside the Tioga Pass Park Entrance in the Tioga Pass Resort. (Details for the resort under Directions to Tioga Pass East Park Entrance.)

LODGING

Lodging Reservations – taken 366 days in advance inside the park. (801) 559-5000. www.yosemitepark.com.

Camping – Thirteen campgrounds inside the park – some are open all year. Information – www.nps.gov/yose/planyourvisit/campground.htm. Reservations – (877) 444-6777 (8am-9pm PST). www.recreation.gov. (24 hrs.)

Tuolumne Meadows Campground – Open approximately July to late Sept. (Depends upon snow.) Wheelchair accessible sites. **Note:** Free shuttle stops at campground entrance and travels to various trailheads. Shuttle Information – Tuolumne Meadows Visitor Center. Campground Information – (209) 372-4025. www.nps.gov/yose/planyourvisit/campground.htm.

Tuolumne Meadows Lodge – This is the summer base for many hikers. There are seventy tent-cabins and some sit along the Tuolumne River. They have a common bath and come with breakfast and dinner in a central tent. (Beer and wine are available.) Dinner reservations required, call (209) 372-8413. (Non-guests may also have dinner here with a dinner reservation.) Box lunches available, if requested the day before prior to 8pm. Open June/July to mid-Sept. (Depends upon snow.) Lodge (209) 372-8452. Reservations (801) 559-5000. www.yosemitepark.com. From the Tioga Pass East Park Entrance, travel 6.6 miles to the turnoff for Tuolumne Meadows Lodge and continue beyond the Dog Lake parking area to the lodge.

High Sierra Camps – Five hike-to-camps along a loop trail (6 to 10 miles apart) reached by hiking or horseback. Camps with tent-cabins (two, four or six people). Breakfast and dinner served in a dining tent; box lunches available if requested the day before prior to 8pm. Dinner reservations required, call (801) 559-4884. (Dinner is for guests only.)

Camps mid-June/July to mid-Sept. (Depends upon snow.) Guided hikes – hike or ride a horse to the camps. 9am-5pm. (209) 372-0263. Wilderness Permits – (209) 372-0309. Camp reservations (801) 559-5000. www.yosemitepark. com. (Lottery applications, after Sept 1st for following year.)

The following are the five hike-to camps:

May Lake Camp – Found along May Lake with fishing and swimming. This camp may also be reached by a short hike 1.2 miles from the May Lake parking area off Tioga Road. (Details under May Lake.)

Glen Aulin Camp – Near a waterfall on the Tuolumne River. (No showers.)

Sunrise Camp – Rewarding sunrises at this camp.

Merced Lake Camp – Sits along one of Yosemite's largest lakes.

Vogelsang Camp – Lies along Fletcher Creek. (No showers.)

White Wolf Lodge – Set amid pine trees near the Tuolumne River. Four cabins have private baths and electricity usually from 6am-11pm. Tent-cabins have a common bath. Breakfast and dinner served in a central dining building. Dinner reservations required, call (209) 372-8416. (Non-guests may also have dinner here with a dinner reservation.) Box lunches available if requested the day before prior to 8pm. This is the main base for day hikes to Lukens and Harden Lakes. Mid-June/July to mid-Sept. Lodge (209) 372-8416. Reservations (801) 559-5000. www.yosemitepark.com. White Wolf is located off Tioga Road, 15 miles from Crane Flat.

DIRECTIONS
Three Northern Park Entrances and Lodging Outside the Park.

BIG OAK FLAT – Northwest Park Entrance (west Hwy 120)

From San Francisco, take the Oakland Bay Bridge to Hwy 80 east (8 miles) then take Hwy 580 southeast 50 miles to Hwy 205, and follow it 13 miles to the Golden State Fwy (I-5). Continue north for 2 miles, and exit on Hwy 120. Follow Hwy 120 signs, passing Manteca which is 111 miles from the park. Along the way, visit Groveland (23 miles from the park entrance) and see the Iron Door Saloon built in the early 1900s and the adjoining Groveland Hotel (details below) originally built in 1850. For directions from other areas to Big Oak Flat Park Entrance, check website www.yosemitepark.com. From San Francisco – 184 miles.

Evergreen Lodge & Custom Camping – Cozy, wonderful cabins; all have radios and porches. Adjacent to the cabins is a restaurant/bar and general store. Restaurant – breakfast 7-10:30am, lunch noon-3pm, dinner 5:30-10pm. Cell phones usually don't work here, but the lodge provides a room in their garden (behind the restaurant) where free phone service and Wi-Fi are available. In their nearby campground, everything campers need is provided including tents (already set up), mattresses, bedding, camp chairs, and even campfires. Swimming pool, hot tub, pool bar, yoga, and massages are among the lodge's amenities. In winter, there is snowshoeing and cross-country skiing. Lodge closes few weeks in January. (209) 379-2606. (800) 935-6343. www.evergreenlodge.com. Located 1.2 miles outside the Big Oak Flat Park Entrance. Turn on Evergreen Road and proceed 7 miles to the lodge. Watch for cows on the road. The lodge is a few miles from the Hetch Hetchy Park Entrance.

Note: A few miles from the Evergreen Lodge, a short hiking trail runs along the river to Carlon Falls. To find the trailhead, travel from the lodge toward Hwy 120, and continue beyond a bridge to a second bridge. Here, along the left side of the river, is the trail (1.5 miles) to the falls. (Guided tours available from lodge.)

Yosemite Westgate Lodge – Rooms and suites, heated pool and spa. Wi-Fi. (209) 962-5281. (800) 253-9673. www. yosemitewestgate.com. 7633 Hwy 120, Groveland, 12 miles from the park entrance.

Groveland Hotel – Nicely decorated rooms come with a full breakfast and Wi-Fi. Spa services. Restaurant for dinner on the premises; see menu on website. 5:30-9pm. Dogs okay– even on restaurant's patio. (209) 962-4000. (800) 273-3314. www.groveland.com. 18767 Main Street, Goveland, 23 miles from the park entrance.

ARCH ROCK – West Park Entrance (Hwy 140)

Best winter access to the park. (Lowest elevation.) From Los Angeles, follow Hwy 5 (Golden State Fwy) north. Then, 24 miles south of Bakersfield, take Hwy 99 north to Merced and continue 75 miles on Hwy 140 to the West Park Entrance. Directions from other areas on park's website www. yosemitepark.com.

Yosemite Cedar Lodge Resort – Nice rooms across from the Merced River (short path runs along the river's edge) with a restaurant/gift shop, and heated indoor and outdoor swimming pool/spa. Wi-Fi. (209) 379-2612. (800) 321-5261. www.yosemiteresorts.us. 9966 Hwy 140, El Portal, 8 miles from Yosemite.

Yosemite View Lodge – Stands along the Merced River. Nice rooms with kitchenettes, some with spa tubs. Amenities include three outdoor pools, hot tubs, and an indoor pool.

Restaurant offers breakfast and dinner. Dogs okay. Wi-Fi $10 per day or $25 three days. (209) 379-2681. (888) 742-4371. www. yosemiteresorts.us. Hwy 140, El Portal, 16 miles from Yosemite.

TIOGA PASS – East Park Entrance (east Hwy 120)

From Los Angeles, take Hwy 5 (Golden State Fwy) north to Hwy 14. Turn right (east) toward Palmdale/Lancaster, continue north 68 miles on Hwy 14 to Mojave and keep on Hwy 14 (north) via a right turn out of Mojave. Head toward Bishop, passing Red Rock Park. (If visiting the park, exit at the Visitor Center sign.) Continue north on Hwy 14. It becomes Hwy 395 (in 48 miles) and leads north to Lone Pine in 64 miles with hiking trails to Mt. Whitney. (Information at the Ranger Station, just prior to town.) Continue 55 miles north to Bishop. It's 38 miles further to Mammoth Lakes. From there, continue on Hwy 395 north 25 miles to Lee Vining and Mono Lake. (Details for Mt. Whitney, Bishop, Mammoth Lakes, Lee Vining, Mono Lake in Book One.) To reach Yosemite National Park, .5 mile south of Lee Vining, turn left on Hwy 120 (Mobile gas station and café sit back from the corner), and follow the 12-mile winding mountain road to the Tioga Pass East Park Entrance. Road open May/June to late Sept/Oct (depends upon snow). 327 miles from Los Angeles to Lee Vining and 339 miles to the park entrance. Directions from other areas on park's website www. yosemitepark.com.

Tioga Pass Resort – Year-around cabins (some private baths). Summer only, café, gift shop, and gasoline. Café – B,L,D with great homemade pies 7am-9pm. Great fishing nearby. All cabin reservations by e-mail. No phone. (reservations@ tiogapassresort.com) www.tiogapassresort.com. Hwy 120, 1.9 miles outside the Tioga Pass Park Entrance.

Ellery Lake and Tioga Lake Campgrounds –
The lakes lie outside the Tioga Pass East Park Entrance. (Details under Tioga Pass East Park Entrance.) No camping reservations taken.

Lee Vining – The town overlooks ancient Mono Lake and has eateries, lodgings, gas stations, and a market. (Details for Mono Lake/Lee Vining Lodging under Book One, at the end of section 1.3). To reach Lee Vining travel 12.5 from the park entrance to Hwy 395, turn left, and continue .5 mile.

See photos of the 6 areas listed in this book at: www. CaliforniaVacationPaths.com.

Attraction prices and times listed in this guide are subject to change; call ahead. Information missing or incorrect? Contact author: Pati.Anne@yahoo.com.

KID FAVES

YOSEMITE NATIONAL PARK
SOUTHERN PARK AREA

Note: Details for the following activities are found under main section of Yosemite National Park. (See Table of Contents for page numbers.)

WAWONA AREA

Wawona Covered Bridge/Pioneer History Village
– Kids love crossing the 1800s covered bridge which spans the Merced River and leads to the Pioneer History Village. In summer, there are stagecoach rides along the dusty paths. (Wheelchair/strollers okay on bridge and some of the village paths.)

BRIDALVEIL FALL

Bridalveil Fall – Waterfall is visible from the parking area, and it's a short walk to the base of the fall. Kids like the roar of the waterfall and getting wet from the mist that swirls around the pathway especially in spring and early summer.

YOSEMITE VILLAGE

Yosemite Museum – Outside the museum a short loop trail meanders through a reconstructed Ahwahnee Village where deer frequently wander in to feed. Nearby is Degnan's Loft with great pizza and salad.

YOSEMITE FALLS

Yosemite Falls – Kids and adults are impressed by these spectacular falls which can be seen and heard a long way off. From the bridge close to the base of the falls, visitors get wet from the heavy mist especially in spring and early summer. (Wheelchair/strollers accessible.)

CURRY VILLAGE

Curry Village – Swimming and inner-tube floating (rentals) in the Merced River is a lot of fun at Cathedral and Sentinel Beaches. Take the free shuttle from Yosemite Village or drive to Curry Village.

MIRROR LAKE

Mirror Lake Trail – Paved trail (wheelchair/strollers accessible) meanders along the bubbly-turquoise Tenaya Creek and travels to the tiny lake with a sandy beach. Half Dome reflects its beauty into the lake. Some visitors rent bicycles at Curry Village and bike here instead of taking the free shuttle to the trailhead and walking.

WINTER FUN

Curry Village – Outdoor ice skating. (Skate rentals.)
Badger Pass Ski Area – Skiing, snowboarding, tubing, and snowshoeing. (Rentals and lessons.)

NORTHERN PARK AREA

TUOLUMNE MEADOWS AREA

Lyell Canyon Trail – The trail leads visitors to a pretty area laden with huge boulders and pine trees near twin-wooden bridges crossing the Lyell Fork of the Tuolumne River. This is a great place for kids to swim and wade.

Tuolumne Meadows Horse Stables – Summer horseback riding.

Soda Springs – Short easy trail leads to the springs where clean carbonated water bubbles up from the ground.

TENAYA LAKE

Tenaya Lake – There is a sandy beach with swimming, a picnic area where Steller's jays are plentiful, and a trail that travels around the gorgeous lake of many hues of green and blue.

APPENDIX

YOSEMITE NATIONAL PARK

One of the grandest parks in the world is filled with wondrous, magical events. The music of the park greets all who come, like the song at the beginning of a sports game; it lifts up the spirit and patriotic feelings, and sets up anticipation to witness the great events ahead.

Spring is the showy time of year, when two mighty rivers—the Merced and Tuolumne—now at their fullest, are showing off their multiple shades of blue and turquoise, while hundreds of powerful waterfalls spew misty veils. By August, everything slows down and all of the lakes, creeks, rivers, and waterfalls dwindle. Autumn sends leaves of many hues sailing through crisp air; then winter whirls its white blanket over the park's highest elevations. In every season, it is remarkable so it's no wonder nearly four million people come every year from all over the world to see the grandeur. But most of them gather in the Yosemite Valley area leaving the vast majority, of the nearly 1,200 square-mile park, untouched. Don't follow the crowds, follow this guide into the park and experience the real Yosemite to carry away in a pocketful of memories forever.

HISTORY

Indians of Miwok ancestry were in the Yosemite area for thousands of years before any white man traveled here. *Ahwahnee* (place of a gaping mouth) was the name they gave to Yosemite Valley. Ahwahnee was adopted as the name of the people. The Ahwahnee Hotel, a National Historic Landmark, was built in the valley in 1927. The Yosemite Museum has displays of Miwok life and demonstrations of basket-weaving and beadwork; a reconstructed Indian village lies outside the museum and can be accessed by a short loop trail. The Miwok left behind fascinating legends that are still told today. There are many books filled with stories of their early life and legends. Books and Information – www.archive.org and www.yosemite.ca.us/library.

JOHN MUIR

He was a naturalist, conservationist, and writer who roamed the Yosemite area in the 1800s with his mule, Brownie. He built a cabin along Yosemite Creek and became a sheepherder. But he quickly learned that large herds of sheep can cause tremendous damage to the meadows. Later he fought to keep livestock out of the area and to have it declared a national park. In 1892, he helped organize the Sierra Club and became their first president. Since then, the Sierra Club has helped establish many new national parks. www.yosemite.ca.us/library and www.archive.org and www.sierraclub.org/john_muir_exhibit.

John Muir also fought against the building of the O'Shaughnessy Dam that flooded the Hetch Hetchy Valley part of Yosemite National Park to supply water to the San Francisco area. In 1913, President Woodrow Wilson signed a bill for the dam to be built and it was completed in 1923. Today, hiking trails skirt along the river and the nearby waterfalls. (Details under Northern Park Area, Hetch Hetchy.) Groups like "Restore Hetch Hetchy" www.hetchhetchy.org are showing how (even without the dam) the Tuolumne River could be diverted differently and still provide water for San Francisco.

On December 6, 2006, John Muir was inducted into the California Hall of Fame at the California Museum of History by then California Governor Arnold Schwarzenegger and First Lady Maria Shriver. www.californiamuseum.org.

WAWONA AREA

This area (with an elevation of 4000 feet) is blessed with mild temperatures year around. Many books describe the Wawona area and Wawona Hotel. *Wawona's Yesterdays* by Shirley Sargent tells about the covered bridge built across the South Fork of the Merced River (near the hotel) and *The Wawona Hotel and Thomas Hill Studio* by Laura E. Harrison tells about the architecture of the hotel and the adjacent visitor center. www.yosemite.ca.us/library. (Details of the Wawona area under Southern Park, Wawona.)

PIONEER CEMETERY

A guide to Yosemite's Pioneer Cemetery of American Indians and others buried here is available at the Yosemite Valley Visitor Center. (Details under Southern Park Area, Visitor Centers.) The cemetery is located near the visitor center.

YOSEMITE GUIDE

This guide is free (with paid admissions) at all park entrances but, to obtain a copy in advance, call one of the visitor centers. Abundant park information is found in the guide with descriptions of the park areas including photos displaying the magnificence of the park. It lists religious services, lodging, dining, camping, post offices, wildlife information, and much more.

This is the place to find walks and talks, and even campfire stories scheduled with the park rangers. Look for kid activities like the *Wee Wild Ones* (6 and under) or find out how kids (in different age ranges) can earn a Junior Ranger badge. (More information at the visitor centers.) There are many tours like the *Moonlight Tour* in an open-air tram on full-moon nights and the *Twilight Stroll*. Information – (209) 372-1240. Reservations – (209) 372-4FUN (4386). www.yosemitepark. com/activities.aspx.

The guide also contains a park map and maps of specific areas like Wawona, which includes the Wawona Hotel, Pioneer History Center, stables, and the gas station; Yosemite Village, which encompasses restaurants, the Village Market, Yosemite Museum and Visitor Center/Bookstore. The Yosemite Lodge area map includes the post office, bicycle rentals, and the Yosemite Falls trails. Curry Village has stables, and bicycle/raft rentals. The Tuolumne Meadows area includes a post office, visitor center, wilderness center, and Tuolumne Meadows Lodge and Campground.

SHUTTLE & HIKERS' BUS

Summer daily hikers' bus from Yosemite Lodge to Tuolumne Meadows. Reservations/Information – (209) 372-1240. Shuttle Buses of Yosemite Valley (accessible) – Free – See the shuttle map in the Yosemite Guide. It tells of summer routes and year round routes. There is a daily shuttle from the Wawona Hotel (and Wawona Store) to Yosemite Lodge near Yosemite Falls and Yosemite Village. Information – Wawona Hotel (209) 375-6556 or Yosemite Lodge (209) 372-1274. (Details for hotels under Southern Park Area, Lodging.)

Free summer shuttle buses run in the Tuolumne Meadows area (Northern Park Area). Information at the Tuolumne Meadows Visitor Center (209) 372-0263.

HALF DOME & WILDERNESS PERMITS

Note: A permit is required for all overnight hiking and for Half Dome climbs.

Half Dome permits – Service fee: $1.50. www.recreation. gov. (Click *Permits* at top of the page.) No permits available in the park.

Advance wilderness permit reservations – taken from May thru Sept from 24 weeks to 2 days prior to start of a trip. Free, if obtained in person; $5 per person for advance reservations. (209) 372-0740.

SOUTHERN PARK WILDERNESS PERMITS

Wawona Visitor Center – mid-May to mid-Oct. (209) 375-9531. Adjacent to the Wawona Hotel.

Yosemite Village Wilderness Center – (209) 372-0745. Located in Yosemite Village.

NORTHERN PARK WILDERNESS PERMITS

Tuolumne Meadows Wilderness Center – Summer only. (209) 372-0309. It's near the Tuolumne Meadows Lodge.

Big Oak Flat Information Station – mid-May thru Oct (depends upon snow). (209) 379-1899. Just inside the Big Oak Flat Park Entrance.

Hetch Hetchy Park Entrance – (209) 379-1899.

INTERNET ACCESS

Access is available in the park at the following: Yosemite Lodge (non guests pay $5.95 per day) and Degnan's Café in

Yosemite Village. Guest rooms in the Ahwahnee Hotel come with Wi-Fi. (Southern Park Area.) Guests of the Evergreen Lodge and their custom camping have access to Wi-Fi in a room found in the garden behind the restaurant. The lodge isn't inside the park, but it's located close to the Hetch Hetchy Park Entrance.

POST OFFICES

Yosemite Village – Mon-Fri 8:30am-5pm and Sat 10am-noon. Information – Yosemite Valley Visitor Center. (209) 372-0298.

Yosemite Lodge – Mon-Fri 12:30pm-2:45pm. Information – Yosemite Lodge (209) 372-1274.

Wawona – Mon-Fri 9am-5pm and Sat 9am-noon. Information – Wawona Hotel (209) 375-6556.

Tuolumne Meadows – Mon-Fri summer 9am-5pm and Sat 9am-1pm. Information – Tuolumne Meadows Visitor Center (209) 372-0263.

ALTITUDE SICKNESS

Acclimate over a few days especially before hiking in high elevations. Headaches, nausea, shortness of breath, and fatigue are signs of altitude sickness. When experiencing any of these symptoms, descend to a lower elevation or visit the Yosemite Medical Clinic near Yosemite Village. (209) 372-4637. (Details for clinic under Southern Park Area, Information.) **Note:** To avoid heat exhaustion and dehydration be sure to bring plenty of water on all hikes or day walks.

BEARS

Many bears are killed by motorist exceeding the speed limit. Black bears, prevalent in Yosemite (no grizzly bears in park), come in many shades of brown and black. Bears recognize bags and coolers and have a strong sense of smell. Even a tiny candy wrapper left in the trunk of a car, is enough to entice them to break in. Please use the bear resistant canisters provided in the parking areas. If a bear is encountered in the wild, make noise, yell, and pick up small children. Don't run; a bear can run a football field in about six seconds. Report bear sightings (209) 372-0322.

KENNELS

Yosemite Valley Stable – Southern Park Area

Only gentle dogs over 6 months old accepted. If dog under 20 pounds, owner must provide a crate or kennel. Proof of license and immunizations required. Reservation advised. Open Memorial Day to Labor Day, 8am-4:30pm. (209) 372-8348.

WHEELCHAIR ACCESSIBLE ACTIVITIES

Note: See Table of Contents for page numbers of activities.

Many of the park's activities are wheelchair accessible. Wheelchairs and bicycles may be rented in the Southern Park Area at Yosemite Lodge and Curry Village. (Details under Southern Park Area, Summer Fun-Bicycle Rentals.) Bicycle/wheelchair trail maps available at rentals. Wheelchair rentals are also available at Yosemite Medical Clinic in Yosemite Village. (Details under Southern Park Area, Information.)

Accessible Campgrounds – (Details under Southern and Northern Park, Lodging.)

Accessibility Guide – www.yosemitepark.com/accessibility. aspx.

Note: TTY pay phones available: Yosemite Valley Visitor Center, Yosemite Lodge, and The Ahwahnee Hotel.

YOSEMITE SOUTHERN PARK AREA

Activities listed below are wheelchair accessible:

Mariposa Grove in Wawona – Accessible tram travels through grove; also cars with placards may follow tram and listen to tour narration.

Wawona – Pioneer History Village – Village path crosses a covered bridge over the Merced River.

Glacier Point Trail – Short paved trail leads to breathtaking views and sunset ranger talks.

Badger Pass Ski Area – Winter sit-ski lessons. (209) 372-8430.

Bridalveil Waterfall – Waterfall is visible from parking area. Short paved trail to base of the fall has a few steep inclines.

Yosemite Museum – Don't miss Indian Village Path behind museum.

Short path from Yosemite Village – Travels to Yosemite Falls and Yosemite Lodge or take shuttle bus from Yosemite Valley Visitor Center.

Lower Yosemite Falls – Paved path to falls under the mist.

Paved Bicycle/Wheelchair Paths – From Yosemite Lodge and Curry Village. (Bicycle/wheelchair rentals.)

Happy Isles Nature Center – Short trail leads out to islands.

Mirror Lake – Trail begins paved, then compacted gravel.

Note: Details of above activities are listed in the Southern Park Area in consecutive order. (See Table of Contents for page number of activities.)

National Park Ranger service is available to provide American Sign Language interpretation for Ranger programs. Information – Wawona or Yosemite Valley Visitor Centers. Temporary accessibility placards that allow cars to be driven on roads usually prohibited to private vehicles are available at all park entrances and visitor centers.

YOSEMITE NORTHERN PARK AREA

Tenaya Lake – At the eastern beach, a wheelchair accessible boardwalk is in the planning stages.

Tuolumne Meadows Campground – Accessible sites available.

RESOURCES/INFORMATION

Yosemite Public Relations – (209) 372-0248.

Wawona Visitor Center – (209) 375-9531. Adjacent to Wawona Hotel.

Yosemite Valley Visitor Center & Bookstore – (209) 372-0298. Located in Yosemite Village.

Tuolumne Meadows Visitor Center – (209) 372-0263. Located in Tuolumne Meadows.

Big Oak Flat Information Station – (209) 379-1899. Located near the Big Oak Flat Park Entrance.

Mono Basin National Forest Scenic Area Visitor Center – (760) 647-3044. www.fs.usda.gov/inyo. Located in Lee Vining, outside Yosemite's East Park Entrance.

Yosemite Sierra Visitor Bureau – (559) 683-4636. Oakhurst, outside Yosemite's South Park Entrance.

WEBSITES

www.yosemitepark.com
www.nps.gov/yose
www.hetchhetchy.org
www.yosemitetours.us
www.yosemite.ca.us/library

Sequoias in the Forest

Majestic sequoias live in the forest, one of the
largest and oldest of all living things.
Branching only at the top, their heads are
held high befitting the kings.
With thick protective bark, in a forest fire,
they won't despair.
While other trees fall, they survive,
with long life so rare.
They live thousands of years,
triumphant over all.

Pati Anne

Book
THREE

Sequoia and
Kings Canyon
National Parks

Visitors should walk the park's trails to fully enjoy the picturesque scenery which shows off waterfalls, lakes, rivers, and mountains in unique settings. Those who stand among the thousand-year-old sequoia trees while inhaling the pine-scented air will surely feel dwarfed and awed by the majestic giants. The massive sequoia trees have extremely thick bark that allows them to survive even forest fires.

Abundant wildlife wanders throughout the park. The sound of squawking blue jays and the tapping of red-headed woodpeckers are distinctly heard above the chirping of smaller birds. Gentle mule deer allow quiet observers to see them up close; black bears may be found in the forest and meadows; marmots (akin to ground squirrels) and bighorn sheep are found in the higher elevations. (Feeding wildlife prohibited.)

It seems like the ubiquitous sound of rushing rivers and waterfalls and the wondrous sights of wildlife and wildflowers amid the giant sequoia trees is just nature showing off. The majestic beauty extends throughout Sequoia National Park, the Sequoia National Forest, and through the adjoining Kings Canyon National Park.

3.1 Sequoia National Park Near Ash Mountain Entrance
What To Do & See

MINERAL KING
Remote area of Sequoia National Park –
Prior to ASH MOUNTAIN PARK ENTRANCE

This is one of the most remote and picturesque areas of Sequoia National Park. Here the summer heat brings out the squirrel-like marmots—notorious for eating radiator hoses and the wiring in parked cars. Lengthy hiking trails, popular with backpackers, pass by small lakes leading to wondrous vistas. The first trail along the entrance road to the park is the Atwell Mill Trail which is reached in 20 miles. It begins at the Atwell Mill Campground (first-come-first served) and leads visitors through the forest to tumbling waterfalls and the Kaweah River in 1 mile. For the less-than-hardy, this is a good turning around point. For more trail information, contact the Mineral King Ranger Station. (Maps of Mineral King available.) Memorial Day to mid-Sept. (Depends upon snow.) 8am-4pm. (559) 565-3768. Park entrance fees may be paid at the ranger station or at the pay-station machine located at Lookout Point, 11 miles along the entrance road. No trailers or RVs. No gasoline. **Silver City Mountain Resort** (Details under Eateries/ Lodging Sequoia National Park Area.) The Mineral King area is reached from Hwy 198, four miles northeast of the town, Three Rivers; two miles south of the Ash Mountain Park Entrance. A small sign marks the right-hand turn coming toward the park from Three Rivers. The narrow, twisting access road is twenty-five miles long (90 percent paved) and takes approximately 1.5 hours one way.

The following park attractions are listed in sequential order beginning at the Ash Mountain Park Entrance (the closest entrance from Los Angeles) and continuing through Sequoia National Park and National Forest, and into Kings Canyon National Park.

ASH MOUNTAIN – Sequoia Park Main Entrance

The **Foothills Visitor Center** (details under Visitor Centers) is one mile from the Ash Mountain Park Entrance. Park map free at entrances. This area is 15-20 degrees warmer than most of the park, which is at higher elevations. (Details for park entrance fees under Park Information.) Just north of Bakersfield, take Hwy 65 north to Hwy 198, which travels 25.5 miles east and becomes Generals Hwy at the park entrance. (Details under Sequoia Park Directions.) Sequoia National Park may also be reached by traveling through Kings Canyon National Park. (Details under Kings Canyon National Park Directions.)

INDIAN HEAD RIVER TRAIL

From the east side of the parking area a short path leads down to the Kaweah River. Many visitors swim here in late summer, but it's not recommended. (No swimming allowed in early spring and summer when the river is full and the current is swift.) Warning: slippery rocks and cold water cause drowning in the park every year. Trail: Easy .25 mile. Located .1 mile from the Ash Mountain Park Entrance. Parking area is on the right-hand side of road marked with a carved Indian head.

MARBLE FALLS TRAIL

This rocky trail winds mostly uphill in and out of shady spots. The trail is extremely warm in summer, but early mornings it's mostly shaded. After almost 2.5 miles, there is a view of a creek below. It's another uphill 1.4 miles to reach the falls. Pieces of sparkling white marble are scattered all along the path. The trail eventually leads to a creek that must be forded before the final ascent. The magnificent falls, located on the Marble Fork of the Kaweah River, are at their peak in springtime. For the less-than-hardy, this may be a hike to skip. Wildflowers abundant in spring. Information – Foothills Visitor Center. (559) 565- 4212. Mosquitoes: Early/late day, especially May to July. Trail: Moderately-strenuous 3.7 miles one way. Located in the Potwisha Campground, 2.7 miles north of the Foothills Visitor Center. Visitors should park across the road from the campground. Begin the hike near campsite #14, and follow the dirt road until it crosses a concrete ditch. Soon a sign marks the trailhead.

HOSPITAL ROCK – Picnic Area

The trees—even telephone poles—are full of holes that noisy red-headed woodpeckers drill and stuff with acorns. Across the main road from the picnic area, observe pictographs on enormous quartzite Hospital Rock. These pictographs have never been deciphered. From there, cross over the narrow side road to find the round grinding holes in the boulders which were created by Indians grinding acorns into meal. (Potwisha Indians once lived in this area.) Follow the short path signed *trail* (near grinding holes) down to the Kaweah River for a powerful display of the river crashing over gigantic boulders. It's especially impressive in the spring and early summer when the river is bursting with energy. No swimming or wading; treacherous water. Dangerous area for children. In the southern area is a lookout point and adjacent to it is a cave-like entrance in the rocky hillside. The path through the entrance leads (in approximately 8 yards) to a large pool. Visitors do swim here in late summer (when the river is low), although it's not recommended. Located 2.2 miles north of the Potwisha Campground, 5 miles north of the Foothill Visitor Center. Parking is in the Hospital Rock Picnic Area, across the road from Hospital Rock.

PARADISE CREEK TRAIL

The trail begins with a short walk (.25 mile) through the forest to the Middle Fork of the Kaweah River. A walk along the river reveals a small waterfall. Above the falls, take the footbridge that crosses over the river. Follow the path that travels straight ahead (along Paradise Creek) and then turns left and climbs up lending fine views of the creek below. The river and creek have extremely strong currents; no swimming or wading. The buckeye trees found in this area produce a large shiny-brown nut in spring which is poisonous to humans and many animals. (Details under Appendix, Seasonal Information.) There is no easy trail access because there is no nearby parking except for those who are camping in the Buckeye Flat Campground. (Details for campground under Eateries/Lodging.) Visitors may park in the Hospital Rock picnic area and walk down 1.5 miles along the narrow, winding road to the campground. Trailhead is on the immediate left of the campground entrance. Trail: Easy 1.5 miles one way.

CRYSTAL CAVE

Down in the cave, visitors will witness many actively growing stalactites and stalagmites. The 45-minute summer tours are daily on-the-half hour; in spring (from mid-May) and in autumn (until mid-Oct), Fri/Sat/Sun on-the-hour. (Closed in winter.) Caves open 11am-4pm. Adults $15, seniors $13, children $7, under 6 $3. **Note:** Tickets must be purchased in advance from the Lodgepole or Foothill Visitor Centers. No wheelchairs, strollers, or tripods. Temperature, a constant 48 degrees. Bring jackets. (559) 565-4489. Entrance road is 8.2 miles north of Hospital Rock on the left; 7 miles via winding Crystal Cave Road to the cave parking area. No vehicles over 20 ft. From the parking area, a steep trail leads .25 mile along Cascade Creek, down to the entrance.

3.2 Giant Forest, Crescent Meadow
What To Do & See

GIANT FOREST AREA

GIANT FOREST MUSEUM

The many displays include one showing different sized pinecones from a variety of trees while another describes the growth of the forest. The museum and some of the trails that begin near the museum are wheelchair/stroller accessible. Trail information is found inside the museum and at the information center kiosk located outside the museum. Museum 9am-6pm. Open approximately May to mid-Oct. (Depends upon weather.) (Closed in winter.) Information, maps, and gifts available. Admission is free. Restrooms outside the museum. (559) 565-4480. Located on Generals Hwy, 2 miles north of the turnoff to Crystal Cave, 4.5 miles south of the Lodgepole Visitor Center. Handicapped parking is alongside the museum; other visitor parking is located across the road from the museum on the hillside.

BEETLE ROCK & BEETLE ROCK TRAIL

On clear days, amazing views are seen from Beetle Rock. Climbing atop the many smooth gigantic granite slabs and boulders is exhilarating, and allows visitors to see many miles off in the distance. Keep young children by the hand. The .5 mile loop trail (wheelchair/stroller accessible) begins at the parking area, passes Beetle Rock, and loops back to the parking area. (Details for Accessible Activities under Appendix.) Located across the road from the Giant Forest Museum; follow the short path uphill behind the parking area.

BIG TREES TRAIL

A short path through the forest begins near the Giant Forest Museum (from the outdoor trail information center kiosk), crosses Generals Hwy, and skirts the handicapped parking area. It then meets the beginning of the paved loop path (wheelchair/stroller accessible) which travels around Round Meadow. This is a peaceful and beautiful area surrounded by magnificent trees, wildflowers, ferns, and other greenery. Sequoias tower far above the other trees and their reddish-brown color gleams brightly in the sunshine. The path passes over small wooden bridges as it encircles the marshy meadow. There are benches along the way to sit and absorb some of the beauty. Interpretive signs posted along the trail give information about the trees and the meadow. Information – Lodgepole Visitor Center. (559) 565-4436. Trail: Easy one mile from Giant Forest Museum, Loop trail from handicapped parking area is .6 mile. Trailhead is found near the Giant Forest Museum on Generals Hwy. Parking area is across the road from the museum. Handicapped parking is .2 mile north of the museum on the left, near the Loop Trail Entrance. (Location of winter parking varies; depends upon snow plowing.)

CRESCENT MEADOW AREA

CRESCENT MEADOW ROAD

Cars squeeze between the tall (300 feet or more) reddish-brown barked sequoias that touch the edge of the narrow road as it meanders through the forest. Visitors can stand among the giant beauties, feel their rough bark, and marvel at their immense size. **Note:** Vehicle access on Crescent Meadow Road may be limited during the summer season when a free shuttle operates from the Giant Forest Museum and the Lodgepole Visitor Center. (Shuttle details under Transportation.) In winter, the road is closed to traffic, but snowshoeing and cross-country skiing are allowed. Rentals at the Wuksachi Village Lodge. (559) 565-4070. The 3-mile road begins along the south side of the Giant Forest Museum and leads to the base of Moro Rock (details under Moro Rock). It then travels through Tunnel Log (a giant sequoia which fell in 1937 and was cut large enough for a car to pass through it) and continues on to Crescent Meadow (picnic area, restrooms, and trailheads) at the end of the road. Reach Tharp's Log from the trail that begins here. (Details under Crescent Meadow and Tharp's Log.)

HANGING ROCK

A narrow dirt path amid tall green ferns takes visitors up to a lookout point a short distance away. From here, the path continues uphill to the Hanging Rock lookout point where a huge boulder sits atop a massive granite slab. There is a fine view of Moro Rock and the valley below. Travel 1.3 miles on Crescent Meadow Road. (The road begins along the south side of the Giant Forest Museum.) Keep to the right at all intersections. Just .2 mile prior to the large parking area for Moro Rock, is a tiny parking area signed *Hanging Rock*.

MORO ROCK

Moro Rock juts upward with a steep .25 mile climb to reach the summit. Nearly 400 steps and many resting seats are carved into the granite for an easy ascent. Once at the top, sensational panoramic views are revealed. Not recommended for people with heart conditions. Directions are given above under Hanging Rock. When leaving, continue along the road (to the right) and follow signs for Crescent Meadow.

CRESCENT MEADOW

This lovely meadow comes alive in spring and summer when the wildflowers are blooming, and tiny pools in the marshy meadow are filled with singing frogs and teeny fish. The surrounding trees add to the beauty, especially when the white dogwood flowers blossom among the greenery. There are no trails into the meadow; just peer into pools from the path and bridges. A picnic area and restrooms are found near the parking area. Follow the signed *Crescent Meadow* trail (wheelchair/stroller accessible) which crosses a couple of tiny wooden-plank bridges while curving along the meadow. A signed right turn along the paved path, on the far side of the meadow, heads out to Tharp's Log. (Details under Tharp's Log.) Trail: Easy .3 mile around meadow; path including Tharp's Log .8 mile one way. Parking is at the end of Crescent Meadow Road, 1.5 miles from Moro Rock. Trailheads are found near right side of the restrooms.

THARP'S LOG

Hale Tharp, the first (recorded) white man in this area, established his home inside this enormous fallen sequoia in the late 1800s, and lived there during the summertime. The tiny room he built with a stone fireplace and a window with a wooden shade is still visible by peering inside the log. To reach Tharp's Log, take Crescent Meadow Trail from the end-of-road parking area. (Trailhead found right of restrooms.) Follow this paved (wheelchair/stroller accessible) path around Crescent Meadow to a right turn signed *Tharp's Log*. This paved path has a slight incline and passes by a long meadow where there is a bench to rest and observe the beauty. As the meadow diminishes, the path ascends a short distance to the log. Return on the same paved trail or continue on the dirt trail as it loops back behind the log house, (to the left) to Chimney Tree in .3 mile. It then continues .2 mile to Crescent Meadow and the parking area. Trail: Easy .8 mile to Tharp's Log one way, additional .5 mile on dirt trail includes Chimney Tree. The trail to Tharp's Log is found along the Crescent Meadow Trail. (Details under Crescent Meadow above.)

GENERAL SHERMAN TREE

The world's largest tree is more than 2,000 years old. Although it is 274.9 feet tall, not the tallest tree, it is the largest in volume. It weighs approximately 1,400 tons (enough wood to build about 40 houses) and it's still growing. The redwoods in northern California are taller, but not as large. (Information under Trees in Appendix.) From the parking area, a wide cement pathway (with huge steps) travels steeply downhill .5 mile to the tree. The Congress Trail (details below) begins near the General Sherman Tree. Anyone who can't walk the steep pathway (from the regular parking area) may apply at the visitor centers for a one-day pass and park in the handicapped parking area. From there it's a short flat walk to the General Sherman Tree. **Note:** From Memorial Day to shortly after Labor Day, visitors can take the free accessible shuttle which runs every 15 minutes from the Lodgepole Visitor Center and the Giant Forest Museum to both the upper and lower (handicapped) entrances. (Details for shuttle under Transportation.) Handicapped parking area is plowed in most winters, but the trails are usually snow-covered. Snowshoeing is fun around the General Sherman Tree and on the adjoining Congress Trail. (Snowshoe rentals at Wuksachi Village Lodge.) (559) 565-4070. Trail: Steep .5 mile to tree, one way; easy level (wheelchair/stroller accessible) path from handicapped parking area. **Note:** Path may be covered in snow in winter. The parking area for the General Sherman Tree and the connecting Congress Trail is located via the turnoff road signed *Wolverton/General Sherman Tree* (1.5 miles to parking area) found 2.5 miles north of the Giant Forest Museum (.5 mile north of the handicapped parking area), and 1.5 miles south of the turnoff for the Lodgepole Visitor Center. Handicapped parking is on Generals Hwy at the signed parking area 2 miles north of the Giant Forest Museum and .5 mile south of the Wolverton/General Sherman Tree turnout.

CONGRESS TRAIL

Some of the special trees encountered along this trail are named the President's, the House, and the Senate trees. This is one of the park's most popular and astonishing trails where majestic trees dwarf everything around them. This paved trail is wheelchair/stroller accessible.(Some assistance may be needed.) Open year-round. In winter the trails are covered in snow; snowshoeing is fun on the trail. (Snowshoe rentals at Wuksachi Village Lodge.) Trail: Easy 2-mile paved loop. See directions above to the General Sherman Tree where the trailhead to the Congress Trail is reached.

3.3 Wolverton & Lodgepole Areas
What To Do & See

WOLVERTON

The Wolverton Picnic Area offers daily summer outdoor barbeques beginning mid-June. (Call ahead for current times and rates.) Tickets may be purchased from the market next to the Lodgepole Visitor Center or the Wuksachi Lodge. In winter Wolverton offers sledding, snowshoeing, and cross-country skiing. Call ahead for snow conditions. Information – Lodgepole Visitor Center (559) 565-4436. Ski/snowshoe rentals at Wuksachi Village Lodge. (559) 565-4070. (Details for lodge under Lodging and Eateries.) Take the Wolverton turnoff road located 3 miles north of the Giant Forest Museum and 1.5 miles south of the Lodgepole Visitor Center, (details under Lodgepole) and continue 2 miles to end of the road.

LODGEPOLE

LODGEPOLE VISITOR CENTER

Information, trail maps, gift shop, books, and Crystal Cave tickets. (Details under Crystal Cave.) Wilderness permits – summer 7am-3:30pm (closes for lunch; times vary). Winter permits – self-registration. Free accessible summer shuttle runs from here to the main park attractions. (Details under Transportation.) Adjacent to the Visitor Center is a grill, deli, and market/gift shop. Grill, summer 9am-8pm; fall and spring 9am-6pm. (Closed in winter.) Laundry and showers available spring thru fall. (Closed in winter.) Nearby is the post office (open all year, Mon-Fri) and the Lodgepole Campground (details under Eateries/Lodging). Call ahead for ranger-led winter snowshoe walks. Visitor center open all year. Open daily beginning April 1st through fall. Call for spring hours. Summer – 7am-7pm, after Labor Day 8am-5pm until late Sept, then 9am-4:30pm until winter. (Call for winter days open and hours.) (559) 565-4436. www.nps.gov/seki. **Note:** Call ahead; in some winters many roads may not be plowed, therefore, the visitor center and the surrounding areas may be closed. Located 1.5 miles north of the Wolverton turnoff, one hour drive from the Ash Mountain Park Entrance and a 45-minute drive from Grant Grove Village in Kings Canyon National Park.

TOKOPAH FALLS TRAIL

One of the loveliest paths in Sequoia Park begins with a short walk from the far end of the campers' parking area and crosses a bridge where the trailhead is found. At the start, the dirt trail hugs the river where robins and blue jays call out and bears are sometimes seen. Soon the trail leaves the river's edge and comes to gigantic boulders blocking the trail. Turn up away from the river, and pick up the trail on the other side.

The path follows along the showy mint-green Kaweah River, which is full of white-water cascades and is especially attractive in spring and early summer when the water level is high. There are many spots to stop and watch the cold water passing by. (No swimming or wading; treacherous water.) Rock-hop or walk over small wooden bridges in order to cross the many tiny streams.

Near the end of the trail, the soft dirt path becomes extremely rocky and climbs up a granite hill without any trees for shade. Then it levels out with a pleasant short walk to the falls. Small marmots sun themselves on the huge boulders near the base of the picturesque cascading falls which rush through the gorge. (Feeding marmots is prohibited.) The mist swirls around the boulders at the end of the trail; sitting near them has a cooling effect. Visitors should not climb on the rocks around the falls as they are slippery and dangerous. Patches of last season's snow may still linger along the top of the gorge even in June. Falls are best in late spring and early summer. Trail: Moderate 3.5 miles round trip. To locate the trailhead, follow the road beyond the Lodgepole Visitor Center through the entrance gate for the Lodgepole Campground (which lies along the Kaweah River) to the far end of the parking area. **Note:** No fee for hikers entering the campground.

3.4 Sequoia National Park
PARK INFORMATION

PARK ENTRANCE FEES – (Subject to change.)

Seven-day Pass: $20 per vehicle; $10 walk-ins, motorcycles.
Annual Pass: $30.
National Park Annual Pass: $80 (Admittance to all national parks.)
Senior Pass: $10 (Age 62+ for lifetime.)
Access Pass: Free for U.S. citizens with permanent disabilities.

Note: Passes available at park entrances and the pay-station machine along Mineral King Road. Pay station accepts only credit cards.

Mail-in application forms are available online for Senior and Access passes. www.nps.gov/seki. (Under search, type entrances fees.)

The park offers several "free" days per year:

Martin Luther King, Jr. weekend in January, National Park Week in April, Get Outdoors Day in June, National Public Lands Day in September, and Veteran's Day weekend in November. (Subject to change.) Information – www.nps.gov/seki.

VISITOR CENTERS

Foothills Visitor Center – Information, trail maps, bear canisters, and Crystal Cave tickets are available. (Details under Crystal Cave.) Open all year. Summer 8am–4:30pm. (559) 565-4212. Located 1 mile from the Ash Mountain Park Entrance. (Details under Sequoia National Park Directions.)

Wilderness Center – Summer permits Mon-Fri 8am-4:30pm, after mid-Sept self-registration. Located near the Foothills Visitor Center. (559) 565-3766.

Lodgepole Visitor Center – Information, trail maps, wilderness permits (7am-3:30pm), gift shop, and Crystal Cave tickets. (Details under Crystal Cave.) Free accessible summer shuttle runs from here to main park attractions. (Details under Transportation.) Visitor center open all year. Open daily beginning April 1st thru fall. Call for spring hours. Summer – 7am-7pm, after Labor Day 8am-5pm until late Sept, then 9am-4:30pm until winter. (Call for winter days open and hours.) Closed 11am-noon for lunch. (559) 565-4436. Call ahead; in some winters, roads may not be plowed. **Note:** See Lodgepole for details on the grill, deli, market/gift shop, laundry, and showers adjacent to the visitor center. Located 1.5 miles north of the Wolverton turnoff, 1 hour drive from the Ash Mountain Park Entrance and a 45-minute drive from Grant Grove Village in Kings Canyon National Park.

INFORMATION

Sequoia National Park – 635 sq. miles.

Emergency – Dial 911. (No coins needed within the park.)

California Road Conditions – Caltrans (800) 427-7623. Delays for winter snowplows could be half a day or more.

Park Information/Weather – 24 hrs. (559) 565-3341. (Press 1,1 for weather/road conditions.) Road closures due to snow storms – (888) 252-5757. www.nps.gov/seki.

Eateries/Lodging/Camping – (Details under Eateries/Lodging.) www.visitsequoia.com and www.nps.gov/seki.

Seasonal Information – (Details under Appendix.)

Park History & Information – (Details under Appendix.)

Drowning – (Details under Appendix.)

Junior Ranger – Kids earn patches to become a Junior Ranger. (Details at the visitor centers.)

National Forest Information – (559) 338-2251.

Mineral King Ranger Station – 8am-4pm. (Closed in winter.) Call ahead, times are subject to change. (559) 565-3768.

Wilderness Permits – (Details under each visitor center and Appendix.)

Horseback Riding – (Details under Kings Canyon Park.)

Bears – (Details under Appendix.)

Park Guide – www.nps.gov/seki. (Under *Plan Your Visit*, click on *Brochures*. Then click on, *View current and back issues* of the park newspaper or *Park Map*.)

Accessibility Guide – www.nps.gov/seki. (Under *Plan Your Visit*, click on Accessibility Information (on the right-hand side of the page).

Wheelchair Accessible Activities – (Details under Appendix.)

GASOLINE/TOWING – Sequoia Park & National Forest

Stony Creek Lodge – Gas 24 hrs. with credit card. Open late May to early Oct. (559) 565-3909. Located in the National Forest, 3.7 miles east of Montecito-Sequoia Lodge, 13.3 miles west of the Lodgepole Visitor Center.

AAA – 24 hrs. – (800) 400-4222.

SNOW PLAY

Ranger-led winter snowshoe walks – Sign ups at the Lodgepole Visitor Center. (559) 565-4436. (Call ahead, subject to change.)

Wolverton – Cross-country skiing and snowshoeing. (Rentals from Wuksachi Lodge.) (559) 565-4070. (Call ahead, subject to change.) Directions under Wolverton.

Montecito-Sequoia Lodge – Ice skating on a private lake, cross-country skiing, and snowshoeing lessons/rentals. www.mslodge.com. (Details for lodge under Lodging between Sequoia National and Kings Canyon National Parks.)

FISHING

California fishing license required, age 16 and older. Park fishing regulations are available at the visitor centers. The

Lodgepole Market, near the Lodgepole Visitor Center, sells fishing gear and licenses.

PETS

National Parks – Dogs allowed in picnic areas and campgrounds, not on park trails.

National Forest – Dogs okay on trails and Big Meadows Campground. (Details under Sequoia National Forest.)

TRANSPORTATION

Park Shuttle – Free accessible summer shuttle runs from 9am-6pm and leaves from Dorst Campground, Wuksachi Village Lodge & Restaurant, and the Lodgepole Visitor Center. It continues to the General Sherman Tree (upper and lower parking areas), Giant Forest Museum, Moro Rock, and Crescent Meadow. Runs approximately Memorial Day to shortly after Labor Day every 15 minutes. Information – Lodgepole Visitor Center (559) 565-4436. Giant Forest Museum (559) 565-4480.

Sequoia Shuttle Bus – Round trip from Visalia $15. Information call Visalia Visitor Bureau. Mon-Fri 8am-5pm. (559) 334-0141. Reservations (877) 287-4453. www.sequoiashuttle.com.

AIRPORTS

Visalia Airport – Information (559) 713-4201. 40 miles from Sequoia National Park.

Fresno Yosemite Int'l Airport – 53 miles west of Kings Canyon National Park.

EATERIES/LODGING – Sequoia National Park Area

Note: Also see Eateries/Lodging Kings Canyon National Park Area and Sequoia National Forest Area.

Camping

Reservations – Most are first-come, first-served: make reservations for Lodgepole and Dorst Creek Campgrounds. (877) 444-6777 (8am-9pm PST). www.recreation.gov. (24 hrs.) (Enter Sequoia and Kings Canyon National Park on website.) Information for all Sequoia and Kings Canyon National Parks campgrounds – www.nps.gov/seki/planyourvisit/campgrounds.htm.

Lodgepole Campground – Scenic camping along Kaweah River. Open May thru Nov. Tents and limited RVs. Information – (559) 565-4436. Located behind the Lodgepole Visitor Center. (Directions under Lodgepole Visitor Center.)

Dorst Creek Campground – Open late-June to Sept (weather permitting). Some wheelchair accessible sites. Main entrance for Dorst Creek Camping and trailheads, 8.3 miles west of Lodgepole, 5 miles east of Stony Creek Lodge.

Note: Free accessible summer shuttle from Lodgepole Visitor Center, Dorst Creek Campground, and Wuksachi Village Lodge & Restaurant to main park attractions. (Details under Transportation.)

Buckeye Flat Campground – Nice quiet area for tent camping. No RVs. Open early-April thru Sept. One wheelchair accessible site. First-come-first served. Located one mile down a narrow winding paved road across from Hospital Rock Picnic Area. (Directions under Hospital Rock Picnic Area.)

Wuksachi Village Lodge/Restaurant – Gift shop, lounge, cross-country skis, and snowshoe rentals. (Winter trails nearby.) Wi-Fi. Weddings. **Wuksachi Restaurant** – Breakfast 7am-10am, Lunch 11:30-2:30pm, Dinner 5pm-10pm. (Winter until 8:30pm.) Dinner reservations required. Menu includes pizza and soups to steaks, chicken, and fish. Children's menu. Lodge open all year, lower winter rates. (559) 565-4070. Reservations (888) 252-5757. www.visitsequoia. com. It's 1.5 miles west of the Lodgepole Visitor Center, 11.5 miles east of Stony Creek Lodge. (Details under National Forest Lodging, Eateries/Lodging.)

Silver City Mountain Resort – Chalets/cabins, restaurants, and bakery/store. No gasoline. June to mid-Oct. (559) 561-3223. www.silvercityresort.com. Located near the remote Mineral King area of park, 21 miles from the town of Three Rivers. (Directions for Mineral King under Mineral King.)

Sequoia High Sierra Camp – Summer splendor in the wilderness. Great meals, tent-cabins with fine linens, reading lanterns, and a bathhouse with flush toilets/hot showers. Mid-June to mid-Sept. (866) 654-2877. www. sequoiahighsierracamp.com. Hike one mile from Big Meadows Horse Corral Road to the camp. (Directions on website.)

EATERIES/LODGING – Sequoia National Forest
Between Sequoia and Kings Canyon National Parks

Montecito-Sequoia Lodge – The lodge sits on the shore of their private lake in a scenic setting surrounded by pine trees. Rooms and cabins (some cabins share bath) include all meals (buffet-style). A trail lunch is available if staff is notified the night before. Wi-Fi, books, and games are available in the lobby/dining room which is enhanced by two huge stone fireplaces. A large-screen TV is available at no fee in a building adjacent to the lodge. At the lake in summer, there are canoes, paddleboats, sailboats, and swimming from the sandy beach. (Lessons for adults and kids.) There is an outdoor spa, swimming pool, and nightly campfire sing-alongs. In winter, there is cross-country skiing, snowboarding, snowshoeing, and ice skating on the lake. Family Camp (6-night stays) mid-June to late Aug. (One night non-camp stays on Saturday during this time.) **Note:** Camp is only 4 night stays the last 2 weeks in Aug. (Sept until mid-June no minimum night stays) There are supervised kids' programs (all ages) that allow parents free time. Open all year (closed two weeks after Thanksgiving). Winter access from the Kings Canyon Park Entrance. (Heavy snowstorm escort service to and from the lodge.) Chains required Nov to May. Front desk and road conditions – (559) 565-3388. Reservations – (800) 227-9900. Information/snow report check website. www.mslodge. com. Located off Generals Hwy, between the Sequoia National Park and Kings Canyon National Park in the Sequoia National Forest. It's 7.8 miles east of the intersection of Hwy180 and Generals Hwy in Kings Canyon National Park, (intersection is 1.5 miles south of Grant Grove Village) and 17 miles west of the Lodgepole Visitor Center in Sequoia National Park.

Stony Creek Lodge and Restaurant – A stone fireplace adorns the lobby, nice rooms with baths, TV, continental breakfast, and Wi-Fi. Restaurant (pizza and salad) market/gift shop, and gasoline late May to early Oct. Hikers' showers available. Front desk (559) 565-3909. Reservations (866) 522-6966 (for both Stony Creek and Montecito Lodges). www.sequoia-kingscanyon. com. Located between Sequoia National Park and Kings Canyon National Park in the Sequoia National Forest; 3.7 miles east of the Montecito-Sequoia Lodge turnoff road, 13.3 miles west of the Lodgepole Visitor Center in Sequoia National Park.

EATERIES/LODGING – Outside Sequoia National Park

Towns like Visalia, Lemon Cove, and the cozy Three Rivers, provide restaurants, lodging, and, at Lake Kaweah, swimming, fishing, and houseboat/fishing boat rentals. The lake is about 7 miles long in summer. Mon-Fri 8am-4:30pm, Sat/Sun 8am-7pm. (559) 597-2526. Lake Kaweah is located between Lemon Cove and Three Rivers. **Note:** Temperatures in these towns are 15 to 20 degrees warmer than the higher elevations in the park. Information: **Visalia Visitor Bureau** – Area information Mon-Fri 8am-5pm. (559) 334-0141. www.visitvisalia.org. 425 Oak Avenue, 3rd floor, Visalia. **Note: Sequoia Shuttle Bus** to Sequoia National Park leaves from the visitor bureau, the convention center (303 E. Aceuuia Street), and from many hotels. (Check website for hotel locations.) $15. Wheelchair accessible. Reservations (877) 287-4453. www.sequoiashuttle.com.

Plantation B/B – *Gone With the Wind* themed-rooms and gourmet breakfast indoors or on outdoor patio. Nice grounds, swimming pool, and hot tub. Check for specials online. (They allow older children only.) (559) 597-2555. www.theplantation.net. Hwy 198, Lemon Cove, 17 miles from Sequoia National Park.

Lazy J Ranch Motel – (America's Best Value Inn) Cottages with full kitchens close to the Kaweah River. There's an outdoor swimming pool and nice grounds with a children's play area. Continental breakfast. Wi-Fi. Dogs okay. (559) 561-4449. (888) 315-2378. www.americasbestvalueinn.com. Located at 39625 Sierra Drive (Hwy 198), Three Rivers, 8 miles from the park's entrance.

Comfort Inn and Suites – Nice rooms, some with a whirlpool and all with refrigerators, microwaves, and Wi-Fi. Outdoor pool/spa. Continental breakfast. Dogs Okay. (559) 561-9000. (800) 331-2140. www.choicehotels.com. 40820 Sierra Drive (Hwy 198), Three Rivers, 6.5 miles from the Sequoia National Park Entrance.

Sierra Subs and Salads – A variety of subs, salads and soups. Outside tables along the Kaweah River provide a pleasant eating area. Menu on website. Tues-Sat. 10:30am-6pm, Sun 10:30-5pm. (Closed Mon.) (559) 561-4810. www.sierrasubsandsalads.com. 41717 Sierra Drive (Hwy 198), Three Rivers. (Just past the Comfort Inn.)

Crystal Cove Inn – One romantic room with a small kitchen (fine china) tucked amid a lush garden. The garden path meanders down to an outdoor patio overlooking the stunning Kaweah River and a waterfall. The fireplace is nice in the winter, and river swimming allowed June - Sept. This is a rare find! Two-night minimum. (559) 280-5853. www.californiaweekendgetaway.com. 40846 Sierra Drive, Three Rivers.

We Three Bakery – B,L – American cuisine – fresh breads and pastries. 7am-2:30pm. Fri/Sat/Sun B,L,D 7am-9pm. (After Labor Day closes 2:30pm.) Patio dining available. (559) 561-4761. 43368 Sierra Drive (Hwy 198), Three Rivers.

Sequoia Village Inn – Chalets and cottages; some have kitchens. Outdoor pool. Dogs okay. Open all year. Wi-Fi. (559) 561-3652. www.sequoiavillageinn.com. 41717 Sierra Drive (Hwy 198), Three Rivers, across the road from the Gateway Restaurant, .25 mile from the park's main entrance.

Gateway Restaurant and Lodge – Restaurant with outdoor patio dining (summer reservations) overlooks boulder-strewn Kaweah River and the 1922 Pumpkin Hollow Bridge. Vast variety of cuisines; menu on website. Mon-Fri 11am-9pm. Sun 8am-9pm. Winter 8:30pm; bar until midnight. Weddings. Cabins and suites are available along the river's edge. Wi-Fi. (See rooms online.) Small dogs okay. Open all year. (559) 561-4133. www.gateway-sequoia.com. Hwy 198, .25 mile from the park's main entrance.

DIRECTIONS – Sequoia National Park

From Los Angeles, travel north on the Golden State Fwy (5). Just north of Bakersfield, take Hwy 99 north. In 3 miles, exit onto Hwy 65 north (exit #30, signed *Sequoia National Park*) and continue 45 miles to Porterville. A few miles beyond Porterville, turn right (at stoplight) to stay on Hwy 65. Continue 16 miles north to the quaint town of **Exeter** with hotels, restaurants, antique shops, and gas stations. **Note:** To see the striking murals painted on the side of the buildings, turn left at the tall water tower onto Pine Street. At the end of the street, turn around and drive back toward Hwy 65 to see the murals on the other side of the buildings.

From Exeter, continue two miles north, and turn right on Hwy 198. To reach the Sequoia National Park Entrance, continue 25.5 miles. Tiny **Lemon Cove**, endowed with hundreds of citrus trees, is reached in 8.5 miles and offers lodging at the Plantation B/B. Seven miles prior to the park entrance is the town of **Three Rivers** with restaurants, markets, gasoline, and lodging. (Details for Lemon Cove and Three Rivers under Lodging Outside the Park.) Continue northeast on Hwy 198 passing the turnoff for **Mineral King** (the remote park area) to the Ash Mountain Entrance, which is the park's main entrance. From here, Hwy 198 becomes Generals Hwy, and travels through Sequoia National Park, parts of the Sequoia National Forest, and eventually connects to Kings Canyon National Park. Los Angeles to Sequoia National Park – 233 miles.

Note: To reach Sequoia National Park in winter or when driving from Fresno or the San Francisco area, enter through Kings Canyon National Park which connects to Sequoia National Park. Vehicles longer than 22 feet must always enter Sequoia Park through Kings Canyon Park. All vehicles (including 4-wheel drive) may be required to have chains in snowy weather. (Directions under Kings Canyon National Park Directions.)

To reach Kings Canyon National Park from within Sequoia National Park, travel from the Ash Mountain Park Entrance to Lodgepole (one-hour drive from park entrance), continue west 24.8 miles, on Generals Hwy, to intersection with Hwy 180 in Kings Canyon Park. Turn right and in 1.5 miles Grant Grove Village in Kings Canyon National Park is reached.

3.5 KINGS CANYON NATIONAL PARK
Near Big Stump Entrance
What To Do & See

Inspirations and lasting memories are created here. Spring's warmth melts winter's snow, which fills creeks and rivers to the brim with raging waters in swirls of aqua-green and blue. By autumn, the creeks and rivers flow gently between rocks never seen while they are raging. Walk a winter's trail, beneath giant trees and in the quiet, listen for the sound of the wind brushing snow off tree branches. Journey to the canyons of the Cedar Grove area, where in spring and early summer, thunderous waterfalls caressed by cool white mist are heard from a long way off. The park is filled with adventures and visions so perfect, it's hard to believe they are not illusions.

The following attractions are listed in sequential order beginning at the Big Stump Park Entrance and continuing, beyond Grant Grove Village, through the park on Hwy 180 to the end of the road. This area, called Road's End, is the site for many trailheads. Visitors must then journey back through the park to Grant Grove Village. **Note:** To reach Sequoia National Park from Grant Grove Village, continue 1.5 miles and turn left onto Generals Hwy. This leads to the Sequoia National Forest trails and eventually connects to Sequoia National Park.

BIG STUMP – Kings Canyon National Park Entrance

It's accessed by Hwy 180, which stretches east from Fresno and runs throughout the park as Kings Canyon Road. (Details under Park Directions.) Entrance fees are paid at the Big Stump Park Entrance. (Details for park entrance fees under Park Information.) To reach Grant Grove Village from the park entrance, continue .6 mile to the Big Stump Picnic Area (restrooms and trailheads are found here), continue past the intersection with Generals Hwy (leading into Sequoia National Park) in 1 mile. From here, proceed 1.5 miles, and turn right into Grant Grove Village. The Kings Canyon Visitor Center is located here.

BIG STUMP TRAIL (PICNIC AREA)

The trail passes by stumps that were cut by loggers in the 1880s. The unmarked, paved trail travels down the left side of the restrooms and shortly becomes soft as it is covered with crushed pine needles. It descends through the forest where ferns and tiny new pine trees grow among sequoia stumps. At the trail split, take the left turn onto the upper path that narrows and meanders amid the ferns. Along the trail edge is the tall Burnt Monarch Tree. The huge meadow ahead, laden with stumps, was the site of an 1880s lumber mill. The trail merges with the lower path and continues to the left, crossing a stream on a tiny wooden bridge. (It's dry by end of July.) At the edge of the next meadow is the

Mark Twain Stump where a ladder is provided for visitors to climb atop the stump to witness it's width. From here, the trail begins to climb then crosses the highway and continues to the left for the return part of the loop. The path winds in and out of shade between tall pines. A signed right turn leads 100 yards up a steep climb to the Sawed Tree where saw marks are visible, but are not deep enough to kill the tree. Returning downhill to the main path, turn right and walk through the forest. Ahead, the path descends to a tunnel under the highway. When exiting the tunnel, turn left to reach the parking area. The best time to visit is late spring when wildflowers bloom or in autumn when the foliage is colorful. Trail: Easy/moderate 1-mile loop. Parking is in the Big Stump Picnic Area, .6 mile from the Big Stump Park Entrance. Look for the paved trail along the left side of the restrooms.

HITCHCOCK MEADOW TRAIL

From the trail sign, bear to the left onto the soft forest-carpeted path surrounded by lush delicate ferns and many cut tree stumps leftover from the 1800s logging days. The path creeps downhill under the conifers and soon reaches the meadow. Return on the same path or continue past the meadow, with some vigorous uphill climbing, to reach Viola Falls in 1.5 miles. (Falls dwindle by mid-July.) Best time for falls is in May and June. Trail Information – Kings Canyon Visitor Center. (559) 565-4307. Trail: Easy .8 mile one way. Parking is in the Big Stump Picnic Area. Trailhead is signed, and is located just inside the entrance to the Big Stump Picnic Area.

Note: To reach the main part of the park and the Kings Canyon Visitor Center in Grant Grove Village, turn left when leaving the Big Stump Picnic Area and follow Hwy 180. Travel beyond the intersection (reached in 1 mile) with Generals Hwy which leads to the Sequoia National Forest and Sequoia National Park. Continue another 1.5 miles, and turn right into Grant Grove Village.

GRANT GROVE VILLAGE

A restaurant, gift shop, restrooms, post office, and a market that, in winter, rents snowshoes and cross-country skis, are located in the village, as well as the following:

Kings Canyon Visitor Center (also called Grant Grove Visitor Center) – Information, books, and trail maps are available. Summer 8am-6pm. Spring and fall hours vary; usually 8am-5pm. Winter 9am-4:30pm. Ranger-led winter snowshoe walks. (Depends upon snow level.) Open all year. (559) 565-4307. Located 2.5 miles beyond the Big Stump Picnic Area, 1.5 miles past the intersection with Generals Hwy coming from the National Forest area and Sequoia National Park.

John Muir Lodge and Grant Grove Cabins – Rooms and cabins. (Details under Lodging.) Summer hiking trails and winter cross-country skiing trails are close by. (Details for trails below.)

PANORAMIC POINT

On a clear day, there are great views of Kings Canyon from Panoramic Point. (This is the starting point for the Park Ridge Trail.) It is reached by walking 300 yards from the parking area up a paved trail covered in pine needles. (Directions under Park Ridge Trail.)

PARK RIDGE TRAIL

A dirt trail begins to the right of Panoramic Point and follows switchbacks uphill, along clusters of wildflowers in spring, until it meets the fire road. Follow the road to the left for about 50 yards, to pick up the trail. Then follow it along the ridge until it meets the fire road again. Take this road .1 mile to reach the fire lookout. Several trails lead to the fire lookout. (Information at Kings Canyon Visitor Center.) Trail: Easy/moderate 2.4 miles one way to fire lookout from Panoramic Point. To reach Panoramic Point's parking area from the Kings Canyon Visitor Center, follow the road through the parking area .1 mile, and turn right along the side of John Muir Lodge. The road winds uphill 2.2 miles. No trailers allowed on road leading up to the parking area.

GENERAL GRANT LOOP TRAIL

Follow the path to the left where the **Fallen Monarch Tree** lies. Walking inside the tree gives a real feel of its vastness. Then, facing each other across the path, are the **California Tree** and the **Oregon Tree**. Next along the path is the **Gamlin Cabin** built in 1872. In the early 1900s it served as the quarters for the first park ranger. The path to the left of the cabin climbs up steeply to a lookout point. Traveling downhill from the cabin, visitors will find the famous **General Grant Tree** which has been designated our nation's Christmas tree. A tree ceremony is held, with a choir singing Christmas carols, on the second Sunday in December. The tree is approximately 1,700 years old, and is the third largest tree in the world. (268 feet tall, with a circumference at the base of 107 feet.) Information is under Trees in Appendix. While walking along the trail in winter when the trees are blanketed in snow and tiny snowflakes float through the air, visitors will be treated to a lovely surreal winter scene. The snow is usually packed down on most of the trail for easy walking. For an adventurous walk, rent snowshoes from the Grant Grove Village Market. This paved loop is wheelchair/stroller accessible in good weather. (Details for Accessible Activities under Appendix.) Trail: Easy .5-mile paved loop. (Directions under North Grove & Dead Giant Loop Trails.) Trailhead is found in the center of the parking area, between the auto and bus/RV parking areas.

NORTH GROVE & DEAD GIANT LOOP TRAILS

Beyond the metal gate, the path meanders among the trees and follows an old road, where white dogwood bloom in springtime, and the leaves turn magenta in autumn. At the junction, turn left. (The right turn is the dusty half of the North Grove Loop where many trees have been injured by fire, but the fertile soil here has provided a nursery for hundreds of new trees.) Continue on the dirt road down among the giant trees to the far end of the loop. Here, a trail meanders .25 miles to the left leading to a .6 mile loop. Visitors beginning on the left will come to the Sequoia Lake Overlook first (a private lake), and those beginning the right will see the Dead Giant Tree first. (Ax cuts deep into the nutrient system caused this tree to die.) Return back up the .25 mile trail to the North Grove Loop. Enter the loop to the right to return on the shortest route back to the parking area. Information – Kings Canyon Visitor Center. (559) 565-4307. Trail: Moderately-Steep North Grove Loop 1.5 miles, combined with the Sequoia Lake/Dead Giant Loop 2.2 miles. To find the trails, travel north of Grant Grove Village and in .2 mile turn left. Continue past the Columbine Picnic Area, to the Dead Giant parking area. Trailhead is located at the far left end of the parking area at the metal gate.

HUME LAKE

The lake provides swimming and fishing with nearby camping, picnicking, hiking, and boat/bicycle rentals. There is also a market, 24-hour laundry, and gasoline that can be purchased with a credit card. From the campground, an easy trail winds 2.5 miles around the lake. Hume Lake is in the Sequoia National Forest. **Hume Lake Christian Camps** – (559) 305-7770. (Details under Lodging.) Ranger station (559) 338-2251. Access via a narrow paved road 6 miles from Grant Grove Village. The winding Hume Lake Road lends entrance to the lake in 12 miles. Road is plowed in winter. Another paved winding entrance road (10 miles) is located off Generals Hwy, 3.5 miles from the intersection of Hwy 180 and Generals Hwy.

Note: North of the Hume Lake turnoff, Hwy 180 turns drastically into a u-turn eastward and heads out 25 miles to Road's End. Road closed mid-Nov to May. (Depends upon weather and rockfall.) Beyond Boyden Cavern, it descends, zigzagging along the Kings River, (raging and spectacular in spring) down into the depths of the canyon (deepest canyon in U.S.).

3.6 North of Hume Lake Turnoff
What To Do & See

BOYDEN CAVERN

Marble stalactites and stalagmites are viewed during the 45-minute tour. Tickets can be purchased at the cavern.

Constant 55 degrees; bring jacket. Tours on-the-hour, 10am-5pm May to mid-Sept. 11am-4pm mid-Sept to mid-Oct. Call for current prices; senior discounts, under 3 free. From the ticket area there is a steep 5-minute walk to reach the cave entrance. Snack Bar and gift shop. Information (559) 338-0959. www.caverntours.com. Take Hwy 180, 13.5 miles from the Hume Lake turnoff, 19.5 miles from Grant Grove Village.

GRIZZLY FALLS

This impressive waterfall flows down into the mighty Kings River. It's reached by a short walk (approximately 50 yards) from the picnic area off Hwy 180. The waterfall can be heard from the parking area (especially in spring and early summer) and can be seen from some of the picnic tables. The parking area for the waterfall is signed *Grizzly Falls Picnic Area*, and is located 5 miles beyond Boyden Cavern on the left-hand side of the road, 4.3 miles prior to the turnout for the Cedar Grove Visitor Center.

CEDAR GROVE PACK STATION

Summer overnight rides. (559) 565-3464. Located 7.5 miles from Boyden Cavern, one mile prior to Cedar Grove Village.

CEDAR GROVE VILLAGE

Note: The Cedar Grove area (4,600 ft elevation) is usually 10-20 degrees warmer, in summer, than Grant Grove (6,600 ft elevation). (Closed in winter.)

Cedar Grove Visitor Center – Open Memorial weekend thru Labor Day. 9am-5pm. (559) 565-3793. (Details under Visitor Centers.) Village located 9 miles from Boyden Cavern,

28 miles from Grant Grove Village. Take the first left turn on the entrance road off Hwy 180 to reach the visitor center.

Cedar Grove Lodge – Market/gift shop, showers, laundry, and a grill (B,L,D) with counter service. Memorial Day to mid-Oct. (559) 565-3096. (Details under Eateries/ Lodging.)

KNAPP'S CABIN

Knapp's Cabin was built in the 1920s and can be reached via a short walk from the parking area. Located two miles past the turnoff for Cedar Grove Village where a small sign on the left-hand side of the road marks the parking area.

ROARING RIVER FALLS & RIVER TRAIL

The falls flow into the canyon with a mighty force in spring and early summer lending a spectacular display. They can be reached by a 5-minute lovely walk from the parking area on paved **Roaring River Falls Trail**. (Wheelchair/stroller accessible.) A short trail leads down to the base of the falls.

Another option to reach the falls, is to follow the beginning of the **Zumwalt Meadow Trail** to the bridge crossing over the river. (Details for the trail below.) Turn right (left for Zumwalt Meadow), and follow the **River Trail**, which is strewn with massive boulders and oak and pine trees along the forceful south fork of the Kings River. It's especially beautiful in autumn, when the red and honey-colored oak leaves provide a vivid contrast among the green pines. The river is low in the fall and reveals many huge boulders, but the current is still strong. No swimming or wading; treacherous water. Roaring River Falls Trail: Easy 5-minute walk; River Trail from Zumwalt Meadow: Easy 1.6 miles one way. The parking area for the 5-minute walk is located .9 mile from the Knapp's Cabin turnout, just beyond the Roaring River Bridge on the right-hand side of the road. To access the River Trail from the Zumwalt Meadow parking area, follow directions under Zumwalt Meadow.

ZUMWALT MEADOW

From the parking area, a sandy path follows the south fork of the pale green Kings River downstream and crosses the river on a sturdy bridge. The path immediately meets a sign indicating the River Trail to the right, which leads along the river 1.6 miles to Roaring River Falls. (Details for the falls above.)

Follow the Zumwalt Meadow walk to the left upstream to a split in the path. (Numbered signs, from 1 to 18, show the way and describe the trees and foliage. Numbered maps are available at the trailhead and in the visitor centers for $1.50.) Take the loop path to the right, passing by white fir trees and then through an outcropping of boulders. Soon the trail begins looping back around the meadow passing by marshy areas filled with cattails and willows. Here swallows and pretty red-breasted robins are seen. Continue around the meadow where, in early summer, colorful wildflowers blossom. The path meanders along the river to another marshy area and crosses a long wooden walkway. The surrounding area is filled with trees that, in autumn, turn lemon-yellow, orange and red. Return back to the bridge crossing the river, and then turn right toward the parking area. No swimming or wading; treacherous water. **Note:** In springtime, the river may overflow and flood some of this area. Trail: Easy 1.5-mile loop. Located 1.5 miles beyond the Roaring River Falls turnout, 1.1 mile prior to Road's End. (It is 33.5 miles from the Kings Canyon Visitor Center.)

ROAD'S END

MUIR ROCK

A massive flat monolith sitting along the edge of the mighty Kings River stretches over the water, providing a place for visitors to rest and partake in awe-inspiring river views. It was named after John Muir who gave talks from this giant rock about preservation of this area. It is not advisable to swim in the river or to jump off the massive rock. Located in Road's End lower parking area, prior to the wilderness permit station. A small plaque near the edge of the parking area marks the very short trail to the rock. (1 mile from Zumwalt Meadow.)

ROAD'S END WILDERNESS PERMIT STATION

Information, trail maps, and bear canister rentals available. Many trailheads are found here. Summer 7am-3pm. (Wilderness permits until 2:30.) No telephone. Road's End, 1.1 mile from Zumwalt Meadow, 34.6 miles from Grant Grove Village.

MIST FALLS

One of the most memorable walks in the park begins on a trail which eventually reaches the largest waterfall in the area. The sandy path along the side of the wilderness permit station begins winding through a burned area of trees, and shortly crosses a small creek on a wooden bridge. It then crosses tiny streams to be forded using small rocks and logs strewn across them, and passes by massive boulders. (Streams usually dry by mid-summer.) After passing in and out of shaded areas for about a mile, the path heads into the shade of the dense forest where birds are calling to each other. Along the path are hundreds of reeds, tall grasses, and ferns. Soon the roar of a powerful creek is heard as the path meets Bubbs Creek.

At the Bubbs Creek Bridge, the signed path begins climbing the 2.6 miles to Mist Falls. For the less-than-hardy this is a good turning around point. Soon the path levels out and runs close to the pale turquoise bubbly river. Visitors will be treated to views of the magnificent frothing river cascading over hundreds of gray granite boulders. (By late summer, the boulders are quite visible as the water is low.) Further along the trail, hikers will reach the granite switchbacks. Hikers may find this to be a strenuous climb, especially in warm weather, as there is no shade at all. At the top of the switchbacks, the trail levels out then runs along the river. From this point, one can hear the thunderous waterfall and within minutes, it comes into view. The vast stunning cascades give off a tremendous mist providing a cooling effect. The falls are best in late spring and early summer. Begin early morning to avoid the high temperatures. (It's 15 to 20 degrees warmer than Grant Grove Village.) Walking just part of the trail is extremely rewarding. No swimming or wading; the rocks along the river and below the waterfall are extremely slippery and dangerous. **Note:** During spring/ early summer, mosquitoes are prevalent especially early and late in the day. Bring lots of water. Trail: Easy 2 miles to Bubbs Creek; moderate 2.6 miles from bridge to the falls one way. Visitors should park in Road's End upper parking area, close to the wilderness permit station. Trailhead is along side of the wilderness permit station at Road's End.

3.7 Sequoia National Forest – Generals Hwy Area
What To Do & See

GENERALS HWY – Connects the two national parks

From Grant Grove Village (to reach Sequoia National Park), continue 1.5 miles south of the village and turn left on Generals Hwy. It's 24.8 miles to the Lodgepole Visitor Center in Sequoia National Park. Along the way, in the Sequoia National Forest are hiking trails, lodging, and gasoline. (Details under Lodging, and Gasoline/Towing; hiking trails listed below.)

REDWOOD CANYON TRAIL

An isolated trail with large sequoia groves begins downhill and soon splits. Take the path to the right among the sequoias and wildflowers following Redwood Creek. (Creek dry by mid-summer.) In May, enjoy white dogwood blossoms among the giant trees. In July, the pink azaleas bloom, and in autumn the dogwood leaves turn deep scarlet. Continue ahead to the creek crossing (no bridge) and return on the same trail. Trail Information – Kings Canyon Visitor Center or Lodgepole Visitor Center. Trail: Easy 2 miles one way. Off Generals Hwy, 3.5 miles east of Hwy 180, across from the Hume Lake turnoff road. Trailhead and parking area via a narrow winding 1.5 mile dirt road.

BIG MEADOWS AREA

BIG MEADOWS CAMPGROUND

Hiking trails, and guided horseback rides are found here. No reservations. Open June thru Sept. (Depends upon snow.) The summer days are a cool (60-70 degrees). **Horse Corral Pack Station** – 9am-4pm. (559) 565-3404. Located in the Sequoia National Forest. Directions under Weaver Lake Trail.

WEAVER LAKE TRAIL

A narrow soft gravel path meanders among the pines and crosses a creek on a small wooden bridge. (Creek nearly dry by mid-summer.) The partially shaded path begins climbing, and in .75 mile some rock-hopping is needed to cross the second creek. The path becomes rocky and climbs up more steeply to reach a meadow with fallen logs and cut stumps. Beyond the meadow, the path climbs up .5 mile to a signed trail junction. Follow the trail to the left, and it soon crosses another creek and continues out to the warm swimming lake. All around the lake are pretty damselflies which are much like tiny dragonflies. Visitors who look closely may discover small frogs along the shore. Good fishing. The lake sits at the base of Shell Mountain. Some years the trail opens Memorial Day and other years in mid-June. (Depends upon snow.) Dogs okay. Mosquitoes are gone by end of July, but lots of bees hang around in August and September. Information – Ranger Office (559) 338-2251. Trail: Moderate 3.5 miles one way. Located in the Sequoia National Forest off Generals Hwy, at the signed *Big Meadows/Pack Station* turnoff. (6.8 miles east of the intersection with Hwy 180 in Kings Canyon Park.) It is 3.2 miles east of the Redwood Canyon Trail turnoff and 1 mile west of the Montecito-Sequoia Lodge turnoff. Follow the Big

Meadows turnoff road 3.8 miles (making no turns) to the large Big Meadows Trail sign; go to the uphill parking area where a small trailhead sign is found.

3.8 Kings Canyon National Park
PARK INFORMATION

PARK ENTRANCE FEES – (Subject to change.)

Seven-day Pass: $20 per vehicle; $10 walk-ins, motorcycles.
Annual Pass: $30.
National Park Annual Pass: $80 (Admittance to all national parks.)
Senior Pass: $10 (Age 62+ for lifetime.)
Access Pass: Free for U.S. citizens with permanent disabilities.

Note: All passes available at park entrances. Mail-in application forms are available online for Senior and Access passes. www.nps.gov/seki. (Under search, type entrances fees.)

The park offers several "free" days per year:

Martin Luther King, Jr. weekend in Jan, National Park week in April, Get Outdoors Day in June, National Public Lands Day in Sept, and Veteran's Day weekend in Nov. (Subject to change.) Information – www.nps.gov/seki.

VISITOR CENTERS

Kings Canyon Visitor Center – (aka – Grant Grove Visitor Center) Summer 8am-6pm. (Spring/autumn/winter hours vary, usually 9am-5pm.) **Note:** Wilderness permits until 4pm. (559)

565-4307. Located in Grant Grove Village, 2.5 miles from the Big Stump picnic area, 2.7 miles from the park entrance.

Cedar Grove Visitor Center – Open Memorial weekend thru Labor Day. 9am-5pm. Then weekends only thru Sept. (Depends upon weather, call ahead.) (559) 565-3793. Located 9 miles from Boyden Cavern, 28 miles from Grant Grove Village. **Note:** From Hwy 180, take the first left turn on the entrance road.

INFORMATION

Kings Canyon National Park – 717 sq. miles.

Emergency – Dial 911. (No coins needed.)

California Road Conditions – Caltrans (800) 427-7623. Delays for winter snowplows can be half a day or more.

Park Information/Weather – 24 hrs. (559) 565-3341. (Press 1,1 for weather/road conditions.) Road closures due to snow storms – (888) 252-5757. www.nps.gov/seki.

Eateries/Lodging/Camping – (Details under Eateries/Lodging.) www.sequoia-kingscanyon.com.

Mineral King Information – (559) 565-3768.

Seasonal Information & Facts about Kings Canyon – (Details under Appendix.)

Drowning – (Details under Appendix.)

Junior Ranger – Kids earn patches to become a Junior Ranger. (Details at the visitor centers.)

Lodging Reservations – Cedar Grove, Wuksachi Village Lodge, and John Muir Lodge. (888) 252-5757.

Cedar Grove Ranger Station – (559) 565-3790.

Hume Lake Area Information – (559) 338-2251.

Wilderness Permits – Mon-Fri 8am-4:30pm. Closes mid-Sept. (559) 565-3766. (Details under Appendix.)

Bears – (Details under Appendix.)

Park Guide – www.nps.gov/seki. (Under Plan Your Visit, click on Brochures. Then click on, View current and back issues of the park newspaper or Park Map.)

Accessibility Guide – www.nps.gov/seki. (Under *Plan Your Visit*, click on Accessibility Information (on the right-hand side of the page).

Wheelchair Accessible Activities – (Details under Appendix.)

AIRPORTS

Visalia Airport – Information (559) 713-4201. Located 40 miles from Sequoia National Park.

Fresno Yosemite Int'l Airport – Located 53 miles west of Kings Canyon National Park.

GASOLINE/TOWING – Kings Canyon Park & Sequoia National Forest

Hume Lake – Gas 24 hrs. with credit card. (559) 305-7770. (Directions under Hume Lake.)

Kings Canyon Lodge – May to mid-Oct/Nov. (Depends upon weather.) (559) 335-2405. Along Hwy 180, 13 miles east of Grant Grove Village.

Stony Creek Lodge – Gas 24 hrs. with credit card. Late May to early Oct. (559) 565-3909. Located on Generals Hwy in the Sequoia National Forest, 3.7 miles east of Montecito-Sequoia Lodge, 13.3 miles west of the Lodgepole Visitor Center.

AAA – 24 hrs. – (800) 4000-4222.

SNOW PLAY

Grant Grove Village – The market rents snowshoes and cross-country skis for the nearby trails. Information at Kings Canyon Visitor Center. (559) 565-4307.

Montecito-Sequoia Resort – Ice skating on their private lake, cross-country skiing, and snowshoeing lessons/rentals. (559) 565-3388. www.mslodge.com. (Details for lodge under Lodging between Sequoia National and Kings Canyon National Parks.)

FISHING

California fishing license required, age 16 and older. Park fishing regulations are available at the visitor centers. The Cedar Grove Market and the Grant Grove Market sell fishing gear and licenses.

HORSEBACK RIDING

Grant Grove Stables – .25 mile from Grant Grove Village. (559) 335-9292.

Cedar Grove Pack Station – Open 8am-4pm. Overnight rides. Kings Canyon Park. (559) 565-3464.

Horse Corral – Open 10am-4pm. Memorial weekend to

mid-Sept. From Generals Hwy, take the *Big Meadows/Pack Station* turnoff. It's located in the Sequoia National Forest between Sequoia National Park and Kings Canyon National Parks. (6.8 miles east of the intersection with Hwy 180 in Kings Canyon Park and 3.2 miles east of the Redwood Canyon Trail turnoff. (1 mile west of Montecito-Sequoia Lodge turnoff.) (559) 565-3404.

PETS

National Parks – Dogs allowed in picnic areas and campgrounds, not on park trails.

National Forest – Dogs okay on trails. The Big Meadows Campground is a nice area for dogs. (Details under Sequoia National Forest.)

EATERIES/LODGING – Kings Canyon National Park Area

Note: Also see Eateries/Lodging under Sequoia National Park and Sequoia National Forest.

Camping

Note: Information for all Sequoia and Kings Canyon National Parks campgrounds – www.nps.gov/seki/planyourvisit/campgrounds.htm.

Crystal Springs Campground – First come-first served. One site is wheelchair accessible. Open late May to mid-June. Close to Grant Grove Village. (Directions under Grant Grove Village.)

Big Meadows Campground – 45 campsites on Big

Meadow Creek. Good fishing. 7600 feet elevation. May-Sept. No reservations. No fee. Information - (559) 338-2251.

Hume Lake Christian Camp – Sequoia National Forest – See rooms on website, breakfast buffet is included; lunch and dinner buffets are available. Open all year. (559) 305-7770. www.humelake.org. Located at Hume Lake via narrow winding roads. (Two entrance roads to the lake; directions under Hume Lake.)

John Muir Lodge – Lodge has motel-type rooms with views of the forest. Rooms have telephones and coffeemakers. The lobby is adorned by a large stone fireplace with cozy seating and there are books, games, and puzzles. Wi-Fi – Common area in lodge. Weddings. Open all year. Front Desk – (559) 335-2314. Reservations – (888) 252-5757 www. sequoia-kingscanyon.com. Located off Hwy 180 in Grant Grove Village, three miles from the park entrance.

Grant Grove Cabins – Some cabins open all year with private baths. Rustic cabins and tent cabins are open mid-May to mid-Oct with a shared bathhouse. See cabin descriptions on website. Bring flashlight for walking at night. Wi-Fi – near the restaurant. **Note:** Near the John Muir Lodge and Grant Grove Cabins there is a restaurant (family dining – B,L,D – with free Wi-Fi.). Open daily in summer, call for fall/winter schedule. Adjacent to the restaurant is a gift shop and a market. Registration for both the lodge and cabins is in the gift shop. Lodge/Cabins Front Desk – (559) 335-2314. Reservations – (888) 252-5757. www.sequoia-kingscanyon.com. Located off Hwy 180 in Grant Grove Village, three miles from the park entrance.

Cedar Grove Lodge – The hotel rooms have showers, telephones, and some have air-conditioning and a patio. There are views of the amazing Kings River from the hotel's deck. Snack bar (in the hotel) offers light meals indoors or on the outdoor patio. There is a market, gift shop, and laundry facilities. Wi-Fi – limited. Memorial Day to mid-Oct. (Depends upon snow.) (559) 565-3096. Reservations – (888) 252-5757. www. sequoia-kingscanyon.com Cedar Grove Village, 28 miles east of Grant Grove Village.

EATERIES/LODGING – Sequoia National Forest

Between Sequoia and Kings Canyon National Parks.

Montecito-Sequoia Lodge – The lodge sits on the shore of their private lake in a scenic setting surrounded by pine trees. Rooms and cabins (some cabins share bath) include all meals (buffet-style). A trail lunch is available if staff is notified the night before. Wi-Fi, books, and games are available in the lobby/dining room which is enhanced by two huge stone fireplaces. A large-screen TV is available at no fee in a building adjacent to the lodge. At the lake in summer, there are canoes, paddleboats, sailboats, and swimming from the sandy beach. (Lessons for adults and kids.) There is an outdoor spa, swimming pool, and nightly campfire sing-alongs. In winter, there is cross-country skiing, snowboarding, snowshoeing, and ice skating on the lake. Family Camp (6-night stays) mid-June to late Aug. (One night non-camp stays on Saturday during this time.) **Note:** Camp is only 4 night stays the last 2 weeks in Aug. (Sept until mid-June no minimum night stays) There are supervised kids' programs (all ages) that allow parents free time. Open all year (closed two weeks after Thanksgiving). Winter access from the Kings Canyon Park Entrance. (Heavy snowstorm escort service to and from the lodge.) Chains required Nov to May. Front desk and road conditions – (559) 565-3388. Reservations – (800) 227-9900. Information/snow report check website. www.mslodge.com. Located off Generals Hwy, between the Sequoia National Park and Kings Canyon National Park in the Sequoia National Forest. It's 7.8 miles east of the intersection of Hwy180 and

Generals Hwy in Kings Canyon National Park, (intersection is 1.5 miles south of Grant Grove Village) and 17 miles west of the Lodgepole Visitor Center in Sequoia National Park.

Stony Creek Lodge and Restaurant – A stone fireplace adorns the lobby, nice rooms with baths, TV, continental breakfast, and Wi-Fi. Restaurant (pizza and salad) market/ gift shop, and gasoline late May to early Oct. Hikers' showers available. Front desk (559) 565-3909. Reservations (866) 522-6966 (for both Stony Creek and Montecito Lodges). www. sequoia-kingscanyon.com. Located between Sequoia National Park and Kings Canyon National Park in the Sequoia National Forest; 3.7 miles east of the Montecito-Sequoia Lodge turnoff road, 13.3 miles west of the Lodgepole Visitor Center in Sequoia National Park.

LODGING – Outside Kings Canyon National Park – Fresno & Sanger

Best Western Plus – Outdoor pool and whirlpool. Continental breakfast. Wi-Fi. Dogs okay. (559) 226-2110. (800) 528-1234. www.bestwestern.com. 3110 N. Blackstone Avenue, Fresno. From Hwy 41, exit Shields Avenue, 2.5 hour drive from Kings Canyon Park.

Ramada Northwest – Outdoor pool. Continental breakfast. Wi-Fi. Dogs okay. (559) 277-5700. 800 2-ramada. www.ramada.com. 5046 N. Barcus, Fresno. From Hwy 99 exit Shaw Avenue.

Holiday Inn – Fresno Airport – Indoor and outdoor pool, whirlpool, exercise room. Wi-Fi. Restaurant and lounge on premises. (559) 252-3611. (800) 465-4329. www.ihg.com. 5090 E. Clinton Avenue, Fresno. From Hwy 41, exit McKinley.

DIRECTIONS – Kings Canyon National Park

From Los Angeles – Take Hwy 5 (Golden State Fwy) north. Just north of Bakersfield, take Hwy 99 north to Fresno; exit on Clovis Ave. Turn east on winding Hwy 180 (Kings Canyon Road) and continue 52 miles to Kings Canyon Big Stump Park Entrance. Los Angeles to Fresno – 216 miles.

From San Francisco – Take Hwy 80 (Bay Bridge) east 8 miles to Hwy 580, and continue east for 50 miles to Hwy 205 south and take it 17 miles. Then travel Hwy 5 north for two miles to reach Hwy 120 east. Continue on Hwy 120 for 6 miles and take Hwy 99 south 54 miles to Merced. From Merced travel on Hwy 59 south 2 miles to reach Hwy 99 and continue south 56 miles to Fresno. Turn east on winding Hwy 180 (Kings Canyon Road) and continue 52 miles to Kings Canyon Big Stump Park Entrance. (Details under www.nps.gov/seki) San Francisco to Fresno – 202 miles; Fresno to Park – 52 miles.

Note: To reach Sequoia National Park from Kings Canyon National Park – 1.5 miles north of the Big Stump Park Entrance, (1.5 miles south of Kings Canyon Visitor Center) turn right at intersection onto Generals Hwy. Continue past Montecito-Sequoia Lodge and Stony Creek Lodge to Sequoia National Park. (24.8 miles).

To reach Morro Bay from Sequoia and Kings Canyon National Parks take Hwy 41 west from Fresno 135 miles.

TOWNS NORTH OF KINGS CANYON PARK
Leading to Yosemite National Park's Southern Entrance.

Visitors traveling to Yosemite National Park from Kings Canyon National Park should follow winding Hwy 180 west for 53 miles (toward Fresno) to Hwy 41 north. It's signed

Yosemite National Park. Then continue ahead 47 miles to the town of **Oakhurst** and nearby **Bass Lake**. This is a great stopping-off place before driving the final 15 miles to reach Yosemite's South Park Entrance.

In **Oakhurst**, visitors will find lodging, restaurants, gas stations, Starbucks, and a variety of shops. Close by is an 18-hole golf course. The lovely **Bass Lake** provides a quiet setting for swimming, boating, fishing, and camping. Nestled along the north shore is the Pines Resort with cottages, a heated swimming pool, boat rentals, jet skis, and tennis courts. The resort has two restaurants; one with casual outdoor patio dining overlooking the lake. **Pines Resort** – (559) 642-3121. (800) 350-7463. www.basslake.com. Oakhurst and Bass Lake Information – Yosemite Sierra Visitor Bureau. (559) 683-4636.

Note: Details for Oakhurst and Bass Lake under Yosemite National Park, Towns Outside South Park Entrance.

See photos of the 6 areas listed in this book at: www. CaliforniaVacationPaths.com.

Attraction prices and times listed in this guide are subject to change; call ahead. Information missing or incorrect? Contact author: Pati.Anne@yahoo.com.

KID FAVES

SEQUOIA NATIONAL PARK

Note: Details for the following activities are found under main sections of Sequoia and Kings Canyon National Parks. (See Table of Contents for page numbers.)

CRESCENT MEADOW

Tharp's Log – The enormous hollow log has a room built into it with a window and a stone fireplace. It is reached by a walk around marshy Crescent Meadow where kids can look into the meadow's pools filled with tiny fish and frogs. (The path around the meadow is wheelchair/stroller accessible.)

GENERAL SHERMAN'S TREE & CONGRESS TRAIL

General Sherman's Tree – The world's largest tree is 275 feet tall. The trail is lined with other spectacular trees. There's a free shuttle from Lodgepole Visitor Center which brings visitors up close to the tree. (The paths are wheelchair/stroller accessible.)

FAMILY CAMP

Montecito-Sequoia Lodge – Private lake for swimming, paddle boats and sailboats, as well as a swimming pool and hot tub. (Sailing lessons available.) There is a great kids playground (staff watches kids while parents have free time), nightly campfire sing-alongs, and a room with computers and a large-screen TV. Winter activities and lessons include cross-country skiing and ice skating. **Note:** All meals (buffet style) come with rooms.

KINGS CANYON NATIONAL PARK

BIG STUMP PICNIC AREA

Big Stump Trail – Along the trail, at the Mark Twain stump a ladder is provided to climb atop the stump so that visitors can realize the immense size. Just walking part of this trail is worthwhile. (1 mile loop.)

GENERAL GRANT TREE

General Grant Loop Trail – Kids can walk inside the Fallen Monarch Tree, and see the General Grant Tree. It's the world's third largest tree, and has been designated our nation's Christmas tree. (Wheelchair/stroller accessible .5 mile loop trail.)

GRIZZLY FALLS

The picnic tables here are real close to the falls. (50 yards from the parking area.)

KNAPP'S CABIN

This 1920s cabin can be reached via a short walk from the parking area.

ROARING RIVER FALLS

River Trail – A 3-minute walk along this (wheelchair/stroller accessible) trail brings visitors to the impressive falls which flow into the canyon with a mighty force in spring and early summer. Older kids can take the short path down to the base of the falls.

JUNIOR RANGER

Become a Junior Ranger - Earn a patch like the Jay Award for kids 5 to 8 years old or the Raven Award for kids 9 to 12 years old, and those over 12 can earn a senior patch. (Details at the visitor centers.)

APPENDIX

SEQUOIA AND KINGS CANYON NATIONAL PARKS

SEASONAL INFORMATION

Springtime comes alive in the park with an abundance of wildflowers and greenish-yellow blossoms hang on the tall buckeye trees found in the Buckeye Campground and along Paradise Creek Trail. (Sequoia National Park.) In autumn, large shiny brown nut-like seeds fall from the pods hanging in these trees. The squirrels love them, but they are poisonous to humans and to many other animals. Native Americans blanched them to remove the tannic acid for use with leather. (Details for Paradise Creek Trail under Sequoia National Park.) In May, the white dogwood bloom and in July the pink azaleas mingle among the green hues of the forest. Beware of the poison oak with its shiny-green three-leaf clusters, white berries, and leaves that turn a pretty red in fall.

Summer brings a lot of visitors and many of the wildlife found in the park is visible especially the foxes, squirrels, mule deer, and black bears. (By September, young bear cubs, set free by their mothers, are seen alone rummaging for food.) Once bears have contact with human food, they will search campgrounds and break into cars for even a discarded candy wrapper. Please use designated animal-proof containers in the parking areas to store all food.

Winter is a quiet, peaceful time in the park. An accessible and beautiful area, especially when snow is draped over the trees, is found along the General Grant Trail. It's near the Kings Canyon Visitor Center where ranger-led snowshoe walks begin. (Snowshoe rentals at the market in Grant Grove Village.) Call the visitor centers for park road closures due to snow storms.

HISTORY

The Monachee (Western Mono) Indians lived in the lower regions of Sequoia National Park. The Potwisha Indians (small band) spoke the same language as the Monachee and lived near the Potwisha Campground. They left behind pictographs in nearby Hospital Rock. (Details under Hospital Rock picnic area, Sequoia National Park.) Pictographs are painted with a mineral substance combined with either blood or fat, instead of etched or carved into the rocks like petroglyphs. Hospital Rock was named by an early white settler who was injured near here, and camped among the boulders until he recovered.

In the 1800s, a white settler, Hale Tharp, built his home in a fallen sequoia tree, (hollowed out by fire) in the Giant Forest, near Crescent Meadow. (Details under Tharp's Log, Sequoia Park.) His friend, John Muir, who was studying the canyons to the north, now Kings Canyon National Park, visited him here. At that time, loggers were cutting down many of the beautiful giant sequoia trees. It was quite a feat, using only axes and cross-cut saws, as there were no power chainsaws. Tharp and Muir, who wanted to save the giants for future generations to enjoy, battled against logging in the area, Thousands of large sequoias were cut down before the Giant Forest area was incorporated into the Sequoia National Park in 1890.

NATIONAL PARKS ESTABLISHED

Sequoia National Park was the second national park established (1890) in the United States. Also established in 1890, was General Grant National Park. It was later expanded, and, in 1940, became Kings Canyon National Park. The Cedar Grove area was added to Kings Canyon Park in 1965 and the Mineral King area was added to Sequoia National Park in 1978.

Kings Canyon National Park forms the northern area and Sequoia National Park forms the southern area. They are administered together as one park, by the U.S. National Park Service. Most of the park (nearly 97 percent) is set aside as wilderness and is protected by the Wilderness Act of 1964. The wilderness area is accessible only by foot or horseback. Combined together, they stretch over 865,000 acres. More than 1.6 million visitors visit the park each year.

TREES

In Sequoia National Park, in the Giant Forest area, stands the majestic General Sherman Tree. It's the largest tree in the world (in volume not height). The President's Tree (second largest tree) is also found here.

In Kings Canyon National Park, in the General Grant Grove, is the famous General Grant Tree, the third largest tree in the world. It has been designated our nation's Christmas Tree. (Details under General Grant Trail in Kings Canyon National Park.)

The giant sequoias are a member of the redwood family which also has cinnamon-colored bark. Unlike the sequoias, that lose their lower limbs while their trunks expand and their bark thickens, the redwoods are more slender and shaped like conifers.

KINGS CANYON

In the eastern part of Kings Canyon National Park, lies Kings Canyon. (Per the Guinness Book of World Records, it reaches a depth of 8,200 feet, making it the deepest canyon in the United States.) The 34.6 mile road, beginning at Grant Grove Village, descends beyond Boyden Cavern along the forceful Kings River through Kings Canyon to Road's End. (Some of the park's best trails begin here.) It's a spectacular drive, especially in spring and early summer, when the wild turquoise river throws white spindrifts up in the air. (Details under Road's End, Kings Canyon National Park.) The Kings River was named by Spanish explorers in 1806 as "Rio de los Santos" (River of the Holy Kings).

CAVES

There are over 200 caves in the two parks, but only Crystal Cave, located in Sequoia National Park, and Boyden Cavern located in the national forest near Kings Canyon National Park are open seasonally to the public. (Details under Sequoia National Park and Kings Canyon National Park.)

WILDERNESS PERMITS
Permits are required for all overnight hikes.

Wilderness and Permit Office – Advance permits daily – Summer Mon-Fri 8am to 4:30pm. Closes mid-Sept. Information – (559) 565-3766. www.nps.gov/seki/planyourvisit.htm. (Under the Trip Planning, click Permits.)

SEQUOIA NATIONAL PARK WILDERNESS PERMITS
(Times subject to change.)

Lodgepole Visitor Center – Summer permits 7am-3:30pm; closes for lunch 11am-noon. Winter self-registration. (559) 565-4436. One hour drive from the Ash Mountain Park Entrance.

Wilderness Center – Summer permits Mon-Fri 8am-4:30pm. Self-registration after mid-Sept. (559) 565-3766. Near the Foothills Visitor Center, 1 mile from the Ash Mountain Park Entrance.

KINGS CANYON PARK WILDERNESS PERMITS
(Times are subject to change.)

Road's End Wilderness Permit Station – Summer permits 7am-3:45pm. No phone; for information call the Cedar Grove Visitor Center. (559) 565-3793. Permit Station located 5 miles from Visitor Center.

Kings Canyon Visitor Center – (Also called Grant Grove Visitor Center) Summer permits 8am-4pm, winter self-registration. (559) 565-4307. Located in Grant Grove Village.

MINERAL KING WILDERNESS PERMITS

Summer permits 8am-4pm. Information – (559) 565-3768. Reservations – (559) 565-3766.

BEARS

Bears are killed or injured each year by motorist exceeding the speed limit. Please obey the speed limit. Black bears come in various colors and are prevalent in the park. (No grizzly bears in the park.) Bears recognize picnic bags and coolers and have a strong sense of smell. Even a tiny candy wrapper left in the trunk of a car is enough to cause them to break in. Please use the bear containers provided in parking areas to store food and scented items. **Note:** If a bear is encountered in the wild, make noise, yell, and pick up small children. Don't run; a bear can run a football field in about six seconds.

DROWNING

Drowning is the number one cause of death in the park. Stand back from any swiftly moving water, and use caution near any creeks or rivers. Rocks tend to be very slippery in and around water, and the water is extremely cold with strong currents. No swimming is advised in the rivers or creeks in Sequoia and Kings Canyon National Parks.

WHEELCHAIR ACCESSIBLE ACTIVITIES

Note: See Table of Contents for page numbers of activities.

The activities listed below in Sequoia National Park and Kings Canyon National Park are wheelchair accessible. Wheelchairs can be borrowed (as available) at Lodgepole Visitor Center, Giant Forest Museum, and the Kings Canyon Visitor Center. **Note:** All park shuttles run from approximately Memorial Day weekend to mid-Sept and are wheelchair accessible.

Details of activities listed are in consecutive order based on entering Sequoia National Park on Hwy 198, and entering Kings Canyon National Park on Hwy 180, or coming through Sequoia Park on Generals Hwy. Temporary accessibility placards are available at all park visitor centers.

SEQUOIA NATIONAL PARK

Giant Forest Museum – Handicapped parking located alongside the museum.

Big Trees Trail – Close to Giant Forest Museum.

General Sherman's Trail – Close to Lodgepole Visitor Center.

The following do not meet ADA standards for wheelchair accessibility, but may be accessible with assistance:

Congress Trail – Connects to the General Sherman's Trail.

Beetle Rock Trail – Across from the Giant Forest Museum.

KINGS CANYON NATIONAL PARK

Zumwalt Meadow Trail – Portion of the trail coming from the parking area to boardwalk. Located in Cedar Grove.

The following do not meet ADA standards for wheelchair accessibility, but may be accessible with assistance:

General Grant Loop Trail – Close to Kings Canyon Visitor Center.

Roaring River Fall Trail – Short trail to waterfall. Located in Cedar Grove.

RESOURCES/INFORMATION

Foothills Visitor Center – (559) 565-4212.

Lodgepole Visitor Center – (559) 565-4436.

Kings Canyon Visitor Center – (559) 565-4307.

Cedar Grove Visitor Center – (559) 565-3793.

National Forest Information – Mon-Fri 8am-4:30pm. (559) 338-2251.

Park Information – (559) 565-3341. www.nps.gov/seki.

Mineral King Ranger Station – Mon-Fri 8am-4:30pm. (559) 565-3768.

WEBSITES
www.nps.gov/seki
www.sequoia.national-park.com/
www.visitsequoia.com/sequoia-history.aspx

Rekindle by the Sea

Chase waves of the sea as they
roll over shiny wet sand.
Long-legged sea birds cast
reflections side by side.
Footprints along the sea's edge are
swept away with incoming tide.
Outgoing tide uncovers colorful sea
creatures like starfish so grand.
Spending time by the sea
will rekindle the soul.

Pati Anne

Book
FOUR

Santa Barbara

A lovely, sparkling seaside town, bursting with excitement and charm, meanders down to the harbor and Stearns Wharf supplying the backdrop for an irresistible playground for adults and kids. The allure is magnified by beaches sprawling out for miles, the gentle roll of ocean waves upon wheat-colored sand, and mild breezes that tame the sunshine into perfect year-round weather.

4.1 Santa Barbara – Stearns Wharf, Bicycles, & Arts/Crafts
What To Do & See

STEARNS WHARF

Stearns Wharf offers superb dining, fishing, shopping, and wine tasting. To feel the special charm of the pier, stroll out over the water and watch the pelicans with their over-sized bills, the people in their varied costumes, and the sailboats bobbing in the glistening bay. Leashed dogs okay. The wheelchair/stroller accessible pier has 90-minute free parking with merchant validation. (Information under Appendix.) www.stearnswharf. org, www.stearnswharf.com.

The following are in successive order on Stearns Wharf:

Harbor Restaurant – Fine dining. Here the emphasis is on steak, fresh seafood and the view. Window seats overlook the boats in the marina. Lunch 11:30am-2:30pm, Sat/Sun 10am-4pm. Dinner Mon-Fri 5-10pm, Sat/Sun 4-10pm. Sat/Sun Brunch 10am-2pm (805) 963-3311. www.stearnswharf.org

Longboard's Grill – Grab a handful of peanuts, throw the shells on the floor; it's expected. The casual dining and sensational ocean views add to the party atmosphere inside and outside on the glass-enclosed patio. The menu includes: fish/chips, salads, hamburgers, and cocktails. (Kid's menu.) Mon-Thurs 11:30am-10pm, Fri/Sat 11pm; Sun until 10pm. (805) 963-3311. It's upstairs, over the Harbor Restaurant. **Note:** Elevator for Longboard's inside Harbor Restaurant.

Ty Warner Sea Center – Kids adore this place; they can climb through a huge water tank tunnel to view sea life, and have fun with the Touch-Tanks. Open 10am-5pm. Adults $8, Seniors and teens 13 to 17 $7, age 2-12 $5, and under two free. (Closed Thanksgiving, Christmas, Christmas Eve at noon, and New Year's Day.) (Wheelchair/stroller accessible.) (805) 962-2526. www.sbnature.org It's across from the Harbor Restaurant.

Old Wharf Trading Company – Nautical gifts and decorating items, also toys and books. Summer 9am-9pm. Winter until 7pm, Sat 8pm. (805) 962-4118. On the wharf, beyond the Ty Warner Sea Center.

Coastal Treasures – Lovely jewelry, gifts, handbags, hats, and travel books. Open 11am-6pm. (805) 966-7643. Located upstairs over the Old Wharf Trading Company, adjacent to the Deep Sea Wine Tasting Room.

Deep Sea Wine Tasting Room – This fine wine tasting room offers California wines and great harbor views. Outdoor patio. Mon-Wed noon-8pm, Thurs-Sun noon-9pm. After Labor Day noon-8pm every day. (805) 618-1185. www.stearnswharf.org. Located upstairs, adjacent Coastal Treasures, over the Old Wharf Trading Company.

Char West – A tiny, but popular restaurant. Fish and Chips and char-burgers. – (Indoor and outdoor seating.) 9am-7pm. Winter 10am-5pm, Sat/Sun 9am-7pm. (805) 962-5631 Located next to the Old Wharf Trading Company, behind the Mother Stearns Candy Co.

Moby Dick Restaurant – Nice harbor views from inside or from the outdoor patio. Happy hour, Mon-Fri 4-7pm. (Kids' menu.) B,L,D – The menu includes: seafood, steak, sandwiches, salads, and cocktails. 7am-9:30pm. Winter until 9pm. (805) 965-0549.

Celebration – 42-passenger yacht – Harbor cruises, parties, brunch, and whale watching. Sunset cruises with apetizers. Gray whale watching (mid-Feb to mid-May). Reservations (888) 316-9363. www.celebrationsantabarbara.com. Across from Moby Dick Restaurant.

Water Taxi – The *Little Toot Tugboat* runs between Stearns Wharf and the Santa Barbara Harbor. Fare one way: Adults $4, children under 12 $1. Noon to 6pm, weather permitting. Autumn closed Wed. Winter, until Memorial Day, Fri/Sat/Sun only. (805) 896-6900. (888) 316-9363. www.sbwatertaxi.com. Across from Moby Dick Restaurant.

Santa Barbara Shellfish Company – A small seafood bar with take-out. (Indoor and outdoor seating.) The shrimp, clams, mussels, and oysters are mighty fine and the beer is cold. 11am-9 or 10pm. Winter until 8 or 9pm. (805) 966-6676. www.sbshellfishco.com. Near the end of the wharf.

Stearns Wharf Bait & Tackle Shop – Sales and rentals. 8am-8pm; autumn/winter until 5pm. (805) 965-1333. It's at the end of the wharf, where the fishermen hang out.

DIRECTIONS – Stearns Wharf

Northbound traffic exit Hwy 101 at (96b) Garden Street. (Signed *Garden/Laguna Streets*.) The off-ramp splits with Garden Street to the left and Laguna Street to the right. Follow the *Garden Street* sign to the left and proceed to the beach (visitor center is on the right corner). Then turn right along the waterfront (Cabrillo Boulevard) and continue 2 blocks to reach the wharf. Southbound traffic exit Hwy 101 on Castillo, and travel south toward the sea. At the beach, (Cabrillo Boulevard) turn left and continue .2 mile to the wharf.

BICYCLES & ARTS/CRAFTS – Near wharf entrance

The paved walkway (wheelchair/stroller accessible) bordered by hundreds of palm trees swaying in the ocean breeze is a popular place to rollerblade or ride a bicycle (built-for-two, four or six) along the edge of the sea. (Details for bicycle rentals under Information.) Every Sunday and July 4th (except rainy and cold windy days) local artists exhibit their paintings and wares along Cabrillo Boulevard (in front of the walkway and palm trees) on the mile-long grassy area that runs east of the wharf entrance. 10am-6pm, winter 4 or 5pm.

4.2 East of wharf, West of wharf, West of Santa Barbara Harbor
What To Do & See

EAST OF STEARNS WHARF

CHASE PALM PARK

The park has a wonderful children's play area and an antique merry-go-round which is open 11am-9pm. Winter 11am-6pm.(Closed Christmas.) Kids $2. Paths circle around ponds (filled with ducks, turtles, and pretty koi) and grassy areas with lots of park benches where visitors can sit and listen to the birds. Concerts held Thursdays 6-8:30pm from the end of June thru mid-Aug. Merry-go-round – (805) 722-4021. Information – (805) 965-3021. 323 E. Cabrillo Boulevard, two blocks east of wharf.

EAST BEACH

Volleyball nets are set up on a wide expanse of the beach alongside an old bathhouse that now houses a lifeguard station, public showers, lockers, and the **East Beach Grill**. The grill opens with breakfast dishes, and from then on it's hamburgers, fries, burritos, and beer/wine. Open 6am-6pm. (805) 965-8805. The beach is found along E. Cabrillo Boulevard (east of Chase Palms Park), across the street from the Hyatt Santa Barbara Hotel.

SANTA BARBARA ZOO

This charming zoo, in a garden setting, claims over 500 animals from around the world. Feed the giraffes ($6), and see the fascinating gorillas, monkeys, elephants, lions, leopards, pink flamingos, and penguins. **Note:** Call ahead for giraffe feeding times. The call of the vibrant macaws is heard over everything. A miniature train ride around the zoo (wheelchair accessible) shows off the plants, trees, and a few animals. Train rides: Adults/seniors $5.00, 2-12 yrs. $4.50, under 2 free. Wheelchair/stroller rentals $6. (Closed Christmas; closes 3pm Thanksgiving and Christmas Eve.) Zoo admittance: Age 13-64 $15, kids 2 to 12 $10, and seniors $12, under 2 free. Parking fee $6. Open 10am-5pm. Last tickets sold 4pm. (805) 962-5339 Mon-Fri, (805) 963-5695 Sat/Sun. www.santabarbarazoo.org. From Hwy 101, follow directions to Andree Clark Bird Refuge. Continue beyond the Refuge and lagoon to Cabrillo Boulevard along the beachfront. Across the road from East Beach take Ninos Drive. It's just beyond the Hyatt Santa Barbara Hotel.

ANDREE CLARK BIRD REFUGE

This scenic lagoon is home to ducks, egrets, herons, and frogs. A short nature path winds along the north side of the lagoon where butterflies and dragonflies gather. The path begins at the parking area. Leashed dogs okay. From Hwy 101, northbound traffic, exit left on (94c) Cabrillo Boulevard, turn left and travel under the overpass and turn right on Los Patos Way. Southbound, exit left (94b) on Cabrillo Boulevard, turn right at stop sign, and right on Los Patos. Parking at the lagoon.

Eateries across from the Bird Refuge:

Café del Sol – Mexican fare. 11am-10pm, Sun 10am-10pm. Sunday brunch 10am-3pm. (805) 969-0448.

Stella Mare's – French cuisine served in a cozy atmosphere. Lunch Tues-Fri 11:30am-2:30pm, Sat/Sun 10am-2:30pm.

Dinner 5-9pm. Brunch Sat/Sun 10am-2:30pm. (Closed Mon.) Jazz music from 7pm on Wed. (805) 969-6705.

WEST OF STEARNS WHARF

SANTA BARBARA HARBOR

The cement breakwater around the harbor creates an enticing walkway (wheelchair/stroller accessible) between the sea and the harbor. When the sea is rough, expect a few waves to come splashing up onto the walkway.

Santa Barbara Maritime Museum – Kids love it for the interactive fun that includes: a sport fishing simulator, a submarine periscope, hands-on objects from real shipwrecks, and they can play with puppets. The museum and gift shop open 10am-6pm, after Labor Day until 5pm. (Closed every Wed and Thanksgiving, Christmas, New Years Day, and first Friday in August for the Fiesta Parade.) Adults $7, seniors & age 6-17 $4, 1-5 years $2, and under 1 free. Military in uniform, free. Visitors free on third Thurs of month. Museum is wheelchair accessible. (805) 962-8404. www.sbmm.org. 113 Harbor Way, in large white building facing the harbor.

Outdoors Santa Barbara Visitor Center – Wonderful views from here show off the city, beaches, harbor, Stearns Wharf, and offshore islands. The outside deck has interpretive displays and a telescope for viewing wildlife. Information available on outdoor activities like: hiking, diving, kayaking, fishing, snorkeling, tide pooling, boating, and backpacking. Wheelchair accessible. Open 11am-5pm. (805) 456-8752. www.outdoorsb.noaa.gov. Located at 113 Harbor Way. It's located above the Santa Barbara Maritime Museum. (Take the elevator inside the building to the 4th floor.)

Santa Barbara Sailing – Learn to sail or rent a kayak or power boat. There are catamarans available for parties and whale watching. Dinner sails Saturdays, April thru mid-Sept. Open 9am-6pm. 133 Harbor Way. (805) 962-2826. www. sbsail.com.

Sunset Kidd Sailing – Sail on a 41 foot sailing yacht. Choose serene morning sails, fast exhilarating afternoon sails, or romantic sunset sails. Open 8am-6:30 or 7pm. 125 Harbor Way, #13. (805) 962-8222. www.sunsetkidd.com.

Sea Landing – Diving trips, sports fishing, and whale watching. The whale watching tours include: Gray Whales Dec-April (calves in April), Humpback Whales May-Aug, and Blue Whales July to mid-Oct. They also have jet skis and stand-up paddleboards for rent. Open 7:30am-6pm. 301 W. Cabrillo Boulevard. (805) 963-3564. (888) 77whale. www. sealanding.net.

EATERIES – Santa Barbara Harbor

Breakwater Restaurant – Egg dishes available for breakfast, the rest of the day salads, sandwiches, and seafood are served. Early bird specials from 4-6pm. (Kids' menu.) Open 7am-8pm, Fri/Sat 9pm. Winter closes an hour earlier. (805) 965-1557. Located at 107 Harbor Way.

Chuck's Waterfront Grill – The restaurant offers fine views of the sailboats in the bay. Specialties are: fresh seafood, steak, and pasta. Lunch 11:30am-3pm. Dinner 5:30-10pm. Free valet parking. (805) 564-1200. Located at 113 Harbor Way.

The Endless Summer Café & Bar – This casual café sits above the Waterfront Grill, and the outside patio overlooks the harbor. (Kids' menu.) Lunch 11:30am-3pm, dinner 5:30-10pm. (805) 564-4666.

Brophy Bros. – The huge cocktail/oyster bar is overlooking the harbor. Here the fresh fish and shell fish are very popular. Open 11am-10pm, Fri/Sat 11pm. (805) 966-4418. Located at 119 Harbor Way, upstairs, over the shops.

DIRECTIONS – Santa Barbara Harbor

From Stearns Wharf, take the *Little Toot* water taxi. (Details under Stearns Wharf.) When driving from Stearns Wharf, travel west on Cabrillo Boulevard (becomes Shoreline Drive) and, in .7 mile turn left onto Harbor Way. To reach the harbor from Hwy 101 (southbound), exit on Castillo Street and continue to the beach. Turn right on Cabrillo Boulevard, and in .5 mile turn left onto Harbor Way.

WEST OF SANTA BARBARA HARBOR

LEADBETTER BEACH PARK

This is an ideal beach for summer swimming in the gentle surf (lifeguards on duty) and soaking up sunshine on the pale honey-gold sand while watching showy windsurfers soar up like giant birds in the bay. In the grassy park, at the edge of the sand, are picnic tables with barbeque pits where dogs are welcome. There is pay parking, or walk half a mile down from Shoreline Park (details below) where the parking is free. (Leadbetter Beach is located three miles northwest of Santa Barbara Harbor.)

Shoreline Beach Café – Enjoy tables with beach umbrellas right out on the sand or tables on the glass-enclosed patio. There are breakfast foods, seafood, sandwiches, and fish tacos. (Kids' menu.) Summer 9am-8pm, Sat/Sun 8am-8:30pm. Winter 10am to sunset; Sat/Sun 8am-6pm. Happy Hour – Mon-Fri 4-6pm. (805) 568-0064.

SHORELINE PARK

Hugging the bluff top is a grassy park with benches, restrooms, picnic tables, and a children's play area. A paved walkway (wheelchair/stroller accessible) runs through the middle of the park. (Walkway continues .5 mile to Leadbetter Beach.) The best viewing spot for gray whales (mid-Feb to mid-May) is near the bronze whale's tail statue. Beneath the small wooden arch, stairs zigzag down to a secluded beach strewn with rocks that present tide pooling at low tide. A mile up the beach (west of the stairs) a small lighthouse sits on the bluff blinking over the sea. (To find the beach stairs, walk from the parking area, beyond the restrooms about 100 yards to a huge eucalyptus tree.) **Note:** At nearby Leadbetter Beach, the parking area is level with beach. (No stairs to climb.) Free parking at Shoreline Park. Shoreline Park is .5 mile west of Leadbetter Beach.

ARROYO BURRO BEACH

This beach cove is popular with dog owners because dogs are allowed on the beach. This is also a good place to hunt for seashells especially at low tide; and, there is a restaurant and free parking.

The Boat House – The sand tumbles up to the restaurant's front door. B,L,D. Restaurant specialties are steak, seafood, and chicken. (Kid's menu.) 7:30am-10pm. Winter 9pm. (805) 898-2628. From Shoreline Park, travel west on Shoreline Drive (becomes Meigs Road); turn left on Cliff Drive (Hwy 225), and continue one mile to the beach.

WATERFRONT EATERIES – East & West of Wharf

Eateries east of the wharf include:

El Torito – Mexican cuisine. Open 11am-9:30pm, Fri/

Sat 10pm. Sunday brunch 9:30am-2pm. Sunday until 9pm. (Winter, closes an hour earlier.) Happy Hour Mon-Fri 4-8pm. (805) 963-1968. Located at 29 E. Cabrillo Boulevard, just east of the wharf.

Santa Barbara FisHouse – Popular items are fresh seafood, steak, and soups/salads. (Kids' menu.) Lunch 11:30am-3pm. Dinner 5-9:30pm. Sunday breakfast 9:30am-2 pm. (805) 966-2112. Located at 101 E. Cabrillo Boulevard.

Rodney's Steakhouse – (Details under the Fess Parker's Doubletree Resort.)

East Beach Grill – (Details under East Beach.)

Bistro Eleven Eleven Restaurant – (Details under Hyatt Santa Barbara Hotel.)

Note: See Four Seasons Biltmore Hotel (details under Lodging Along the Waterfront) for eateries further east of the wharf.

Eateries west of the wharf include:

Eladio's – B,L,D – Fine Italian cuisine comes with a view of the wharf and harbor. The lunch/dinner menu includes seafood, steak, pasta, soups, pizza, and salads. (Kids' menu.) 7am-9:30pm, Fri/Sat 10pm. Reservations (805) 963-4466. Located at the wharf entrance, corner of Cabrillo Boulevard and State Street.

Sambo's – Breakfast and Lunch. Outdoor patio. (Kids' menu.) Open 6:30am-3:30pm. (805) 965-3269. Located at 216 W. Cabrillo Boulevard.

Toma Restaurant and Bar – Italian and Mediterranean cuisine. This waterfront bistro offers a nice view of the harbor boats. Dinner menu includes: pasta, chicken, and rack of lamb.

5pm-9pm, Fri/Sat/Sun 10pm. (805) 962-0777. Located at 324 W. Cabrillo Boulevard, next to the West Beach Inn.

Note: See Santa Barbara Harbor, Leadbetter Beach, and Arroyo Burro Beach for eateries further west of the wharf.

4.3 State Street and North of State Street
What To Do & See

STATE STREET

This is the place to be for shopping, people-watching, movie theatres, entertainment, and dining (indoor and alfresco) along a busy tree-lined street. In a town where people really do walk the streets, the first mile of State Street extending from the wharf inland, supports an on-going festive atmosphere among countless restaurants and cafés, where colorful umbrellas provide shade for diners and music and laughter spill out onto the street. The restaurants are nestled between chic shops and department stores. Parking is on the side streets and in the 700 block of State Street visitors may use the Macy's parking structure (behind the store). The Santa Barbara Visitor Center has maps available listing the restaurants and shops. (Details under Santa Barbara Information.) Directions from Hwy 101, under Directions, Santa Barbara. From Stearns Wharf, just travel straight ahead as State Street begins at the wharf.

Note: Eateries and shops hugging the street are listed below in order of appearance beginning at Stearns Wharf traveling north up State Street: (Subject to change, call ahead.)

Surf 'n' Wear's Beach House – Here is the place to rent body boards, surfboards, and wetsuits. Ask about referrals for surfing lessons. Open 9am-7pm, Fri/Sat 8pm. Winter closes and hour earlier. (805) 963-1281. Located at 10 State Street.

Enterprise Fish Co. – They have an oyster bar and serve grilled fish and hamburgers. Open 11:30am-9pm, Fri/Sat/Sun 11pm. (805) 962-3313. Located at 225 State Street, in the big red brick building.

Bucatini Trattoria – Italian fare with pizza, gelato, and a full bar. Nice outdoor patio. Daily 11:30am-10pm, Fri/Sat 11pm. (805) 957-4177. Located at 436 State Street.

Santa Barbara Brewing Co. – This sports bar has pizza, sandwiches, burgers, salad, chicken, and steak. 11:30am-11:30pm; Fri/Sat 1am. Winter closes an hour earlier. (805) 730-1040. www.sbbrewco.com. 501 State Street.

Cold Stone Creamery – Terrific ice cream and yogurt is hand mixed with choices of flavors and toppings. Open 11am-10pm, Fri/Sat/Sun 11pm; Sun open 10am. (805) 882-9128. Located at 504 State Street.

Panera Bread - Cafe – Bread, bagels, cookies, pastries, salads, sandwiches, and pastas. Inside and patio seating. Mon-Fri 6am-9pm; Sun 7am. Thurs/Sat until 10pm. (805) 568-1818. 700 State Street, across from Macy's.

Paseo Nuevo Courtyard – It features stores and shops like Macy's, Nordstrom, Gap, and Express. The following restaurants are included: **Nordstrom Café** – 10am-6pm, Sun 11am-5pm. (805) 564-8770. **California Pizza Kitchen** – Great place for kids. 11am-10pm, Fri/Sat 11pm. (805) 962-4648. Enter the courtyard in the 700 block of State Street, along the side of Macy's. Parking is available behind Macy's.

Pascucci – Italian fare with pizza. (Kids' menu.) 11:30am-9:30pm, Fri/Sat 10pm. Radio background music. (805) 963-8123. Located at 729 State Street.

The Andersen's Danish Restaurant & Bakery – B,L,D – Homemade quiches and fine wines and beer. 8am-9pm, Fri/Sat 10pm. (805) 962-5085. Located at 1106 State Street.

La Arcada Courtyard – The entrance is adorned by a tall historic clock. Inside the courtyard there are works of art, shops, and restaurants. Behind the fountain, is the **Cielito Restaurant & Taqueria** – Mexican and Latin American cuisine. Tues-Sun. (closed Monday.) Lunch 11:30am-2:30 pm. Dinner 5-9pm, Thurs/Fri/Sat 10pm. Happy Hour 4-6pm. (805) 965-4770. www.cielitorestaurant.com. Located at 1112 State Street.

La Arcadia Bistro – California cuisine – Salads, sandwiches, burgers, steaks, fish, and pasta. Kids menu. Nice outdoor patio. Breakfast Fri-Sun 9am-1pm. Lunch Mon-Sun 11am-4pm. Dinner Wed-Sun from 4pm. (805) 965-5742. 1112 State Street, located at the courtyard entrance.

Santa Barbara Museum of Art – The museum is housed in an old post office, and displays American, Asian, and European art and rotating exhibits. Museum 11pm-5pm. (Closed on Mon.) Adults $10, kids age 6-17 and students $6, and Seniors $6, under 6 free. (Museum free on Thurs) Wheelchair accessible. **Café** – Tues, Wed & Fri 11am-3pm, Thurs 11am-7pm, Sat/Sun 11am-4pm. Menu includes soups, salads, and sandwiches. (Menu online.) Inside seating and outside tables shaded by umbrellas are available. Wheelchair accessible. (805) 963-4364. www.sbma.net. Located at 1130 State Street.

Santa Barbara County Courthouse – This unique building has hand-painted ceilings, porticos, and gardens where weddings take place. (Free for parties of 15 or fewer.)

Walk or ride up the clock tower (free) for a view of the city, or take a tour of the building. Mon-Fri 8am-5pm, Sat/Sun & holidays 10am-5pm. Free tours everyday at 2pm; Mon/Tues/Weds/Fri 10:30am. Viewing Tower until 4:45pm. Wheelchair accessible. Closed Christmas. (805) 962-6464. Located at 110 Anacapa Street, behind the Santa Barbara Museum of Art.

Jeannine's Bakery & Restaurant – Breakfast (served until 3pm.) and lunch offered amid the scent of freshly baked desserts including muffins, scones, cakes, breads, and cookies. 6:30am-3:30pm. (805) 687-8701. Located at 15 E. Figueroa Street, adjacent to the courthouse.

Tupelo Junction Café – B,L,D – American food with southern influence. Tasty sweet potato fries. Breakfast/lunch 8am-2pm, dinner 5-9pm. (No dinner on Mon.) Happy Hour 5-7pm. (805) 899-3100. Located at 1218 State Street.

Carlitos Cafe and Cantina – Mexican fare – Lovely outdoor patio under umbrellas. Mon-Sat 11am-10pm, Sun 9:30am-10pm. (805) 962-7117. www.carlitos.com. Located at 1324 State Street, across from the Arlington Theater.

NORTH OF STATE STREET

ALAMEDA PARK

In the grassy park under huge bay fig trees is a tree house that stands like a wooden castle (called Kids' World) where children can climb, cross bridges, swing, and go down its slides. Restrooms. Picnic Tables. Free concerts in July on Sundays 3-5:30pm. Information – (805) 965-3021. From State Street, a few blocks north of the Santa Barbara Museum of Art, (1130 State Street), turn right on Micheltorena Street and travel two and a half blocks to the park. From Hwy 101, exit Mission

Street (north of downtown exits), continue northeast five blocks. Turn right on State Street, and in five blocks turn left on Micheltorena Street. Continue two and a half blocks to the park, across from the Alice Keck Garden.

ALICE KECK GARDEN

Turtles swim among orange koi in the lily pond, and sun themselves on rocks at the edge of the pond. A gazebo overlooks the pond; and the surrounding grounds are filled with many trees and flowers. Leashed dogs okay. Paths are wheelchair/stroller accessible. Information – 8am-5pm, Mon-Thurs & every other Fri. (805) 564-5418. Located across from the Alameda Park; detailed directions under Alameda Park.

OLD MISSION SANTA BARBARA

Queen of the Missions – This mission was established in 1786–destroyed by an earthquake in 1812–rebuilt by 1820–damaged by an earthquake in 1925 and restored by 1927. Displayed are Chumash Indian tools, baskets, artwork, musical instruments, and an old missionary's bedroom. Visitors may also look at the church (may be closed for services), and the baptistery. **Note:** The original mission altar is still standing. In late spring and summer, the rose garden across the road is colorful and fragrant. Mission self-guided tours 9am-4:30pm; closes at 5pm. Wheelchair accessible. Adults $7, seniors $5, youth 5-15 yrs. $2, under 4 free. Docent led tours on Thurs/Fri 11am and Sat at 10:30am, $2 with paid admittance. (Closed Easter, Thanksgiving, and Christmas.) **Note:** Restrooms are outside the mission at the top of the parking area. To reach the church for mass and wedding information call (805) 682-4151. For information on the three-day **I Madonnari** (street-painting festival) held during the end of May on the steps of the mission, call (805) 964-4710, ext 4411. Mission (805) 682-

4713. www.santabarbaramission.org. Located at 2201 Laguna Street. From the Santa Barbara Museum of Art, (1130 State Street), continue north on State Street for a mile, turn right on Los Olivos Street (just beyond Mission Street which is signed for the mission but a less direct route) and follow it .4 mile. From Hwy 101, exit Mission Street (north of the downtown exits), continue northeast five blocks and turn left on State Street. Turn right on Los Olivos Street and follow it .4 mile.

ROCKY NOOK PARK

A small oak tree-shaded park with a .3 mile walking path, bordered by huge boulders, runs along a creek. A children's play area, restrooms, and a picnic area with grills is provided; leashed dogs are okay in the park. From the Old Mission Santa Barbara, take Los Olivos Street north .2 mile until it becomes Mission Canyon Road. Turn right at the entrance road signed *Rocky Nook Park.*

MUSEUM OF NATURAL HISTORY

The museum holds displays on Chumash life, the great condor and other birds, and marine life. Short winding paths follow tumbling Mission Creek behind the museum. The museum's Gladwin Planetarium presents shows for kids and adults. (See website for show time and descriptions.) Call for museum special events including: the summertime **"Butterflies Alive,"** the **Santa Barbara Wine Festival** held the last Saturday in June, and many rotating displays. Open 10am-5pm. (Closed Thanksgiving, Christmas, Christmas Eve 3pm, New Years Day, and the last Saturday in June for the wine festival.) Adults $12, seniors and teens 13-17 are $8, under 13 $7, under two free. Price includes exhibitions. (Admission is $1 less in winter.) Museum is wheelchair accessible; one wheelchair is available for use on first come-first served basis. (805) 682-4711. www.sbnature.org. Follow directions to the Old Mission Santa Barbara, take Los Olivos Street north (becomes Mission Canyon Road). The entrance road is on the left just beyond Rocky Nook Park. (Directions from Hwy 101 under Old Mission Santa Barbara.)

SANTA BARBARA BOTANIC GARDEN

A pleasant walk awaits visitors among the desert, meadow, and wooded areas that frame Mission Creek. The aqueduct, along the creek, built in 1806, supplied water to the Old Mission Santa Barbara. Beneath the bridge crossing the creek, a waterfall flows in spring and early summer. There are lovely brazen displays of colorful flowers everywhere, a tiny pond with turtles, and a special area to look for dragonflies. Don't miss the short **Porter Loop Trail**, surrounded with flowers, that lends both mountain and ocean views. It's found uphill from the parking area, across from the entrance gate. A nature-oriented gift shop and picnic tables are on the premises. No food services, except vending machines with water, sodas, and snacks. (Juice and water available in the gift shop.) Open March-Oct, 9am-6pm; Nov-Feb, 9am-5pm. (Closed Thanksgiving, Christmas, Christmas Eve, and New Years Day.) Admittance Fee: Adults $10, seniors and teens 13-17 $8, 2-12 yrs. $6, under two free. (805) 682-4726. www.sbbg.org. Located at 1212 Mission Canyon Road, in the foothills of the Santa Ynez Mountains. Follow directions to the Old Mission Santa Barbara. From the mission, take Los Olivos Street north (becomes Mission Canyon Road). Continue beyond the Museum of Natural History. Turn right on Foothill Road (Hwy 192), and in .2 mile (at stop sign), turn left back onto Mission Canyon Road. At the junction keep right, and follow the signs to the gardens.

4.4 Santa Barbara Area Trails
What to See & Do

TUNNEL TRAIL & SEVEN FALLS TRAILS

The path begins by climbing up a paved un-shaded road. In under a half mile, the path descends and crosses over a bridge on Mission Creek. After crossing the bridge, turn right uphill and follow the old paved road to its end. Take the wide dirt path that continues to climb; eventually it will become narrow and travel close to the creek. Look for a trail sign on the left; the path leads down to the creek bed. This is a special place to savor, where dappled sunlight falls on the creek, and trickling water flows over the rocks. The shallow creek with its tiny pools is a perfect place to cool off on a hot day. **Note:** Just prior to reaching the creek, look for a slim side trail to the left (running alongside the water) which leads to small swimming holes between the boulders. (Swimming holes may dry up in summer.) For the less-than-hardy this is a good turning around point.

The **Tunnel Trail** continues (left of main path descending into the creek) across the creek, and travels up 5 minutes to a view of the ocean. Then the narrow rocky-dirt path ascends and, after traversing a few switch backs (with little shade), continues to Inspiration Point which (on a clear day) provides vast views of Santa Barbara and the ocean. **Note:** It's approximately 30 minutes from the creek.

The old **Seven Falls Trail** has become overgrown, but robust hikers may travel up the creek bed from where Tunnel Trail descends into the creek. This requires serious rock-hopping and boulder-climbing and leads to nice swimming holes, tiny pools where frogs play, and eventually to the Seven Waterfalls.

The creek and falls are dry (in some years) by mid-summer. Sometimes when the creek appears dry, there are still small pools and water in the swimming holes. (Closed on fire-danger days.) Limited trail parking is available along the roadside. Walk .1 mile up to the locked gate and trailhead signed *Tunnel Trail*. **Note:** The closest restrooms are located at the edge of the parking area of Old Mission Santa Barbara. Leashed dogs okay. Information – Santa Barbara Ranger (805) 967-3481. Trail: Easy mile one way to creek. Moderately-strenuous to Inspiration Point (30 minute climb). Strenuous .25 mile climb up rocky creek bed to pools and a little further to Seven Falls. Follow directions to the Old Mission Santa Barbara. From the Mission, take Los Olivos Street north (becomes Mission Canyon Road) for .6 mile. Turn right on Foothill Road (Hwy 192), and in .2 mile at stop sign, turn left back onto Mission Canyon Road. At the junction, turn left onto Tunnel Road and travel to the end (1.1 mile). **Note:** The right turn leads to the Santa Barbara Botanic Garden.

RATTLESNAKE CANYON TRAIL

The trail begins at the edge of the road along the right side of the stone bridge. (Left side is signed *Wilderness Area*; it travels a short distance down to the creek where visitors may cross it and climb up to Rattlesnake Canyon Trail.) At the beginning, visitors must climb over some large rocks to get onto the dirt path. It then levels out beneath tall oaks where chirping birds can be heard; Rattlesnake Creek is on the left. (In some years, the creek is dry by mid-summer.) Soon the path climbs up away from the creek in an area where trees were blackened from a long-ago fire. The terrain is bursting with wildflowers in the springtime. After about half mile, the trail becomes covered in slabs of granite. Beyond this area, left of a triple-trunk oak tree (across from a huge boulder on the right side of the path) a short narrow side path shows the way to a small waterfall tumbling into a placid pool. (It's nearly dry by summer.) Return to the main dirt path, and follow it as it climbs up and rambles close to the creek. When it gets real close to the water, it curves to the right for about 60 yards where it actually runs into the creek. For the less-than-hardy, this is a good turning around point (.75 mile).

Hikers wanting to continue on this trail will need to cross the creek where some rock-hopping is required. The trail climbs to the left and becomes steeper. In 10 minutes, a nice lookout is reached, and, in another 15 minutes, the trail descends and crosses the creek again, and climbs up to a meadow. Return on the same trail. Rattlesnakes are not prevalent here, but poison oak is found near the creek. Leashed dogs okay. **Note:** Skofield Park, just up the road from the trailhead, is a great place for a picnic. 8am to sunset. (Closed Tues/Wed.) Information – Santa Barbara Parks (805) 564-5418. Trail: Easy .75 mile to creek bed, then moderately-strenuous. **Note:** Closest restrooms: **Skofield Park** and at edge of the parking area of Old Mission Santa Barbara. Follow directions to the Old Mission Santa Barbara. From the Mission, take Los Olivos Street north (becomes Mission Canyon Road) for .6 mile. Turn right on Foothill Road (Hwy 192), and in .2 mile at stop sign, turn left back onto Mission Canyon Road. At the junction, keep to the right (do not take Tunnel Road) toward the Santa Barbara Botanic Garden, and in .2 mile make a sharp right-uphill turn on Las Canoas. (Signed *Skofield Park*.) Travel 1.2 miles to the 2nd stone bridge, signed *Rattlesnake Canyon*, and park along the roadside.

COLD SPRINGS & WEST FORK TRAILS

The gravel **Cold Springs Trail** runs slightly uphill, along the right side of the creek, and is shaded by tall trees. Serenity abounds with the sound of the gurgling creek and singing birds. (The creek usually runs year round, but depending upon rainfall, it may be a mere trickle by early summer.) Lush green ferns and vines cover everything, even some trees; and all around, are colorful dragonflies and butterflies. Soon (.1 mile) a short side path, marked by a huge boulder on the left, ushers visitors down to the creek's edge where cool water obliges to refresh both people and dogs. Walking another .1 mile will bring visitors to a trailhead (signed *West Fork Trail*). Sign marks the place to hop across the rocks in the creek to the **West Fork Trail**. Visitors may also cross the creek a few yards further up by climbing over huge boulders surrounding a shallow swimming hole and a tiny waterfall. This is a peaceful place to sit on a wooden bench (Kevin's Bench) at the water's edge, and listen to the trickling water. Cold Springs Trail ends here. For the less-than-hardy, this is a good turning around point. (The East Fork Trail continues ahead, not crossing the creek, but climbing up 1 mile to a lookout point.)

After crossing the creek, the **West Fork Trail** climbs up a few rocky steps and veers off to the right. It begins with a gradual climb traveling under the trees, and follows the creek upstream. At times, the path swings slightly away from the creek, and then swings back close again. Then the path levels out, but it soon climbs some rocky steps hugging the hillside, and the trail becomes narrow and steeper. In a short distance, a small information sign is reached, and the path splits with a gigantic boulder in the center.

Note: The path to the right leads to a stream which may be dry (depends upon rainfall). After crossing the stream, the path leads uphill to the left and continues about a mile to Tangerine Falls. (Named for the orange coloring of some of the rocks surrounding it.) This is a steep-strenuous path which requires scrambling over many slippery rocks. It's treacherous when rocks are wet.

To continue on the **West Fork Trail**, take the path to the left of the boulder. It crosses the creek a few times before reaching an old water tunnel. (It was the main source of water for Santa Barbara in the early 1900s.) The trail climbs and then descends among the shrubs, only to travel back up again to reach the summit at Gibraltar Road. **Note:** Lots of poison oak. Leashed dogs are okay. Best time to visit is in winter after the rainy season begins. Trailhead is on the east edge of the creek, signed *Cold Springs Trail/West Fork Trail.* (Do not take the steep unmarked trail.) The creek will be along the left side of the trail. Parking is along the roadside. Information - Santa Barbara Ranger (805) 967 3481. Trail: Easy .25 mile to Kevin's Bench, Cold Springs Trail. Moderate 1.75 miles one way to Gibraltar Lookout via West Fork Trail. From Hwy 101, in Montecito, (on the southern edge of Santa Barbara) exit (94a) on Olive Mill Road (northbound turn right on Olive Mill Road, southbound turn left) and continue one mile north on Olive Mill Road. (Becomes Hot Springs Road.) Turn left (old church on corner) onto East Valley Road (Hwy 192). In .4 mile, turn right on Sycamore Canyon Road (Hwy 192). Continue .9 mile to a stop sign (small fire station on left); turn right on lovely tree-lined Cold Springs Road. In .4 mile it curves to the right. Stay on Cold Springs Road for .4 mile further. Turn right on East Mountain Drive (.4 mile) and, during the rainy season, drive through the shallow creek water that usually covers the road. Parking pullouts are found beyond the trailhead or park along edge of road.

SAN YSIDRO CANYON TRAIL

This wonderful trail and swimming hole is a place to bring kids or a dog to cool off on a summer day. The trail begins between enormous private estates on a charming tree-lined soft dirt path covered with leaves and bordered by lush greenery. The path travels around an estate home then meets a paved private road. Turn left and walk uphill past the house to pick up the dirt trail on the left side of the paved road. (Signed *Trail*.) Follow the trail uphill as it rambles along the creek until it meets the end of the paved road. Continue straight ahead, beyond the locked gate, on a wide old-dirt road which meanders beside the creek under large oak and eucalyptus trees. Soon it passes another trailhead on the left. Continue on the partially-shaded road beyond another locked gate. After passing a gravel maintenance road on the right, in a short while, look for a small trail sign also on the right.

This narrow tree-lined picturesque path shows off many enticing spots for people and dogs to splash in the creek. It passes small waterfalls, tiny pools, and a small serene shallow pool created where water shoots between two massive boulders surrounded by trees, ferns, and rocks. The rocky path snakes uphill from here to a large swimming hole where kids may be seen jumping off the monstrous boulders into the huge pool. Many people wear bathing suits under their clothes. **Note:** It's dangerous to jump into this pool; the depth of this swimming hole depends upon the rainfall. There's easy access to the pool by walking a few yards beyond it. To the right a steep trail travels (away from the creek) up to a lookout point. Leashed dogs okay. **Note:** Poison oak found along trail. Information, Santa Barbara Ranger (805) 967-3481. Trail: Moderate 1.5 miles one way to large swimming hole. From Hwy 101, in Montecito (just south of Santa Barbara) exit (#93) San Ysidro Road. Follow it north one mile (toward the mountains), turn right on East Valley Road (Hwy 192). Continue .8 mile, turn left on eucalyptus tree-lined Park Lane (.4 mile) and it curves left onto East Mountain Drive. Travel to the end of the road; parking is along the edge of the road. Trailhead is at end of road, signed *San Ysidro Trail*.

Note: A perfect place to find breakfast or lunch before or after taking the Cold Spring/West Fork Trail or the San Ysidro Canyon Trail, is in the small village of Montecito. A local favorite is **Jeannine's Bakery and Restaurant** where breakfast and lunch are served with freshly baked desserts (muffins, scones, cakes, breads, cookies). 6:30am-3:30pm. Pastries/coffee 6:30-7am & 3:30-4pm. (805) 969-7878. Located at 1253 Coast Village Road, west of Olive Mill Road. Exit Hwy 101 on Olive Mill Road, and turn left on Coast Village Road to reach the village. Jeannine's Bakery is in the first block on the left. Coast Village Road is the frontage road skirting Hwy 101, and can be taken (west) when exiting on San Ysidro Road (for the San Ysidro Trail) to reach the village.

4.5 Santa Barbara INFORMATION

GENERAL INFORMATION

Santa Barbara Visitor Center – Maps and information on eateries, lodging, tours, and the following: Art/Crafts Fair every Sunday (details under Stearns Wharf – Bicycles and Art/Crafts), The Old Mission Santa Barbara's Street-Painting Festival (held for three days in May), July 4th parade/fireworks, and the Old Spanish Days Fiesta (held in August) which is celebrated for days with two parades and nights of music, song, and dance. Fiesta Information – www.oldspanishdays-fiesta.org. Visitor center open Feb thru Oct 9am-5pm, Sun 10am-5pm; Nov thru Jan 9am-4pm, Sun 10am-4pm. Free 15-minute parking. (805) 965-3021 or 568-1811. www.santabarbara.com. **Note:** Stearns Wharf is two blocks north of the visitor center.

To reach the Santa Barbara Visitor Center (also the beach and Stearns Wharf) from Hwy 101, exit at Garden Street. At the end of the exit ramp, turn left at the stoplight onto Garden Street, and travel south toward the sea. (Southbound traffic, turn right onto Garden Street.) Garden Street ends at the beach on Cabrillo Boulevard. The visitor center and parking is on the right corner.

Santa Barbara Chamber of Commerce – Mon-Fri 10am-noon & 1-5pm. 104 W. Anapamu Street, Ste. A. (805) 965-3023. www.sbchamber.org.

Outdoors Santa Barbara Visitor Center – Open 11am-5pm. Closed Wed. (805) 456-8752. www.outdoorsb.noaa.gov. Located at 113 Harbor Way. Located above the Santa Barbara Maritime Museum. (Take the elevator inside the building to the 4th floor.) (Details under West of Stearns Wharf – Santa Barbara Harbor.)

City of Santa Barbara Parks & Recreation Dept. – Mon-Fri, 8am-5pm. (805) 564-5418.

Santa Barbara Ranger Station – (805) 967-3481.

Information/History – Santa Barbara. (Details under Appendix.)

Camping – See Carpinteria, El Capitan, and Refugio State Beaches.

Red Tile Walking Tour – Self-guided tour, maps at the Santa Barbara Visitor Center. Tours include Santa Barbara Museum of Art and the beautiful Santa Barbara Courthouse.

Land Shark Tour Bus/Boat – Amphibious bus tours the town and, in summer, cruises the bay. Buy tickets on the bus or at the visitor center. Tours depart at noon, 2pm and 4pm.

Winter noon & 2pm. Adults $30, 10 and under $15, infants free. (805) 683-7600. (Board east side of wharf entrance.)

Wheel Fun Rentals – Bike rentals, even fringed-top bikes for four-or-six people are found here, as well as rollerblade rentals. 8am-8pm, after Labor Day 6pm. **Note:** They will deliver bicycles to hotels and other locations. (805) 966-2282. www.wfrsb.com. 23 E. Cabrillo, half a block east of wharf; also, 22 State Street.

Rentals – Body boards, surfboards, and wetsuits are available. (Details under State Street, Beach House.) Bicycle and rollerblade rentals at Wheel Fun. (Details above.)

Surf Happens – They provide surfboard lessons and surfing camps. Call for an appointment. (805) 966-3613. www. surfhappens.com.

Santa Barbara Sailing Center – (Details under Santa Barbara Harbor.)

Sea Landing – Jet ski and kayak rentals, along with, whale watching tours. (Details under Santa Barbara Harbor.)

Captain Jack's Tours – Exciting tours include horseback riding, kayaking, and wine tours. They will pickup from most hotels for wine tours. (805) 564-1819. www.captainjackstours. com.

Farmer's Market – Every Tuesday in the 500/600 block of State Street, and Saturdays on Santa Barbara and Cota Streets. 8:30am-1pm. (805) 962-5354. www.sbfarmersmarket.org.

Sunsets – To witness gorgeous sunsets visit nearby Goleta Beach located north of Santa Barbara. (Details under Day Trips North of Santa Barbara, Goleta.)

Accessibility Information – (Details under Appendix.)

Wheelchair Accessible Activities – (Details under Appendix.)

TRANSPORTATION

Water Taxi – *Little Toot Tugboat* – runs between Stearns Wharf and Santa Barbara Harbor. Daily noon-6pm. (Closed Wed after Labor Day.) Winter, until Memorial Day, Fri/Sat/Sun only. Fare one way: Adults $4, children under 12 $1. (805) 896-6900. (Details under Stearns Wharf.)

Electric Shuttle Bus – The Downtown Bus travels north up State Street. The turquoise Waterfront Bus travels along the oceanfront and stops at the zoo, waterfront restaurants, and the Santa Barbara Harbor. 10am-6pm, Fri/Sat 9pm. Winter 6pm. Fare one way: $1.75, seniors 85 cents. (Board buses at the wharf entrance.) (805) 963-3366. www.sb.MTD.gov.

Santa Barbara Trolley – A 90-minute narrated trolley-bus city tour with on-off privileges. (See website for variety of tours.) 10am-4pm. Tickets are available on the trolley, from the visitor center, or online. (Board every hour on-the-hour at the Stearns Wharf entrance.) Adults $19, (one child free, 12 and under) additional child 12 and under $8. (805) 965-0353. www.sbtrolley.com.

Santa Barbara Airport – Information – 8am-5pm. Mon-Thurs & every other Fri. (805) 967-7111. www.flysba.com. (Details for the airport and car rentals are under Transportation in the Appendix.) From Hwy 101 northbound travel 7.8 miles north of the Garden Street exit in mid Santa Barbara, and exit onto Hwy 217 (Signed *UCSB/Airport/Hwy 217*.) Head 2 miles south, and exit on Sandspit Road. At the stop sign, turn right, and continue a mile to reach the car rentals. The Santa Barbara Airport lies adjacent to the car rentals.

Southbound traffic exit Hwy 101 on Fairview Avenue, and travel south one mile to the Santa Barbara Airport. Continue beyond the airport to reach the car rentals.

Amtrak Train – There is daily service from San Diego, Union Station in Los Angeles, and several San Francisco locations. (Details for Amtrak and train discounts under Transportation in the Appendix.) Information – (800) 872-7245. www.amtrak.com. Located at 209 State Street, two blocks north of Stearns Wharf.

GOLF COURSES

Santa Barbara Golf Club – An 18-hole, par 70 golf course with twilight discounts in summer after 2pm and, beginning October 1st after 12:30pm. (805) 687-7087. www.sbgolf.com. 3500 Mc Caw Avenue. From Hwy 101 (north end of Santa Barbara) exit on Las Positas Road north, and turn left on McCaw Avenue. **Note:** The golf course is just south of State Street.

Mulligan's Café & Bar – B,L,D – Mexican food, burgers, salads, sandwiches, pasta, chicken, steak, and ribs. Happy Hour Mon-Fri 4-7pm. Sunday dinner-for-two $25. Open 6:30am-8pm, Sat/Sun 9pm. (805) 682-3228. Adjacent to the golf course.

Glen Annie Golf Course – (Details under Goleta Beach.)

Sandpiper Golf Course – (Details under Goleta Beach.)

WINE TASTING

Deep Sea Wine Tasting Room – Wine tasting. (805) 618-1185. (Details under Stearns Wharf.)

Jaffurs Wine Cellar – They make their own wine. Wine tasting daily in summer 11am-5pm, rest of year Fri/Sat/

Sun/Mon. (805) 962-7003. www.jaffurswine.com. 819 E. Montecito Street. Exit Hwy 101 on Milpas Street, continue north, and turn left on Montecito Street.

Santa Barbara Winery – Wine tasting daily 10am-6pm, Fri/Sat 7pm. (805) 963-3633. (800) 225-3633. www.sbwinery. com. 202 Anacapa Street, one block east of State Street.

Santa Barbara Vintners' Assoc. – Information on wine events. Mon-Fri 10am-4pm. (805) 688-0881. www. sbcountywines.com.

Wine Edventures – Guided wine tours. They will pickup from most hotels. (805) 965-9463. www.welovewines.com.

Wine Tasting Tours – Wine Tours. www.santabarbara.com.

EATERIES – Santa Barbara

Eateries under the following areas: Stearns Wharf, East Beach, Santa Barbara Harbor, Leadbetter Beach Park, Arroyo Burro Beach, Waterfront Eateries, State Street.

LODGING – Along the waterfront

Note: Fri/Sat, two-night minimum in July and August.

Four Seasons Resort – Biltmore Santa Barbara – The hotel fronts secluded Butterfly Beach. Elegant rooms and suites overlook the ocean, lush gardens or the pool. (See rooms online.) They include honor bars, terry robes, Wi-Fi, and in-room dining. Hotel amenities include: spa services, bicycles, kids' programs, and Wi-Fi at the pool and in the lobby. The grounds offer magnificent garden settings for weddings, a heated pool, two Jacuzzis, a putting green, and tennis courts. Small dogs okay in cottage rooms. **Bella Vista Restaurant** – B,L,D – American cuisine in a dressy-casual atmosphere.

7am-9pm, Fri/Sat 10pm; winter Tues/Wed until 5pm. Lavish Sunday Brunch 10am-1:30pm. Tea Fri/Sat 2-4pm. Restaurant and Tea Reservations (805) 565-8237. Hotel (805) 969-2261. (888) 424-5866. www.fourseasons.com/santabarbara. 1260 Channel Drive. Exit Hwy 101 on Olive Mill Road (.3 mile southeast of Santa Barbara in Montecito) and turn right on Channel Drive.

Hyatt Santa Barbara – Rooms come with pay Wi-Fi, iHome stereo, and refrigerators. Those with ocean views have a patio or a balcony. Rooms are accompanied by a fitness center, heated pool, Jacuzzi, and spa services. Dogs okay. **Bistro 1111 (Eleven Eleven) Restaurant** – B,L,D – California cuisine with ocean views. Restaurant 6:30am-10pm. Lounge Fri/Sat midnight. (805) 730-1111. Hotel (805) 882-1234. www.hyattsantabarbara.com. 1111 East Cabrillo Boulevard. Sprawled out across from the beach, 1½ blocks from the Santa Barbara Zoo.

Santa Barbara Inn – Striking rooms (some with ocean views) have Wi-Fi, down comforters/pillows, and terry robes. The hotel offers a heated pool/Jacuzzi. Continental breakfast. (805) 966-2285. (800) 231-0431. www.SantaBarbarainn.com. 901 E. Cabrillo Boulevard, across the road from the beach and bay.

Fess Parker's Doubletree Resort – The attractive rooms have ocean, garden, or mountain views, along with honor bars, and pay Wi-Fi. Suites come with Jacuzzis. A beauty salon, spa services, fitness center, putting green, tennis courts, and bicycle rentals are available along with a heated pool/Jacuzzi. Dogs okay. The hotel offers fine dining in **Rodney's Steakhouse.** Tues-Sat 5-10pm. (Closed Sun & Mon.) Weddings are held indoors or on the elaborate grounds. (805) 564-4333. (800) 879-2929. www.fpdtr.com. 633 E. Cabrillo Boulevard, east of the wharf.

Harbor View Inn – Rooms have a view of the harbor or they overlook the pool. The amenities include: room service, terry robes, mini-bars, heated pool and Jacuzzi, poolside food service, a fitness center, spa services, and Wi-Fi. (805) 963-0780. (800) 755-0222. www.harborviewinnsb.com. 28 W. Cabrillo Boulevard, west of wharf, across the road from the beach.

Hotel Oceana – These colorful rooms have views of the ocean, the garden, or the pool. They come with down comforters/pillows, Wi-Fi, flat-screen TV, and continental breakfast. There are two heated swimming pools, Jacuzzi, fitness center, spa treatments, and free use of bicycles. (805) 965-4577. (800) 965-9776. www.hoteloceanasantabarbara. com. 202 W. Cabrillo Boulevard, across the road from beach.

West Beach Inn – Rooms have either an ocean or garden view and come with Wi-Fi, refrigerators, hair dryers, continental breakfast, and a wine and cheese reception. There is a small pool and a Jacuzzi. (805) 963-4277. (800) 716-6199. www.westbeachinn.com. 306 W. Cabrillo Boulevard, across road from beach.

Best Western Plus Beachside Inn – Some rooms have ocean views and others overlook the park or the heated pool; all have Wi-Fi, and come with continental breakfast. $3 parking fee. (805) 965-6556. (800) 932-6556. www.beachsideinn.com. 336 W. Cabrillo Boulevard, across road from the beach.

LODGING – Easy walk to the beach

Old Yacht Club Inn B&B – This was a yacht club in the 1920s. (See the fine rooms online.) Amenities include: whirlpool baths, fireplaces, and Wi-Fi. In addition, there is a gourmet breakfast, a wine social, and bicycles are available.

(805) 962-1277. (800) 549-1676. www.oldyachtclubinn.com. 431Corona Del Mar Drive, one block from beach.

Parkside Inn – These rooms come with room service, Wi-Fi, microwaves and refrigerators. Rooms are non-smoking. Dogs okay. **Note:** This hotel is managed by the Hyatt Santa Barbara, therefore guests are welcome to use the Hyatt swimming pool. (805) 963-0744. www.sbparksideinn.com. 424 Por La Mar, one block from the beach, two blocks from the zoo.

Franciscan Inn – The rooms consist of one or two bedrooms with Wi-Fi. The hotel also provides a heated pool/Jacuzzi, and a continental breakfast. (805) 963-8845. www.franciscaninn. com. 109 Bath Street, half a block from beach.

INEXPENSIVE LODGING

Marina Beach Motel – Selected rooms have Jacuzzi tubs and kitchens; all rooms come with Wi-Fi and continental breakfast. Dogs okay in some rooms. (805) 963-9311. (877) 627-4621. www.marinabeachmotel.com. 21 Bath Street, half block from beach.

Mason Beach Inn – These large rooms include microwaves, refrigerators, and Wi-Fi. Other amenities include a heated pool/Jacuzzi, and continental breakfast. (805) 962-3203. (800) 446-0444. www.masonbeachinn.com. 324 W. Mason Street, half block from beach.

Motel 6 – Modern updated affordable rooms possess a hint of Asian décor. The hotel provides flat-screen TVs, pay Wi-Fi, and an outdoor pool. Dogs stay free. (805) 564-1392. (800) 4motel6. www.motel6.com. 443 Corona Del Mar, 1 block north of E. Cabrillo Boulevard and the beach.

DIRECTIONS – Santa Barbara

From Los Angeles, travel north on Hwy 101, past the cities of Ventura and Carpinteria. Summerland's **Lookout Park** (four miles north of Carpinteria and four miles south of Santa Barbara) is a quiet stopping-off point before reaching Santa Barbara. There's a grassy picnic area and a playground only a short walk from the beach. Leashed dogs okay. Exit (91) on Evans Avenue and follow signs to the park. To reach Santa Barbara from Summerland, continue four miles north on Hwy 101, exit on the left (94c) onto Cabrillo Boulevard, (the first Santa Barbara exit) turn left, and travel under the railroad overpass. Continue to the lagoon, and stop to see the ducks and birds. (Details under Andree Clark Bird Refuge.) From the lagoon, continue south on Cabrillo Boulevard to the beach, zoo, and wharf. (Details under Santa Barbara Zoo, and Stearns Wharf.) 96 miles north of Los Angeles. 337 miles south of San Francisco.

To reach State Street (downtown area), northbound traffic exit Hwy 101 at (96b) Garden Street. (Signed *Garden/Laguna Streets*.) The off ramp splits with Garden Street to the left and Laguna Street to the right. Follow the *Garden Street* sign to the left down to the stoplight. Turn right onto Garden Street (left turn to reach the visitor center, beach, and Stearns Wharf) and then turn left on Gutierrez Street. Proceed three blocks to State Street. (Details under State Street.)

To reach State Street (downtown area), southbound traffic exit Hwy 101 at Carrillo Street and turn left onto Carrillo. (Five blocks to State Street.) To reach the beach, exit on Castillo and travel south toward the sea. At the beach, (Cabrillo Boulevard) turn left for the wharf and right for the harbor. For the Andree Clark Bird Refuge and the Santa Barbara Zoo take left exit (94b) Cabrillo Boulevard and turn right at the stop sign. Continue to Los Patos, turn right, and follow it to the bird refuge and parking. (Details/directions to the zoo under Santa Barbara Zoo and, details for the bird refuge under Andree Clark Bird Refuge.)

4.6 Day Trip South Of Santa Barbara
What to Do & See

CARPINTERIA – (Carp is the local name)

In this small beach town, Linden Avenue is lined with gift and antique shops and some nice restaurants. Travel down Linden Avenue, beyond the shops, to find the fabulous sandy beach with a small free parking area. (Details for directions to Linden Avenue under Carpinteria Directions.)

CARPINTERIA STATE BEACH

This beautiful sun-bronzed sandy beach (popular for swimming and sunbathing) wanders along for miles and passes the edge of the **Carpinteria State Park Campground**. Day use parking fee is $10. (Details for campground/RV park under Carpinteria Lodging.) The embankment running along the beach, at the southern end of the campground, has tar oozing up naturally from the ground. (The Indians used it to waterproof their boats.) South of the last camping site at the edge of the ocean, rocky outcroppings provide a place where sea life is shown off at low tide. (Check at State Beach & Campground entrance for low tide information.) This is also a good place to hunt for seashells. From Carpinteria Avenue, take Palm Avenue. (Details under Carpinteria Directions.)

Note: To find another place to hunt seashells at low tide travel to the end of Linden Avenue, beyond all the shops and restaurants. Then take Sandyland Road to the end. Turn left on Ash Avenue to the beach sand and park along the roadside.

CARPINTERIA BLUFFS & SEAL SANCTUARY

The beaches below the bluff are closed during the seal breeding season and when the young seal pups are left on the beach while mothers search for food. The view from the bluff is quite impressive; the beach is crowded with over a hundred harbor seals lazing in the sunshine. From December to the end of May, the harbor seals stay on the shore most of the day. On June 1st this stretch of the beach opens to the public and, the seals slink into the sea every morning and come on shore only at night. By this time, the pups born in February are nearly as large as their mothers. Best time to view the seals, January thru May. Bring binoculars. **Note:** See Tide Pooling & Harbor Seals below for directions. (805) 684-2247.

TIDE POOLING & HARBOR SEALS

Option One – From Hwy 101, exit #85 (northbound traffic turn left; southbound turn right) onto Bailard Avenue, and head toward the ocean into the parking area. From the middle of the parking area, take the wide dirt path across the meadow heading west (to the right). Walk along the fence beneath the long row of eucalyptus trees. Turn left, carefully crossing over the railroad tracks. Soon up on the bluff a split in the path is reached. To the left, the path, which is covered in places with hardened tar, slithers down to the beach. (Near the end of the path, expect to navigate a few huge slippery rocks.) Turn left on the beach. Here, at low tide, visitors will find fantastic tide pooling. Many starfish and sea anemones of various hues cling to the rocks and hide in tiny pools. Great seashell hunting at low tide. (To protect the seals, the beach to the right is open only June 1ˢᵗ thru Labor Day.) To reach the Seal Sanctuary, walk back up to the bluff top and follow the dirt path .25 mile along the edge of the bluff to the sign stating *Seal Sanctuary.*

Option Two – From Hwy 101, exit at #86 on Casitas Pass Road, and follow the signs for *Carpinteria State Beach* which follows Casitas Pass Road to a right turn on Carpinteria Avenue, and a left turn on Palm Avenue. From the Carpinteria State Beach parking area, walk or ride a bicycle through the campground, and take the scenic walking/bike lane which travels southeast dipping down to the beach, where tar oozes up naturally as it has for thousands of years in this area. Continue on the path beyond the oil refinery parking area and their working pier. Then take the narrow dirt path to the right. It leads along the ocean bluff for a short distance to the signed *Seal Sanctuary.* **Note:** Leashed dogs okay on the bluff paths; no dogs on the beach or at the Seal Sanctuary.

CARPINTERIA VALLEY MUSEUM OF HISTORY

Exhibits recount the area history from Spanish exploration through the Chumash Indian and pioneer periods. The captivating exhibits include Victorian furnishings, a farm house kitchen, and a one-room schoolhouse. Open Tues thru Sat. (Closed Sun and Mon and major holidays.) Gift shop and museum – 1-4pm. Donations appreciated. (805) 684-3112. Located at 956 Maple Avenue, off Carpinteria Avenue, south of Linden Avenue.

INFORMATION

Carpinteria Valley Chamber of Commerce – Information on Independence Day parade, Rods and Roses car show (usually last Saturday in June) and the California Avocado Festival – Arts/crafts, food, live music. Free admittance. Held the first Friday weekend in Oct. Information – (805) 684-5479.

www.avofest.com. Linden Avenue and side streets are closed to traffic for this event. Chamber open Mon-Fri 9am-noon and 1-4pm. (805) 684-5479. www.carpchamber.org. Located at 1056 Eugenia Place #B. (Eugenia Place runs alongside Jack's Bistro at 5050 Carpinteria Avenue.)

Visitor Information at the Kiosk – Memorial Day to Labor Day Fri/Sat/Sun 10am-4pm; 1st Friday of the month, special events and music. 5-8pm. Information – (805) 684-5405 ext. 432. The Visitor Kiosk is located at the seal fountain in the middle of Linden Avenue, between 8th and 9th Streets.

Carpinteria State Beach – Information and low tide times (805) 684-2811. (Bypass the recording by pressing 03.) www.parks.ca.gov. **Note:** Free beach wheelchairs available at entrance. Camping along the Beach – (Details under Carpinteria Lodging.) From Carpinteria Avenue, take Palm Avenue. (Full directions under Carpinteria Directions.)

Rincon Cycles – Bicycle rentals. Open Mon-Sat 10am-5:30pm. (Summer, open some Sundays 11am-2pm.) (805) 684-9466. Located at 5100 Carpinteria Avenue.

Farmer's Market – Thursday; summer 3-6:30pm, winter 3-6pm.(805) 962-5354. The 800 block of Linden Avenue.

Amtrak Train – No station here; the train stops at a large parking area, one block north of the beach. (Details under Transportation in Appendix) (800) 872-7245. www.amtrak. com. 475 Linden Avenue.

EATERIES

Carpinteria Avenue/Casitas Pass Road Eateries

I-Hop Restaurant – B,L,D – great pancakes. Open 6am-

10pm, Fri/Sat 11pm; winter until 9pm. (805) 566-4926. Located at 1114 Casitas Pass Road.

Zookers Café – Lunch 11:30am-3pm with sandwiches and salads. Dinner 5pm-9:30pm with meatloaf, pastas, chicken, and wines. (Closed Sun.) (805) 684-8893. Corner of Casitas Pass Road and Carpinteria Avenue.

Giovanni's – Italian fare with pizza, pasta, salad, and sandwiches. Open 11am-9pm, Fri/Sat 10pm, Sun noon-9pm. Karaoke summer Wednesdays. 5:30-10pm. (805) 684-8288. 5003 Carpinteria Avenue, corner of Linden and Carpinteria.

Clementine's Steak House – Homemade pie comes with dinners. Open Wed-Sun, 4:30-9pm. (Closed Mon/Tues.) (805) 684-5119. 4631 Carpinteria Avenue, close to the Best Western Plus Carpinteria Inn.

Rusty's Pizza Parlor – Kids love it here. Great pizza and salad bar. Open 11am-midnight with delivery service. (805) 564-1111. 5250 Carpinteria Avenue.

Linden Avenue Eateries

The Worker Bee Café – Cute restaurant is popular for breakfast and lunch. Open 6:30am-3pm. Winter 7:30 am-2pm. (805) 745-1828. Located at 973 Linden Avenue.

Corktree Cellars – Wine Bar & Bistro – Popular spot with cheese plates, sandwiches, chicken, fish, tapas, pizzas, salads, and desserts. (Kids' menu.) Outdoor patio. Open 11:30am-9pm, Fri/Sat 10pm. (Closed Mon.) (805) 684-1400. Located at 910 Linden Avenue.

Señor Frogs – Mexican Cuisine. Open Tues-Sat 11am-9pm, Sun 7:30am-9pm. (Closed Mon.) (805) 684-9352. Located at 892 Linden Avenue.

The Palms Restaurant & Bar – Local favorite. Cook your own steak, fish, or chicken; they cook the shrimp and lobster. (Kids' menu.) Dinner 5-10pm, Sunday 4:30pm-10pm. Fri/Sat live bands and dancing. 9pm-1:30am. (805) 684-3811. Located at 701 Linden Avenue.

Sly's – The menu includes: lobster, veal, steaks, salads, and cocktails. Open Mon-Fri 11:30am-10pm. Happy Hour 4-6pm. Brunch Sat/Sun 9am-2:30pm. (805) 684-6666. Located at 686 Linden Avenue.

Giannfranco's Trattoria – Italian fare. Lunch 11am-3pm, Sat/Sun noon-3pm. Dinner 5-9pm. (Closed Tues.) (805) 684-0720. Located at 666 Linden Avenue.

The Spot – Cheeseburgers with grilled onions and chili cheeseburgers are extremely popular. Shakes, fries, cones, and tacos are served also. Outdoor tables. Cash only. Mon 10am-4pm. Tues/Wed/Thurs 10am-6:30pm, Fri/Sat 7pm. (805) 684-6311. Located at 389 Linden Avenue, near the beach.

LODGING

Carpinteria State Beach – Campground & RV Park is along the beautiful swimming beach, and close to walking/ bicycle trails. Many wheelchair sites available. Also free beach wheelchairs at entrance. Leashed dogs okay. **Note:** Raccoons may visit at night. Campground Information and low tide times (805) 684-2811. (Bypass the recording by pressing 03.) Reservations (800) 444-7275. www.reserveamerica.com. From Carpinteria Avenue, take Palm Avenue. (Full directions under Carpinteria Directions.)

Motel 6 – Modern updated affordable rooms possess a hint of Asian décor. The hotel provides flat-screen TVs, pay Wi-Fi, and an outdoor pool. Dogs stay free. (805) 684-8602. (800)

4-Motel 6. www.motel6.com. 5550 Carpinteria Avenue.

Holiday Inn Express – Attractive rooms and suites come with a full breakfast bar, heated swimming pool/spa, fitness room, and Wi-Fi. Dogs okay. (805) 566-9499. (888) 409-8300. www.carpinteriaexpress.com. 5606 Carpinteria Avenue.

Best Western Plus Carpinteria Inn – The hotel entrance is decorated with red bougainvillea, and some of the rooms overlook the picturesque garden courtyard encompassing a small heated pool and spa. **Sunset Grille and Bar** is on-site. Breakfast 7-10:30am, Sat/Sun 11am. Dinner 5-9:30, Fri/Sat 10pm. Bar until midnight. (805) 684-0473. (800) 528-1234. www.chmhotels.com. (click on Santa Barbara) 4558 Carpinteria Avenue.

DIRECTIONS – Carpinteria

From Hwy 101, exit onto Casitas Pass Road (northbound traffic exit 86, southbound exit 86a). Follow it toward the ocean to the stoplight, and turn right on Carpinteria Avenue. Turn left on Palm Avenue to reach the Carpinteria State Beach and campground. (Pay parking.) Continue on Carpinteria Avenue and turn left on Linden Avenue to reach the shops, restaurants, and free beach parking. 86 miles north of Los Angeles. 10 miles south of Santa Barbara.

4.7 Day Trips North Of Santa Barbara
What to Do & See

GOLETA – (Spanish for *schooner*)

GOLETA BEACH

This is the place to watch amazing crimson and gold sunsets melt into the horizon, from the sandy swimming beach or the short fishing pier (no fishing license required on pier) or from the grassy park which has picnic tables and BBQ pits. (Pier is wheelchair accessible.) Dogs are okay on the pier and in the park.

Beachside Café – Dining is indoors or on the glass-enclosed patio with an open top where the birds fly in and out. The ocean view is enhanced by lovely sunsets and the fishing pier. The menu features salads, sandwiches, burgers, fresh grilled seafood, chicken, and steaks. (Kids' menu.) Lunch 11:30am-4:30pm. Dinner 5-9pm, Sat/Sun until 11pm. (805) 964-7881. 5905 Sandspit Road, Goleta Beach. On Hwy 101 (northbound), travel 7.8 miles north of the Garden Street exit in mid Santa Barbara, and exit onto Hwy 217. (Signed *UCSB/Airport/Hwy 217*.) Head 2 miles south and exit on Sandspit Road, turn left at the stop sign (turn right for the Santa Barbara Airport) and continue to a right turn signed *Goleta Beach County Park*. (Southbound traffic exit Hwy 101 on Fairview, and travel south one mile to the Santa Barbara Airport. Continue one mile further to a right turn signed *Goleta Beach County Park*.)

STOW HOUSE

This 1872 Victorian-style home, with a wide veranda and period furnishings is perched on a wonderful lawn, set amongst spring and summer flowers. Huge eucalyptus, palm, Spanish fir, and redwood trees are sprinkled in the garden. This is a lovely setting for weddings. There is a working blacksmith shop behind the house. The **Lake Los Carneros Trail** begins in front of the house paved, but it soon becomes compact dirt. (Details for trail given below.) House open Sat/Sun 1-4pm, house tours – 2 and 3pm. Special events with music and craft shows take place on July 4th and the 2nd weekend in December, when the house is decorated for Christmas. (Closed on all rainy days and Christmas.) Entrance Fee $5, under 12 free. The visitor center has tour tickets, information, and gift shop; it's located in the red barn building across from the Stow House. During the house tour hours the History Education Center in the red barn is open, but visitors must ask the house volunteer to open the door. Wheelchair accessible. Restrooms are behind the gift shop. (805) 681-7216. www.stowhouse. com. 304 N. Los Carneros Road, Goleta. On Hwy 101 from the Garden Street exit in mid Santa Barbara, continue 10.2 miles north and exit onto Los Carneros Road. Travel north .3 mile to a right turn signed *Stow House*. The short road ends in a large parking area for both the Stow House and the South Coast Railroad Museum.

LAKE LOS CARNEROS TRAIL

For a marvelous walk around picturesque Lake Los Carneros, which is encircled by tall reeds, begin from the red barn behind the Stow House. The short path is a partially-paved old road which leads down to the lake. (Some of the trail is wheelchair accessible.) A second entrance is from the paved path in front of the Stow House which immediately becomes compact dirt and leads to the lake. At the lake, turn right; the lake will be on the left. Continue ahead to the south side of the lake where visitors may leave the road and follow the narrow dirt path (to the left) as it meanders close along the lakeshore. Wooden benches provide a place to sit and watch the ducks and birds perform. Great blue herons and egrets may be seen feeding. Continue walking along the path uphill where it meets the old road. Veer left and, just past the lake, take the wide dirt path to the left.

Soon a junction is reached; proceed on the meandering path to the left (toward the lake) and enjoy the spring and early summer wildflowers. In the first part of the morning, bunnies, deer, coyotes, and foxes are sometimes spotted along the paths. Keep to the right at the next junction, and follow the path along the edge of a stand of tall trees. Continue straight ahead (large meadow is on the right side of the path) to a long wooden bridge spanning over a marshy area. Cross the bridge and turn right on the paved road, which ends at the blacksmith shop behind the Stow House. Bear left to reach the Stow House where the trail began. **Note:** Mosquitoes are prevalent especially on early summer mornings, and at dusk. Lake path open sunrise to sunset. Leashed dogs okay. Trail: Easy loop 1.5 miles. (Follow above directions to the Stow House.)

SOUTH COAST RAILROAD MUSEUM

The railroad station, originally built in the early 1900s, is now a train museum. Museum open Thurs/Fri 1-4pm, Sat/Sun 11am-4pm. Closed Mon-Wed. Miniature train rides (must be at least 34 inches tall to ride) $1.50 or 2 rides $2.50. Thurs/Fri 2 to 3:45pm, Sat/Sun 1 to 3:45pm. **Note:** The museum offers day-trips aboard vintage railcars. (Leaving from Santa Barbara.) (805) 964-3540. www.

goletadepot.org. 300 N. Los Carneros Road, Goleta. Follow the directions for the Stow House.

CORONADO BUTTERFLY PRESERVE & ELLWOOD BEACH

Orange and black Monarch Butterflies winter in the eucalyptus trees at the preserve. The first part of the walking path through the preserve, is signed with pictures of butterflies. There are many lovely side paths, but the main path, only a quarter mile long, requires traversing over a stream on a wooden bridge, crossing another stream on a long plank (streams are sometimes dry), and traveling through a ravine covered in leaves and branches. The path ends in the main grove of eucalyptus trees. The butterflies hang together in clusters up in the trees, and fly around only when the sun is out. In the middle of the preserve, a path (with roped guide rail) leads to the left around the border of the preserve. For a walk to the beach, follow this path; walk out of the preserve to a huge grassy meadow and take the wide dirt path to the left. Stay on the main path (there are many narrow paths crisscrossing the meadow) as it leads out to the ocean bluff; turn left (south) and follow the path as it meanders down to the lower part of the bluff. At the tall red-brick marker, look for the wide dirt path (to the right, beneath the trees) that descends down to **Ellwood Beach**. This area of the beach is sprinkled with driftwood, rocks, and unusual seashells. **Warning:** It may be difficult to find the return trail from the beach, but most of the trails at the lower end of the bluff lead back to the bluff top. Trail: Easy .25 mile through the preserve one way, .5 mile extended walk to the beach. Dogs okay. Best time to see the butterflies, December thru February. Donation box is at the preserve entrance. Information – www.sblandtrust.org/coronado.html. To find the preserve, on Hwy 101 travel 10.7 miles north of the Garden Street exit in mid Santa Barbara, exit onto Glen Annie/Storke Road (in Goleta), and turn left over the freeway on Storke Road. Turn right on Hollister Avenue, and follow it 1.1 miles to Coronado Drive which is in a residential area and turn left. Drive one mile to the preserve signed *Coronado Butterfly Preserve.*

GOLETA LEMON FESTIVAL

In **Girsh Park** on the third weekend of October, a host of lemon-based foods are served amid an art/crafts show, with local music, pie-eating contests, a petting zoo, wine tasting, carnival rides, and a car show. Try the lemon beer. Free admission. Sat 10am-6pm, Sun 10am-5pm. Wheelchair accessible. (805) 967-2500 ext.2. www.goletavalley.com. To find Girsh Park, on Hwy 101 travel 10.7 miles north of the Garden Street exit in mid Santa Barbara, exit on Glen Annie/Storke Road (in Goleta), and turn left over the freeway onto Storke Road. Continue beyond the stoplight at Hollister Avenue and beyond Fire Station 11; turn right on Phelps Road.

GOLETA GOLF COURSES

Glen Annie Golf Club – 18 holes of golf (twilight discounts) with ocean views. **Frog Bar & Grill** – Two outdoor patios. Cocktails, and appetizers. The lunch menu includes, fish, steak, tacos, pizzas, sandwiches, and crepes. Mon-Fri 11:30am-2pm. (Closed Sat & Sun.) Weddings. (805) 968-6400. www.glenanniegolf.com. 405 Glen Annie Road, Goleta. On Hwy 101 travel 10.7 miles north of the Garden Street exit in mid Santa Barbara, exit on Glen Annie/Storke Road, and turn right (north) onto Glen Annie Road and continue for .75 mile.

Sandpiper Golf Course – 18 holes of golf with ocean views. **Sandpiper Grill** – B,L – 7am-6pm. Menu includes breakfast items, soups, sandwiches, salads and chili. Outdoor

Weddings. (805) 968-1541. www.sandpipergolf.com 7925 Hollister Avenue, Goleta. 14 miles north of Santa Barbara.

INFORMATION

Goleta Chamber of Commerce – No office; visit the website or call for information. Mon-Fri 9am-5pm. (805) 967-2500. www.goletavalley.com.

Farmer's Market – On the corner of Storke and Hollister (Marketplace Shopping Center). Sun 10am-2pm. At Camino Real Center, 7004 Marketplace Drive, Thur 3-6pm. (805) 962-5354. www.sbfarmersmarket.org.

West Wind Drive-In & Swap Meet – Double-feature movies shown in drive-in theater. Adults $7.50, age 5-11 $1, 4 and under free. Popcorn $5. Call for movie features and times. Sunday swap meets year round. 7am-2pm. Adults $1.25, under 11 free. (805) 964-9050. www.westwinddrivein.com. Located at 907 S. Kellogg Avenue, Goleta.

EATERIES

Hollister Brewing Company – Appetizers, salads, soups, sandwiches, home-made pizzas, chicken dinners, and desserts are served (along with wines and brews) indoors or alfresco in a fun atmosphere. Restaurant 11am-10pm, Sun/Mon 9pm. (805) 968-2810. www.hollisterbrewco.com. 6980 Marketplace Drive. From the Coronado Butterfly Preserve, travel up Coronado Drive to Hollister and turn right. Continue to Camino Real Marketplace Drive (stoplight) and turn right into the Camino Real Marketplace Plaza. Inside the plaza turn left, and continue almost to the end of the road; the restaurant is on the left. To find the restaurant from Santa Barbara, travel 10.5 miles north of the Garden Street exit in mid Santa Barbara, exit on Glen Annie/Storke Road, and turn left over the freeway on Storke Road. Continue to Hollister Avenue (at stoplight) and turn right. Turn left on Camino Real Marketplace Drive (stoplight) into the Camino Real Marketplace Plaza, and turn left. Continue almost to the end of the road; restaurant is on the left.

Outback Steakhouse – Serves steak, chicken, seafood, soups, salads, and desserts. Mon-Thurs 4-9pm, Fri/Sat 9:30pm, Sun noon-9pm. (805) 964-0599. www.outback.com. 5690 Calle Real, Goleta. To find the restaurant from Santa Barbara, travel 7.7 miles north of the Garden St. exit in mid-Santa Barbara. Exit onto Patterson, travel north and turn left onto Calle Real.

Woody's Barbeque – An old west atmosphere with sawdust on the floor. Outdoor patio is shaded with a huge magnolia tree. A variety of barbeque sandwiches are served with good fries. There is also a salad bar, chili, and burgers. (Kids' menu.) Open 11am-9pm, Fri/Sat 10pm. (After Labor Day closes 9pm every day.) (805) 967-3775. www.woodysbbq.com. 5112 Hollister Avenue, Goleta. To find the restaurant from Santa Barbara, travel 7.7 miles north of the Garden Street exit in mid Santa Barbara, exit onto Patterson, and turn left over the freeway. Continue to Hollister Avenue (at stoplight), and turn left. Travel along Hollister Avenue, and turn left at the stoplight into the Magnolia Shopping Center. The restaurant is on the right side of the shopping center, across from Ralph's Grocery Store.

LODGING

Motel 6 – Modern updated affordable rooms possess a hint of Asian décor. The hotel provides flat-screen TVs, pay Wi-Fi, and an outdoor pool. Dogs stay free. (805) 964-3596. (800) 4-Motel 6. www.motel6.com. 5897 Calle Real, Goleta.

Hotel Goleta – Nice rooms and suites come with Wi-Fi and a swimming pool. **Remington Restaurant** on the premises serves breakfast buffet. Patio Bar serves bar grub 5:30-8:30pm. (805) 964-6241. www.GoGoleta.com. 5650 Calle Real, Goleta.

Courtyard by Marriott Santa Barbara Goleta – Pool, room service, Wi-Fi. **The Bistro** – Breakfast, dinner, and drinks. 6-10am, 5-10pm. (805) 968-0500. www.GoGoleta.com. 401 Storke Road, Goleta.

Pacifica Suites Hotel – Pool, Jacuzzi, Wi-Fi. Full breakfast. Small dogs okay. (805) 683-6722. www.GoGoleta.com. 5490 Hollister Avenue, Goleta.

DIRECTIONS – Goleta

See above listed activities for directions from Santa Barbara. The Santa Barbara Airport is located in Goleta. (Details for the airport and car rentals are under Transportation, Santa Barbara and more information is under the Appendix.) From Hwy 101 northbound, travel 7.8 miles north of the Garden Street exit in mid Santa Barbara, and exit onto Hwy 217 (Signed *UCSB/Airport/Hwy 217*.)

EL CAPITAN & REFUGIO STATE BEACHES
Swimming – Camping – Tide Pooling

In **El Capitan Beach**, a bicycle/walking path begins from the parking area near the small store, and leads north along the beach bluffs. It passes along the edge of the campground. At one time, it connected to **Refugio State Beach**, but winter storms have rendered the old connecting path impassable. Great tide pooling is found along the beach. Leashed dogs are okay. Trail: Easy 1 mile one way. The larger of the two state parks, is found at Refugio Beach where a nice grassy area hugs the beach with picnic tables under palm trees.

INFORMATION

El Capitan/Refugio State Beaches day use parking fee $10 per car. Camping and State Park Information – Tues-Fri 10am-4pm. Closed Sat/Sun/Mon. (805) 968-1033. www.parks. ca.gov/.

LODGING

Camping at Beach – El Capitan and Refugio State Beach Campgrounds (800) 444-7275. www.reserveamerica.com.

El Capitan Canyon Tents and Cabins – Amid the trees are cabins with kitchenettes, bathrooms, and some deep tubs; tents are equipped with heaters and electric lights. Hiking trails are nearby. No pets. Reservations (866) 352-2729. www. elcapitancanyon.com.

Ocean Mesa RV and Tent Camping – Central bath houses. Wired for TV and Wi-Fi. The heated swimming pool can be used by Ocean Mesa and El Capitan Canyon guests. Located near Los Padres National Forest. Leashed dogs okay, except not on trails. (866) 410-5783. www.oceanmesa.com. Located next door to El Capitan Canyon.

DIRECTIONS – El Capitan & Refugio Beaches

To reach El Capitan State Beach, from Santa Barbara, travel Hwy 101 north 20.3 miles (don't take first exit signed *El Capitan*) take exit #117 signed *El Capitan State Beach*. To reach Refugio Beach, continue north (on Hwy 101) 2.5 miles past the El Capitan State Beach exit to the signed *Refugio Beach* exit.

HORSEBACK RIDING & COTTAGES
NEAR REFUGIO STATE BEACH

Circle Bar-B Guest Ranch & Stables – Horseback riding along the scenic creek and waterfall. All year. 9am-5pm plus sunset rides. Guest ranch rooms have shower/tubs. Hillside and creek-side cottages showers only. All meals included in room rate. (Lunch is boxed to go.) Local wine served in the full bar, and the game room has a pool table and ping-pong. Outdoor pool and Jacuzzi. Horseback riding – (805) 968-3901. Guest Ranch – (805) 968-1113. www.circlebarb.com. 1800 Refugio Road, Goleta. From Santa Barbara travel 23 miles north, exit at the sign for Refugio State Beach. At the stop sign, head away from the beach 3.5 miles.

See photos of the 6 areas listed in this book at: www. CaliforniaVacationPaths.com.

Attraction prices and times listed in this guide are subject to change; call ahead. Information missing or incorrect? Contact author: Pati.Anne@yahoo.com.

KID FAVES

SANTA BARBARA

Note: Details for the following activities are found under main section of Santa Barbara. (See Table of Contents for page numbers.)

STEARN'S WHARF

Ty Warner Sea Center – Kids can climb through a large tunnel to view sea life and have fun with Touch-Tanks. It's close to the wharf's ice cream store. (Wheelchair/stroller accessible.)

CHASE PALM PARK

Merry-go-Round – it's encircled with grassy areas and paths that wind around ponds (filled with koi, turtles, and ducks) and lead to a playground. (Wheelchair accessible.)

BICYCLE RENTALS

Bicycles – The ones built-for-two, four, or six are popular on the paved way which runs along the oceanfront near the wharf. (Rentals are close to wharf entrance.)

SANTA BARBARA ZOO

Kids get to feed the giraffes and ride a miniature train, as well as see over 500 animals. (Wheelchair/stroller accessible.)

ANDREE CLARK BIRD REFUGE

Lagoon – Home to ducks, egrets, herons, frogs, and lots of dragonflies. Bridges cross the short trail which meanders along the water's edge. Look for frogs under the bridges.

LEADBETTER BEACH

This is a great swimming area with a nice sandy beach. (Lifeguards are on duty.) It is bordered by a grassy picnic area and a cafe with outdoor seating on the sand. The café has a kids' menu, and some tables are on the beach sand. Kids may play in the sand while parents dine.

ALAMEDA PARK

Kids' Park – Under a huge bay fig tree is a tree house where kids can climb, cross bridges, swing and go down its slides.

ALICE KECK GARDEN

Garden & Pond – Turtles swim with orange koi in the pond then sun themselves along the rocky shore.

ROCKY NOOK PARK

Picnic Area – There is a playground and a short trail runs along the creek. (Leashed dogs okay.)

APPENDIX

SANTA BARBARA

HISTORY

The peaceful Chumash Indians inhabited the area for thousands of years. They made plank boats (tomols) similar to those made by the Polynesians, using redwood that drifted down along the coast; but if the supply was low, they used the local pine. The boats were sealed with a mixture of pine pitch and the natural tar that still oozes up along the Carpinteria beaches ten miles south of Santa Barbara.

On December 3, 1602, the Spanish explorer, Sebastian Vizcaino, named the area *Santa Barbara* after he survived a vicious storm in the harbor on the eve of Saint Barbara's feast day. In 1848, after the Mexican-American War, the United States acquired California. In the earthquake of 1925, Santa Barbara was completely destroyed and then it was rebuilt in the Spanish style. A fine example is the County Courthouse built in 1929. (Details for the courthouse under Santa Barbara, State Street.)

STEARNS WHARF

The wharf, built in 1872, was named for its builder John P. Stearns. It was ravaged by an earthquake in 1925, but rebuilt. In 1941, the Harbor Restaurant was constructed and is still going strong today. In spite of its many fires, including the 1998 fire that destroyed the last 150 feet of the wharf, it is still primarily built of wood. The wharf receives approximately five million visitors a year. (Details for the wharf shops and restaurants under Santa Barbara, Stearns Wharf.)

LODGING

Lower hotel rates may apply during the week. Call the hotels direct, and check prices against their website offerings. Reservations can also be made from the hotel listing on the Santa Barbara Visitor Center's website www.sbchamber.org. (Click on *Visitors* and then *Lodging*.) (805) 965-3021.

Note: In the lodgings where dogs are allowed, dog fees vary from hotel to hotel. Motel 6 is one of the few where dogs stay free.

TRANSPORTATION

Santa Barbara Airport (SBA)

There are daily non-stop flights to Santa Barbara from Los Angeles on American Airlines. (800) 433-7300. www.aa.com. United Airlines services both Los Angeles and San Francisco. (800) united1. www.united.com. Airport Information – www.flysba.com. Taxi cabs await visitors at the airport. Airline tickets and rental car reservations are available online at: www.ifly.com/santa-barbara-muni-airport. (Directions from Santa Barbara under Santa Barbara Transportation.)

Airport Car Rentals

Avis – (805) 964-4848. (800) 230-4898.
Budget – (805) 964-6792. (800) 527-0700.
Enterprise – (805) 683-3012. (800) 261-7331.
Hertz – (805) 967-0411. (800) 654-3131.
National – (805) 967-1204. (877) 222-9058.

Amtrak

There is daily train service to Santa Barbara from San Diego and from two locations in Los Angeles. Several San Francisco locations have a combination of bus and train service to Santa Barbara. From the Ferry Building in San Francisco, a 30-minute bus ride to Oakland connects to the train to Santa Barbara. (800) 872-7245. www.amtrak.com. **Note:** To obtain a 20 percent train discount, register free on this website: www.santabarbaracarfree.org. Registered visitors will also receive discounts on bicycle and kayak rentals, cruises, tours, sailing, and some hotels and restaurants in Santa Barbara.

Santa Barbara Amtrak Station

The Santa Barbara train station is located two blocks north of the beach and Stearns Wharf. **Avis Car Rental** – (805) 965-1079.

Carpinteria

Carpinteria (10 miles south of Santa Barbara) has daily Amtrak service from San Diego and Los Angeles. Lodging and restaurants are less expensive than in Santa Barbara; and the swimming beach and campgrounds are sensational. **Note:** No car rentals are available in Carpinteria. (See bus service listed below.)

Santa Barbara Air Bus

Daily buses run between Santa Barbara and Carpinteria. They also connect to the Los Angeles Airport and the cruise ships in Long Beach and San Pedro. (Closed Thanksgiving and Christmas.) (805) 964-7759. (800) 423-1618.

WEATHER

www.santabarbara.com/community/weather/

WHEELCHAIR ACCESSIBLE ACTIVITIES

Note: See Table of Contents for page numbers of activities.

SANTA BARBARA

Stearns Wharf – Ice cream/gift shops, eateries, fishing from wharf.

Walkway along Sunday Arts/Crafts Fair – At wharf entrance.

Bicycle/Walking Path – Along the shoreline, from wharf entrance.

Chase Palm Park – Paved paths and merry-go-round with ramp.

Santa Barbara Zoo – See the animals and feed the giraffes. (Call ahead for feeding times.)

Cement breakwater – Located at the Santa Barbara Harbor. Expect a few waves to come splashing up onto the walkway.

Santa Barbara Maritime Museum – Interactive/ hands-on displays.

Outdoors Santa Barbara Visitor Center – Outstanding views.

Shoreline Park – Paved path meanders through the park.

State Street – Festive atmosphere with music and people-watching.

Santa Barbara Museum of Art – American, Asian, European art.

Santa Barbara County Courthouse – Beautiful unique building.

Alice Keck Garden – Watch turtles swim.

Old Mission Santa Barbara – Chumash Indian tools, and artwork.

Museum of Natural History – Kids especially love the "Butterflies Alive" exhibit.

Santa Barbara Botanic Garden – Paved paths weave among flowers and ponds.

CARPINTERIA – (South of Santa Barbara)

Carpinteria State Beach Campground – There are many wheelchair accessible sites. Free beach wheelchairs available at beach entrance. Information – (805) 684-2811. (Bypass the recording by pressing 03.) Reservations – (Details under Carpinteria Lodging.)

GOLETA – (North of Santa Barbara)

Goleta Beach – Fishing pier is wheelchair accessible (no fishing license required). Enjoy the spectacular sunsets from here.

Stow House Gardens, History Education Center, and Lake Los Carneros Trail – These are located close together and are partially wheelchair accessible, however, the Stow House is not accessible.

Goleta Lemon Festival – Art/crafts, music, and a host of lemon-based foods in Girsh Park, third weekend of October.

RESOURCES/INFORMATION

Santa Barbara Visitor Center – (805) 965-3021 or (805) 568-1811. www.sbchamber.org.

Santa Barbara Ranger Station – (805) 967-3481.

Carpinteria Chamber of Commerce – (805) 684-5479. www.carpchamber.org.

WEBSITES

www.santabarbara.com
www.sbnature.org
www.nps.gov/chis/historyculture/tomolcrossing.htm
www.santabarbara.com/virtual_tour/stearns_wharf/
www.santabarbara.com/points_of_interest/

Beaching

A perfect day for beaching, the air thick
with sand-salty scent.
Hot dry sand burns the bottom of feet.
Wet cold sand, squeezing between toes,
is a treat.
Wind-sifted sand whispers faint mystical
sounds of lament.
Nature's ornaments flaunted daily.

Pati Anne

Book FIVE

Pismo Beach

Spend long lazy sunny days along the magnificent, wheat-colored sand beaches that stretch from the southern part of Pismo Beach into Grover Beach and Oceano. Swimming, building sandcastles, seashell hunting, watching colorful sunsets spread over the sea, and fishing from the Pismo Beach Pier (no license required, gear rented on pier) are among favorite pastimes. To reach the **Pismo Beach Pier** from Dolliver Street (Hwy 1) which runs parallel to Hwy 101, take Pomeroy Street.

5.1 Pismo Beach & Shell Beach
What To Do & See

POMEROY STREET

The heart of Pismo Beach is Pomeroy Street which leads finally to the beach, a parking area, and the Pismo Beach Pier and boardwalk. The street is brimming with activity especially in the summertime. The busiest times are during the special events like: June car show (Father's Day weekend), July 4th fireworks, October Clam Festival, and the Jazz Festival

(Jubilee-by-the-sea) a four-day event held in October. Information – Pismo Beach Visitor Information Center. (Details under Information.) The street holds restaurants (details under Eateries, Pomeroy Street) and shops filled with cotton candy, candied apples, ice cream, seashells, and gifts. Music/dancing is found at Harry's Night Club & Beach Bar. (Details under Information, Music.) Parking along Pomeroy Street is pay-parking and is strictly enforced.

PRICE ANNIVERSARY HOUSE

The grounds of this 1893 California ranch house and windmill are open daily. House tours May-Oct on the first and third Sundays of the month at 1pm. (Closed holidays and rainy days.) Donations accepted. (805) 773-4854. www.pricepark. org. In Pismo Beach, follow Dolliver Street (Hwy 1) one mile south, and turn left on Frady Lane. (It's a small street next to the mobile home park, across from North Beach Campground.)

MONARCH BUTTERFLY GROVE

It's an astonishing sight to see thousands of delicate orange and black butterflies fluttering about. During the sunny part of the day, the butterflies are actively searching for food; but as the day cools down, they return to cluster in the heavily scented eucalyptus trees. Follow the meandering path through the grove and beyond the trees, as it curves to the left. It leads to a boardwalk with ocean views, and ends at the parking area for Grover Beach and **Fin's Restaurant**. (Details under Grover Beach, Eateries/Lodging.) Best time to visit the grove, late October through February. Information (805) 473-7220. www.monarchbutterfly.org. To reach the grove, from the southern end of Pismo Beach follow Dolliver Street (Hwy 1) south, one mile to North Beach Campground.

Just past the campground look for the parking area signed *Monarch Butterflies*. Small roadside parking is near the grove and additional parking is found directly across the road. (Pathway in grove is wheelchair/stroller accessible.) **Another option** is to travel past this entrance (one mile), and turn right on Grand Avenue. Parking is behind Fin's Restaurant. Follow the boardwalk (wheelchair accessible), and enjoy magnificent seascape views. Beyond the boardwalk, the path (not wheelchair/stroller accessible) passes by the campground, keep to the right and enter the butterfly area among the eucalyptus trees.

NORTHERN PISMO BEACH/SHELL BEACH

Sea cliffs extend along the rugged, rocky coastline. One way to enjoy the scenery here is by kayak. (Details for kayak rentals under Information.) Paddle along the shore for an up-close look at caves and coves. Sometimes harbor seals and sea otters are spotted playing offshore.

DINOSAUR CAVES PARK

This park overlooking the sea has a nice playground, and is a great spot for watching dolphins at play. An art and crafts fair takes place here on the first Sunday of each month. It includes food, live music, and children's activities. May thru Nov. 10am-4pm. (805) 704-8128. Leashed dogs okay. Pathway is wheelchair/stroller accessible. From Pismo Beach, take Price Street north (parallel to Hwy 101), and turn left on Cliff Avenue.

MARGO DODD PARK

The park offers an impressive cliff view where offshore sea birds perch atop gigantic rock formations. (Viewing area is wheelchair/stroller accessible.) Three blocks north of the park, find stairs leading down to the sea. Watch for playful harbor seals along the shore, especially between March and May, when the pups are born. Look for the colorful starfish that are displayed at low tide. Leashed dogs okay. Adjacent to Dinosaur Cave Park along Ocean Boulevard.

SPYGLASS PARK

This children's park features a grassy area with picnic tables, playground, ocean views, and beach access. (Wheelchair/ stroller accessible.) From Dinosaur Caves Park or Margo Dodd Park, travel north on Price Street (Price Street becomes Shell Beach Road) and turn left on Spyglass Road. Drive along the south side of Spyglass Inn. Where the road curves to the left, the park is on the right.

BLUFFS COASTAL TRAIL

The one-mile paved trail (wheelchair/stroller accessible) runs along the bluff top that extends from the northern end of Pismo Beach through Shell Beach. The path passes in front of a group of beach homes and runs up to a locked gate with hiker access. The trail meanders uphill to the Cave Landing parking area. From the left side of the parking area, follow the dirt path down to a split; it's signed *Whale's Cave* with an arrow pointing to the right. (To the left is the beach-access path.) Take the short walk to the right which leads up the bluff promontory. Here, perched at the very top, is a cave that opens to the sky and sea. From the cave, visitors will experience a bird's eye view of the vast ocean. Leashed dogs okay. **Note:** On a clear day there are wonderful sea views from the parking area; Avila Bay is to the right and Pismo Beach to the left. To reach the trail from the Spyglass Inn, take Shell

Beach Road north, and turn left on El Portal Street (signed *Coastal Trail*). Turn right on Indio Street; continue to the end for parking.

To skip the mile walk along the bluff and begin the walk at the Cave Landing parking area, continue driving past El Portal Street, north on Shell Beach Road (2.2 miles) to the end. Turn left on Avila Beach Drive, travel past the Sycamore Springs Resort, and turn left on Cave Landing Road (.6 mile to parking).

5.2 Pismo Beach/Shell Beach INFORMATION

GENERAL INFORMATION

Pismo Beach Visitors Center and Chamber of Commerce – Mon-Fri 9am-5pm, Sat 11am-5pm, Sun 10am-2pm. (805) 773-4382. (800) 443-7778. www.classiccalifornia.com and www.pismochamber.com. 581 Dolliver Street (Hwy 1).

State Park Ranger – Mon-Fri 8am-5pm. (805) 473-7220.

Information/weather – (Details under Appendix.)

Farmer's Market – Fresh produce, roasted corn, kettle corn, and homemade items. Wed 3-6pm, Sun 3-7pm. Autumn 3-6pm, Winter 2-5pm. At the Pismo Beach Pier.

Pelicans and Tide Pooling – (Details under Appendix.)

Driving vehicles on-the-beach – (Details under Grover Beach and Oceano.)

Wheelchair Accessible Activities – (Details under Appendix.)

Beach Wheelchairs – Free at beach entrance of Grover Beach and Oceano.

Camping – (Details under Pismo Beach, Inexpensive Lodging.) **Note:** Other camping under nearby Oceano.

Pismo State Beach Golf Course – (Details under Grover Beach.)

Beach Weddings – www.pismoweddings.com.

SCAT – Daily buses provide hourly service from Pismo Beach south to Grover Beach and Oceano. (Most hotels have bus schedules.) Wheelchair Accessible. (805) 541-2277. www.rideshare.org.

Airport and Amtrak Information – (Details under Transportation in Appendix.)

Wheel Fun Rentals – Bicycle rentals include bicycles built-for-six and beach bicycles. Free beach wheelchairs available. 9am-6pm, Sat/Sun 8pm. Winter opens 10am. (805) 773-0197. www.whellfunrentals.com. Located at 150 Hinds Avenue & the beach.

Moondoggies – Surfboard rentals. 9am-6pm. Autumn/ winter 5pm. (805) 773-1995. Dolliver at Main Street.

Central Coast Kayaks – Kayak rentals. Summer 9am-6pm. Fall/winter hours vary; check website for hours. (Closed Weds in autumn and Tue/Wed in winter.) (805) 773-3500. www.centralcoastkayaks.com. Located at 1879 Shell Beach Road, Shell Beach.

Pismo Beach Premium Outlet Stores – 40 stores; call

for list of stores. 10am-9pm; Sun 10am-7pm. (805) 773-4661. From Hwy 101, exit at Five Cities Drive, in the southern end of Pismo Beach.

Music: Call for current information. (Subject to change.) **Harry's Night Club & Beach Bar** – Bands and dancing nightly, except karaoke on Thurs. 9pm-2am, Sat/Sun 3pm-2am. (805) 773-1010. Corner of Cypress & Pomeroy (1 block up from the pier) **Sea Venture Restaurant** – (805) 773-3463. (Details under Lodging/Eateries – Pismo Beach.) **Cliffs Resort's Marisol Restaurant** – Music some afternoons on patio. (805) 773-2511. **F. McLintocks** – Guitar music at dinner; autumn and winter Sat only. (805) 773-1892. (Details under Eateries/Lodging on the Bluff.)

WINE TASTING

Note: The wine tasting tours are fascinating during the grape harvests in September and October.

Breakaway Tours – (805) 783-2929. (800) 799-7657. www.breakaway-tours.com.

Wine Wrangler – (805) 238-5700, (866) 238-6400.

Tastes of the Valleys Bar and Wine Shop – Six pours $10-$20. Mon-Thur noon-9pm, Fri/Sat 10pm. Sun 8pm. (805) 773-8466. www.tastesofthevalleys.com. 911 Price Street, in the Valentina Inn.

Central Coast Limousine Service – Wine tasting by limousine. (805) 503-8850. www.centralcoastlimoservice.com.

EATERIES – Pomeroy Street – near Pismo Beach Pier
Note: Restaurants close about an hour earlier in winter.

Splash Café – Breakfast and pastries. Famous clam chowder served in a homemade bread bowl, as well as burgers, chili, sandwiches, salads, and clams. Beer and wine. 8am-8:30pm, Fri/Sat 9:30pm. (805) 773-4653. www.splashcafe.com. 197 Pomeroy Street.

Mo's Bar-B-Q – Beef, pork, and chicken BBQ sandwiches and ribs, also beer and wine. (Kids' menu.) 11am-9pm, Fri/Sat 10pm. Winter closes an hour earlier. (805) 773-6193. www. mosbbq.com. 221 Pomeroy Street.

Brad's Restaurant – Breakfast menu. They also serve ribs, chicken, steak, beef kabob, seafood, clam chowder. Beer and wine. (Kids' menu.) Inside/outdoor patio. 8am-9pm, Fri/Sat 10pm. (805) 773-6165. Located at 209 Pomeroy Street.

Piz Mo Café –They serve pizza, pasta, salads, and sandwiches. Beer and wine. Open 11-9pm, Fri/Sat 11am-10pm. Winter hours vary, call ahead. (805) 556-0347. www.pizmocafe.com. Located on the corner of Dolliver and Pomeroy, one block up from the Pismo Pier.

EATERIES – Cypress and Price Streets
Near Pismo Beach Pier

Note: Restaurants close about an hour earlier in winter.

Pismo Beach Fish and Chips – They serve fish/chips, steak, and shrimp with beer and wine. (Kids' menu.) 11am-8pm. (Closed Mon.) (805) 773-2853. Located at 505 Cypress Street (runs parallel to the ocean) one block south of the Pismo Beach Pier.

Cracked Crab – A popular place to find fresh seafood, from fish/chips to buckets of crab and shellfish. 11am–9pm, Fri/Sat until 10pm. (805) 773-CRAB (2722). Located at 751 Price Street, south of the pier.

Giuseppe's – Italian fare with pizza, and home-made bread. Lunch 11:30am-3pm. Dinner 4:30-10pm, Fri/Sat 11pm. Delivery service. (805) 773-2870. www.giuseppesrestaurant. com. Located at 891 Price Street.

Honeymoon Café – They are open for breakfast and lunch and serve sandwiches, salads, and desserts. There's also an espresso bar. Open Tues-Fri 7am-3pm, Sat/Sun 8am-2pm. (Closed Mon.) (805) 773-5646. Located at 999 Price Street, north of the pier.

Most lodgings near the pier have stunning sandy beaches unfolding from the sea up to the hotel entrances. At sunset, the sea and the sky are colored in hues of pink and yellow, and the swaying palm trees are silhouetted against the fabulous glow. In summer, hotel rates soar, and there is a two-night minimum for Friday and Saturday stays. Rates are cut drastically in winter.

EATERIES/LODGING – Pismo Beach

Sandcastle Inn – The inn rests on the beach sand. Guests are afforded lovely ocean view rooms with fireplaces and Wi-Fi. Amenities include a spa, sundeck, and continental breakfast. A boardwalk leads from the inn to Pismo Pier. Dogs okay in some rooms. (805) 773-2422. (800) 822-6606. www. sandcastleinn.com. 100 Stimson Avenue, just south of the Pismo Beach Pier.

Sea Venture Resort & Spa – This resort features fine rooms many of which front the beach and have Jacuzzis. A $7 per day resort fee gives use of bicycles, beach chairs, and Wi-Fi. A walkway extends from the resort to Pismo Pier. (805) 773-4994. (800) 662-5545. www.seaventure.

com. 100 Ocean View Avenue, two blocks south of the Pismo Beach Pier.

Sea Venture Restaurant – This eatery features California cuisine specializing in seafood, and steaks. Outdoor patio affords outstanding ocean views. Open 5-9pm, Fri/Sat 9:30pm. Sunday Brunch 10am-2pm. Live music Wed 6-9pm & Sun 3-6pm. (805) 773-3463. Located on the third floor over the Sea Venture Resort.

Kon Tiki Inn – These pleasant rooms open to immense ocean views. On a terrace overlooking the sea with swaying palm trees, a large heated swimming pool and two Jacuzzis are found. From here, there are 112 winding stairs climbing down to the gorgeous sandy beach. The hotel provides a continental breakfast, Wi-Fi, and free admission to a fitness club sporting a fabulous indoor heated swimming pool. (805) 773-4833. (888) 566-8454. www.kontikiinn.com. 1621 Price Street, at lowest level of the bluff.

Steamers Restaurant – The restaurant serves prime rib, steak, pasta, and seafood. Lunch 11:30am-3pm. Dinner 4:30-9pm, Fri/Sat 4-10pm. (805) 773-4711. Adjacent to the Kon Tiki Inn.

INEXPENSIVE LODGING

Pismo State Beach, North Beach Campground – Located inland behind the sand dunes. Wheelchair accessible sites. Information – (805) 473-7220. Reservations – (800) 444-7275. www.reserveamerica.com. From the town of Pismo Beach, travel south 1 mile on Dolliver Street (Hwy 1). It's on the right side of the street.

Pismo Beach Hotel – All of the rooms and suites in this historic hotel have been restored. Suites with ocean views and Jacuzzis are available. There's free Wi-Fi in the lobby.

Continental breakfast. (805) 773-4445. (800) 575-1705. www.thepismobeachhotel.com. 230 Pomeroy Avenue, one block from Pismo Pier.

Sea Gypsy Motel – This motel offers ocean view rooms, kitchenettes, and Wi-Fi. There is a heated pool and spa. Dogs okay. (805) 773-1801. (800) 592-5923. www.seagypsymotel.com. 1020 Cypress, just north of the Pismo Beach Pier.

Motel 6 – All of their hotels are famous for their affordable rooms. This location provides a swimming pool and pay Wi-Fi. It's located close to restaurants and outlet stores. Dogs stay free. (805) 773-2665. (800) 4-motel6. www.motel6.com. Located at 860 4th Street, at Hwy 101.

Oxford Suites – These two-room suites include microwaves, refrigerators, and Wi-Fi. They come with a full breakfast and an evening wine reception (except Sun); and there's a heated outdoor pool and hot tub. Dogs okay. (805) 773-3773. (800) 982-7848. www.oxfordsuitespismobeach.com. Located at 651 Five Cities Drive.

Palomar Inn – Rooms include microwaves, refrigerators, and Wi-Fi; full kitchen rooms are available. Dogs okay in some rooms. The rooms are available on a daily or weekly rate. (805) 773-4204. (888) 384-4004. www.thepalomarinn.com. 1601 Shell Beach Road, in Shell Beach just minutes north of Pismo Beach.

Note: In summer, hotel rates soar, and there is a two-night minimum for Friday and Saturday stays. Rates are cut drastically in winter.

Some of the area's best lodging and restaurants lie along the sea bluffs overlooking the ocean, where whitecaps crash on the rocks below. Long, steep stairways lead down to tiny coves where, at high tide, the beaches disappear into ocean waves.

(Swimming beaches are found near Pismo Pier.) Bluff hotels and restaurants line Price Street (parallel to Hwy 101) in northern Pismo Beach. Further north, Price Street becomes Shell Beach Road (in Shell Beach) with more hotels and restaurants.

EATERIES/LODGING – On the Bluff
North end of Pismo Beach and Shell Beach
Note: Restaurants close about an hour earlier in winter.

Cottage Inn by the Sea – Charming English-country rooms with fireplaces; most rooms have full or partial ocean views. Rooms come with Wi-Fi and deluxe continental breakfast. Heated swimming pool and spa. Dogs okay in some rooms. Beach access from stairs next to the inn. (805) 773-4617. (888) 440-8400. www.cottage-inn.com. 2351 Price Street.

Pismo Lighthouse Suites – These nicely furnished two-bedroom, two-bath suites have ocean views, refrigerators, microwaves, and Wi-Fi. Amenities include a heated pool/hot tub, play deck, putting green, fitness room, massages, and continental breakfast. No beach access from hotel. Dogs okay. (805) 773-2411. (800) 245-2411. www.pismolighthousesuites.com. 2411 Price Street.

Best Western Plus Shore Cliff Lodge – This hotel, perched high above the sea cliffs, lends guests vast ocean views. The picturesque grounds provide perfect settings for weddings. The hotel provides Wi-Fi, a fitness room, and a heated pool/hot tub. Massages available. Continental breakfast. No beach access from hotel. Dogs okay. (805) 773-4671. (800) 441-8885. www.shorecliff.com. 2555 Price Street.

Ventana Grill – Brown pelicans are often seen flying around the perimeters of the restaurant and can be closely observed from the outdoor deck. Restaurant serves burgers, burritos, tacos, salads, steak, chicken, and seafood. 11:30am-9pm; Fri/Sat 10pm, Sun brunch 10am-9pm. Reservations (805) 773-0000. www.ventanagrill.com. Located adjacent to Best Western Plus Shore Cliff Lodge.

F. McLintocks – A popular restaurant with terrific ribs, steaks and seafood. 4:30pm-9pm, Sat 10pm; Sun 10am-9pm. Dinners are approximately $30. Call for current light dinner days and hours which begin at 4pm. Guitar music at dinner daily; autumn and winter Sat only. (805) 773-1892. Located at 750 Mattie Road. From Price Street, near Ventana Grill (Adjacent to Best Western Plus Shore Cliff Lodge.) cross Hwy 101 and head north one mile on Mattie Road.

Best Western Plus Shelter Cove Lodge – Rooms with balconies or patios have vast ocean views from the bluff. The hotel's amenities include, heated pool/spa, Wi-Fi, and continental breakfast. It's a five-minute walk from the bluff to a beach cove via public stairs. Outdoor weddings at oceanfront gazebo. (805) 773-3511. (800) 848-1434. www.bwsheltercove.com. 2651 Price Street, exit Hwy 101 at Price Street.

Spyglass Inn – The inn features nicely furnished bluff-top rooms with ocean views and Wi-Fi. (See rooms on website.) There is a small heated pool/hot tub, and massages are available. No direct beach access, but a path in front of the inn leads (along north side of inn) down to the beach where guests can enjoy tide pooling at low tide. Dogs okay in some rooms. Weddings. (805) 773-4855. (800) 824-2612. www.spyglassinn.com. 2705 Spyglass Drive, Hwy 101 southbound exit Shell Beach Road, northbound exit on Spyglass Drive.

Spyglass Inn Restaurant – B,L,D – Dinner specialties are steak, pasta, and seafood. Nice ocean views from the patio. Open 7am-9pm; Fri/Sat 10pm. (805) 773-1222. Adjacent to Spyglass Inn.

Dolphin Bay Resort & Spa – One and two bedroom suites, ocean view or pool view. Fully equipped kitchens. Fitness center. Heated pool and spa tub. The **Lido Restaurant,** B/L/D, is on the premises. Resort fee $20, includes bicycle rental. Ninety stairs lead down to rocky tidepool area. Dogs okay. (805) 773-4300. www.thedolphinbay.com. 2727 Shell Beach Road.

Cliffs Resort – They boast lovely rooms including marble bathrooms and sweeping ocean views. (See room packages on website.) Amenities include pay Wi-Fi, heated pool/hot tub, and a fitness center with massages. Dogs okay on first floor rooms. Weddings. For tide pooling (at low tide) take the winding path from the hotel down to the beach. (805) 773-5000. (800) 826-7827. www.cliffsresort.com. 2757 Shell Beach Road.

Marisol Restaurant – B,L,D – Ocean view patio dining with California & Latin Cuisine. 7am-9pm, Fri/Sat 10pm, Champagne Sunday Brunch 11am-2pm. Happy Hour Mon-Fri 4-7pm. Music some afternoons on the patio. (805) 773-2511. www.cliffsresort.com. Adjacent to Cliffs Resort.

Alex's BBQ – The local spot for ribs, chicken, and steaks. Open 4-9pm, Fri/Sat 10pm. Bar serves food 11am-9pm. Bar open Fri/Sat 2am. (805) 773-5656. Located at 853 Shell Beach Road. From Pismo Beach, travel north on Price Street, it becomes Shell Beach Road.

Del's – New York style pizza, pasta, and salads are served here. Delivery service available. Daily 4-9pm, Fri/Sat/Sun noon-10pm. Winter until 8:30pm. (805) 773-4438. Located at 401 Shell Beach Road. From Pismo Beach, travel north on Price Street, it becomes Shell Beach Road.

DIRECTIONS – Pismo Beach/Shell Beach

From Los Angeles, take Hwy 101 north (toward Ventura) to Santa Barbara. Take the scenic route in good weather; two miles north of Santa Barbara exit on Hwy 154 (signed *Lake Cachuma/State Street*). It's also called San Marcos Pass.

Note: Scenic Hwy 154 is subject to flooding in the (winter-spring) rainy season, and visitors should then continue on Hwy 101 from Santa Barbara to Gaviota State Park. From here Hwy 101 veers inland (north), and in 10 to 12 miles reaches a turn-off for **Nojoqui (no-Ho-wee) Falls County Park**. This is a lush beautiful place, where chirping birds are heard among the many tall trees and greenery. A creek twists its way along the lovely short path to the falls, and there are benches to sit and absorb the beauty. The falls (over 100 feet tall) bordered with velvet-soft moss and ferns, present an astonishing sight especially from late winter through early summer. The park has picnic tables and grills. No entrance fee. Open 8am-sunset. Information – Mon-Fri 9am-4pm; closed noon-1pm. (805) 568-2461. From Hwy 101 (10 to 12 miles north of Gaviota), look for the *Nojoqui Falls County Park* sign and turn onto Old Coast Road (for 1.5 miles). Then turn left on Alisal Road for .8 mile. Return to Hwy 101, and continue north to Arroyo Grande. (Details on page 306.) Pismo Beach is just 2.5 miles beyond Arroyo Grande.

When following Hwy 154 (San Marcos Pass), it meanders past the 18-hole **San Marcos Golf Course** (805) 683-6334, horse ranches, vineyards, and **Lake Cachuma**. (Boat rentals, fishing, camping, wildlife cruises.) Lake Information (805) 686-5054. www.cachuma.com. Beyond Lake Cachuma (11.5 miles), is the quaint town of **Los Olivos**; a great place to stop for lunch or dinner. (Turn left on Grand Avenue to enter the town.) Surrounded by flowers and trees, it's a peaceful place with gift shops, wine-tasting rooms, and restaurants in historic buildings. Information – www.losolivosca.com.

EATERIES – Los Olivos

Los Olivos Café – Lunch–Dinner–Wine. Open 11:30am-8pm, Sat/Sun 11am-9pm. (805) 688-7265. www.losolivoscafe.com. Located at 2879 Grand Avenue.

Panino – Serves unusual sandwiches. Open daily 11am-4pm. (805) 688-0608. Located at 2900 Grand Avenue.

Mattei's Tavern – Tavern was built in 1800s. Fine dining. Sat/Sun Brunch 11am-4pm. Dinner Weds-Sat 5-10pm, Sun 9pm. Bar Fri/Sat midnight. (Closed Mon/Tues.) (805) 688-3550. www.matteistavern.com. Located on Hwy 154, near corner of Grand Avenue.

Three miles from Los Olivos, Hwy 154 re-joins Hwy 101. Follow Hwy 101 north 42 miles to **Arroyo Grande** where visitors may want to stop-off for a picnic. Exit on Grand Avenue and turn right; continue on Grand until it becomes Branch Street. Turn right on Bridge Street, turn left into **Olohan Alley** (behind all the stores and restaurants), to the walkway above the bubbling creek. Here, colorful wild roosters roam around crowing loudly. There are stairs leading down to the creek and picnic tables with barbeque pits. Above the creek, a pedestrian swinging bridge leads across to historic buildings. See the 1901 **Santa Manuela School** with an old bell tower. Open Sat 12-3pm and Sun 1-4pm. Behind the school, visit an old barn that houses antique carriages. The **Heritage House Museum** offers displays and information on the history of Arroyo Grande. Open Sat 12-3pm and Sun 1-4pm. **Note:** The historic buildings may also be reached by taking Branch Street and turning right on North Mason Street. Information – Chamber of Commerce – Mon-Fri

9:30am-5pm. (805) 489-1488. www.aggbchamber.com. Located at 800 W. Branch Street.

To proceed directly to Pismo Beach and bypass Arroyo Grande, take Hwy 101 north (2.5 miles) and exit on Price Street. Turn left and follow Price Street south crossing over Hwy 1 (Dolliver Street) to Pomeroy Street, and turn right to reach the Pismo Pier area. To find the hotels on the bluffs, exit Hwy 101 on Spyglass Drive. (Southbound traffic exit Shell Beach Road.) San Luis Obispo – 10 miles north of Pismo Beach. Santa Barbara – 96 miles south of Pismo Beach. Los Angeles – 193 miles south of Pismo Beach. San Francisco – 250 miles north of Pismo Beach.

5.3 Day Trips South Of Pismo Beach
What To Do & See

GROVER BEACH

The gorgeous beach here often becomes a roadway laden with vehicles. Cars and trucks are driven, on the wide cream-colored sand down to the very edge of the rolling waves. People can dangle their feet in the surf right from their cars. The excursion begins at Grand Avenue and travels south for 5.5 miles (maximum speed 15mph). To avoid getting stuck, stay on the wet, compact sand. (Details for beach towing under Information.) Free beach wheelchairs are available at the beach entrance. Dogs and beach campfires are okay. Day use 6am-11pm. Entrance fee $5, seniors with pass $4. State Park Ranger – Mon-Fri 8am-5pm. (805) 473-7220.

Note: Many restaurants and shops can be found on Grand Avenue just north of Hwy 1. Visitors with campers, dune buggies, and ATVs must enter the beach at the Oceano entrance (off Hwy 1, one mile south of Grover Beach). (Details for the beach and beach camping under Oceano.)

PISMO STATE BEACH GOLF COURSE

This is a 9-hole par-three course with club rentals. (805) 481-5215. Located at 25 Grand Avenue, at the seashore, in Grover Beach, one mile south of Pismo Beach.

GROVER BEACH BOARDWALK

This boardwalk passes through golden sand dunes laden with greenery and small flowers while flaunting seascapes where the dunes dip low enough. (Wheelchair/stroller accessible.) State Park Ranger – Mon-Fri 8am-5pm. (805) 473-7220. Grand Avenue and the beach. (The boardwalk begins behind Fin's Restaurant parking area.)

INFORMATION

Arroyo Grande and Grover Beach Chamber of Commerce – Mon-Fri 9:30am-5pm. (805) 489-9091. www.aggbchamber.com. 800 A West Branch Steet, Arroyo Grande.

Beach Weddings – www.pismoweddings.com.

State Park Ranger – Information on state beaches, camping, and visitors with disabilities. Mon-Fri 8am-5pm. (805) 473-7220. www.slostateparks.com.

Beach Wheelchairs – Available at the beach entrance. (805) 473-7220.

Kautz Towing – Beach towing 24 hrs. Office Mon-Fri 8am-5pm. (805) 489-2336.

Amtrak Train Station – (Details under Transportation in the Appendix.) (800) USARAIL. (800) 872-7245. www. amtrak.com. Corner of Grand Avenue and Hwy 1.

Arnie's ATVs – Rentals are on the beach in Oceano. (Details under Oceano.)

Steve's ATVs – Rentals on the beach in Oceano. (805) 481-2597. www.stevesatv.com.

EATERIES/ LODGING

Holiday Inn Express – All rooms have Wi-Fi. Hot breakfast included. Outdoor pool/hot tub. (805) 481-4448. (800) holiday. www.holidayinn.com. Located at 775 N. Oak Park Boulevard, two miles from beach, close to Hwy 101.

Fin's Restaurant – Casual dining. Seafood and burgers are served. Live music Fri 6-9pm, also first Sat of month. Open 11am-9pm, Fri/Sat 10pm. Winter 8pm, Fri/Sat 8:30pm. (805) 473-3467. Located at 25 Grand Avenue, at the beach entrance.

Station Grill – Casual foods. 6:30am-8pm, Sunday 7:30 am-3pm. (805) 489-3030. Grand Avenue at Hwy 1, at the Amtrak Train Station, one block north of Grover Beach.

Mongo's Saloon Restaurant – Nice variety of food is served. (Food specials online.) Thurs/Fri DJs from 9pm. Sat dancing to live music; Mon/Tues/Weds karaoke. Top sports games on big screen TVs. Open 10am-2am. (805) 489-3639. www.mongossaloon.com. Located on the corner of Fourth Street and Grand Avenue, .3 mile from Grover Beach.

DIRECTIONS – Grover Beach

From the town of Pismo Beach, take Dolliver Street (Hwy 1) two miles south to Grand Avenue. From Hwy 101, exit 4th Street (2 miles south of Pismo Beach); take 4th Street south 1.5 miles, and turn right on Grand Avenue toward the beach.

OCEANO

Vehicles of every shape and color crisscross the beach all day long. Many adventures await visitors on the impressive **Oceano Dunes**. Ride a dune buggy, ATV, horse, or hike in the dunes for a one-of-a kind experience. Vehicles can be driven on the beach from Pier Avenue, north to Grand Avenue (in Grover Beach), and south of Pier Avenue for miles. ATVs must be transported to the two-mile post to unload; in summer, they are rented here on the beach. (Orange mile-marker signs are located under the 15mph speed limit signs.) The popular and congested **Oceano Dunes Campground** (details under Oceano Eateries/Lodging) begins at mile marker two, amid all the ATV activity, and unfolds along the beach for miles.

Just a few miles south of Pier Avenue (prior to the camping area) Arroyo Grande Creek may overflow during the winter rainy season, and travel down on the beach and into the sea. Before crossing the creek, check the tides; crossing at low tide and with 4-wheel drive vehicles is best. Day use – 6am-11pm. Entrance fee $5, seniors with pass $4. Camping – $10, seniors $8. Dogs okay. Free beach wheelchairs at the beach entrance.

OCEANO DUNES NATURE PRESERVE

Phenomenal sand spindrifts are created in the dunes by wind sending sand particles up in the air and, as with the sea's white frothy spindrifts, quickly spilling them down the crest of the dunes. Hiking the spectacular sandy dunes is like being lost in a vast desert. There are no real paths; one may follow the footprints of others or create new ones. Walking in the sand is difficult, but the view is quite rewarding. From atop tall sand dunes, distant views of whitecaps in the rolling sea are visible. Bring a camera and water. To reach the dune entrance, drive south on the sand from the Pier Avenue beach entrance to mile marker two. Along the way, visitors will notice that part of the dune area is fenced off to protect nesting birds. Park near the mile marker two sign (orange mile-marker signs are located under the 15mph speed limit signs) and walk straight up along the fenced dune area to a small opening in the fence. **Note:** The entrance is almost blocked by a sign stating *Vehicles Prohibited*. This is also the entrance for horseback riders.

GUITON TRAIL

This path begins paved, and becomes gravel as it loops around the Oceano Lagoon. It sits under tall shade trees, and is filled with ducks and turtles. At dusk, beavers may be spotted. Evidence of their branch cutting is found close to the lagoon. Near the end of the loop, muskrats are sometimes seen swimming in the lagoon. Trail maps are available at the start of the trail. Stay on the trail; poison oak is plentiful. Part of the trail and the fishing area are wheelchair/stroller accessible. Street parking is available. Trail: Easy loop 1.5 miles. The trailhead is located on Pier Avenue, 1.5 blocks from the beach alongside the bridge, north of a tiny nature center.

PACIFIC DUNES RANCH

Rent horses, and ride along the beach and amid the sand dunes for a spectacular experience. Fri-Tues 9am-4pm. (Closed Wed/

Thurs, Easter, Christmas, and Christmas Eve.) (805) 489-8100. www.pacificdunesranch.com. From Grand Ave, take Hwy 1 south 1.2 miles, turn right on 22nd Street, continue to the end of the street.

INFORMATION

State Park Ranger – Information on state beaches, camping, and visitors with disabilities. Mon-Fri 8am-5pm. (805) 473-7220. www.slostateparks.com.

Beach Wheelchairs – Available at the beach entrance. (805) 473-7220.

Kautz Towing – Grover and Oceano beaches towing. 24 hrs. (805) 489-2336.

Camping – On the beach. (800) 444-7275. www.reserveamerica.com.

Angello's ATVs – All terrain vehicle rentals. Rentals on the beach. (805) 481-0355. Office at 307 Pier Avenue.

Arnie's ATVs – All terrain vehicle rentals. Rentals on the beach. Summer daily. (Closed Tues/Wed in winter, open daily holiday weeks.) (805) 473-1610. www.arniesatvrentals.com. Office at 311 Pier Avenue.

Sun Buggies – Dune buggy rentals on the beach. (805) 432-1788.

Steve's ATVs – Rentals on the beach. (805) 481-2597. www.stevesatv.com. Office at 332 Pier Avenue, Oceano.

Note: Rentals 8am or 9am (depends upon weather) to sunset. Closed when the beach creek floods, usually a few weeks in January. Take the Oceano Beach entrance south to mile marker two. (The orange mile-marker signs are located under the 15mph speed limit signs.)

EATERIES/LODGING

Old Juan's Cantina – Mexican cuisine. 11:30am to 9pm, Fri/Sat 11am-9:30pm. Winter closes half an hour earlier. Sunday Brunch 10am to 2pm. (805) 489-5680. Pier Avenue at Hwy 1.

Pismo State Beach, Oceano Campground – It's close to the beach and the lovely Oceano Lagoon. (Details under Guiton Trail above.) Wheelchair accessible sites. Information – (805) 473-7220 ext. 0. Reservations – (800) 444-7275. www.reserveamerica.com. Located at 555 Pier Avenue. Entrance is in Oceano, 3 miles south from the town of Pismo Beach via Dolliver Street (Hwy 1). Turn right on Pier Avenue.

Oceano Dunes SVRA (State Vehicular Recreation Area) – Very popular camping on the beach amid all-terrain vehicles and dune buggies. Wheelchairs available at beach entrance. Information – (805) 473-7220. Reservations – (800) 444-7275. www.reserveamerica.com. Located 3 miles south of Pismo Beach via Dolliver Street (Hwy 1). Turn right on Pier Avenue.

Pacific Plaza Resort Hotel – This hotel offers one and two bedroom condos with kitchens and Wi-Fi. Outdoor hot tub. (805) 473-6989. www.pacificplazaresort.com. Located at 444 Pier Ave, one block from the Oceano Beach.

DIRECTIONS – Oceano

From Grand Avenue in Grover Beach, take Dolliver Street (Hwy 1) and drive 1 mile south. Turn right on Pier Avenue.

From Hwy 101, exit on 4th Street, (2 miles south of Pismo Beach) and head south 1.5 miles. Turn right on Grand Avenue, heading toward the beach, and turn left on Hwy 1. Continue south 1 mile, and turn right on Pier Avenue.

OSO FLACO LAKE STATE PARK

A tranquil path leads visitors to a boardwalk, which travels across the lake and the beach sand to the sea. A secluded willow-lined lane begins at the parking area, and leads in .3 mile to a left turn that connects to a boardwalk. Here birds sing while frogs and ducks frolic in the lake; and the fishing is fine. The boardwalk crosses over the main part of the lake, and continues over sand dunes scattered with clusters of colorful springtime wildflowers. In .5 mile, a right turn leads to the restrooms. The main beach boardwalk unfolds down toward the edge of the sea, where the sound of ocean waves running ashore breaks the stillness.

Near the end of the pathway, a left turn leads to a lookout over the sea. From the turn, the boardwalk continues a short distance to the beach sand. Beware, especially in summer, of billowing fog rolling off the sea, making it difficult to find the return path. Rare terns and snowy plover birds nest on the sand March 1st through September 30th. To protect them, nesting areas are fenced off. Boardwalk is wheelchair accessible. No dogs. Fishing is okay with a license. Open sunrise to sunset. Entrance fee $5, seniors with pass $4. State Beach Rangers (805) 773-7170 ext. 0. Trail: Easy 1.3 miles one way.

DIRECTIONS – Oso Flaco Lake

From Oceano, follow Hwy 1 south 8.5 miles to turn-off, (signed *Oso Flaco Lake State Park*). Turn right on the farm road, and travel three miles to the end. (3.5 miles north of Guadalupe.)

GUADALUPE

GUADALUPE DUNES CENTER

The center provides information and free guided walks on the dunes and around the town. Open Wed thru Sun 10am-4pm. (Closed Mon/Tues.) (805) 343-2455. www.dunescenter.org. Located at 1055 Guadalupe Street (Hwy 1). From Oso Flaco Lake State Park, follow Hwy 1 for 3 miles to reach the Dunes Center.

RANCHO GUADALUPE DUNES COUNTY PRESERVE – Hiking the dunes

To see the wonder of nature, follow the meandering road through the pristine white sand dunes to a parking area. From here, the thunder of ocean waves reverberating through the dunes is amazing. Explore the impressive sand dunes which enhance the beach for miles. No designated paths. Turn right (north) on the beach to observe a variety of migrating birds, in a small lagoon, from October 1st to end of February. (Most of the dunes are fenced off to protect nesting plover birds March 1st through September 30th.) To explore the tall dunes south of the beach entrance, from October 1st to end of February, walk 2.3 miles to Mussel Rock, aka Mussel Point. This dune (approximately 450 feet tall) affords fantastic views; but climbing to the top is difficult. The surf along this area is extremely dangerous. Preserve is open sunrise to sunset. No RVs. Donation box near entrance gate. Information – (805) 343-2455. To reach the County Preserve from Oso Flaco Lake State Park, follow Hwy 1 south 3.7 miles (Hwy 1 becomes Guadalupe Street), and turn right at the old cemetery onto Main Street (signed Guadalupe Beach). Travel down the country road 4.8 miles to the Guadalupe Dunes County Preserve; it's at the end of the road.

315

Note: To reach Hwy 101 from the Preserve, take Main Street (Hwy 166) northeast, and (after crossing Hwy 1); continue 8.8 miles to Santa Maria.

5.4 Day Trips North Of Pismo Beach
What To Do & See

A unique place to stop along the way from Pismo Beach/ Shell Beach to Avila is the Avila Valley Barn.

AVILA VALLEY BARN

Adults and kids will enjoy the hayrides and barnyard animals. There are wonderful fruits, vegetables, freshly baked pies, and homemade jams and sauces for sale. Wheelchair accessible. In October and November plenty of pumpkins, cider, and apples are available. December brings out Christmas trees and decorations. Summer 9am-6pm. Winter 9am-5pm. (Closed Christmas Eve and day.) (805) 595-2816. www.avilavalleybarn.com. Located at 560 Avila Beach Drive. From Pismo Beach, travel on Price Street north until it becomes Shell Beach Road; follow it to the end. Continue as the road curves to the left and becomes Avila Beach Drive. Drive a quarter mile to the Avila Hot Springs Resort. Just beyond this is the Avila Valley Barn. The entrance is on the right, nearly hidden by green brush and flowers.

AVILA

The small village sits, tucked away from it all, in a quaint seaside setting. It fronts Avila State Beach where waves slip like silk onto the shore, and the turquoise bay is filled with sailboats and fishing boats. The tiny Avila Pier, embraced by a sandy beach, is great for fishing (no license needed on pier) and watching colorful sunsets slink into the bay. (Wheelchair accessible.) No dogs are allowed on the pier, but okay (leashed) on the beach before 10am and after 5pm. Across the road from the pier and the beach is Front Street, where no cars are allowed.

AVILA BEACH COMMUNITY PARK

The park, with its wonderful grassy play area, picnic tables, and barbeques, lies close to the beach. From Avila Beach Drive, turn left on First Street, then turn right on San Juan Street alongside the Avila Lighthouse Suites.

AVILA BEACH RESORT GOLF COURSE

The course has 18 holes, par 71, a driving range, and a putting green. Twilight discounts are available. There is a paved path (wheelchair accessible) leading to the Bob Jones Bicycle/Walking Trail (details under Bob Jones Bicycle/Walking Trail) beyond the clubhouse. (805) 595-4000. www.avilabeachresort.com. Golf course entrance in located between Avila Village and the Harford Pier.

Mulligan's Bar & Grill – Lunch – sandwiches and burgers. Open 7am-7pm. Winter 5pm. Weddings. (805) 595-4171. Adjacent to Avila Beach Resort Golf Course.

EATERIES/SHOPS

Sea Barn – The store sells shorts, sandals, and bathing suits, and offers boogie board and wetsuit rentals. 10am-7pm. (805) 595-2142. Located at 444 Front Street.

Old Custom House Restaurant – B,L,D – Hors d'oeuvres, salads, steak, and seafood. Open 8am-9pm, Thurs/Fri/Sat 10pm. (Kids' menu.) Dining inside or alfresco. (805) 595-7555. www.oldcustomhouse.com. 404 Front Street, across from the Avila Pier.

Mr. Rick's Beach Bar & Nightclub – Serves sandwiches, pizza, burgers, salads, clam chowder. (See website for full menu.) Open from noon Mon-Thurs, from 11am Fri/Sat/Sun. Happy Hour Mon-Thurs 4-7pm. Weds DJs and karaoke. Live bands/dancing Fri/Sat from 9pm, and Sunday 2-6pm on patio. (805) 595-7425. www.mrricks.com. Adjacent to Old Custom House Restaurant.

Mission Pizza – Variety of pizzas – 11:30am-9pm. (805) 595-7555. Located on San Miguel Street, just around the corner from the Old Custom House Restaurant at 404 Front Street.

Hula Hut – B,L,D – Deli cuisine – Coffee drinks, fruit smoothies, ice cream, sandwiches, salads, chowder, and fish tacos. (Kids' menu.) Indoor/outdoor seating. Summer 8am-9pm, Fri/Sat/Sun 10pm. Winter closes earlier. (805) 627-0488. Located at 380 Front Street.

Avila Grocery & Deli – B,L,D – Deli cuisine and groceries. Food served Sun-Thurs 8am-8:30pm, Fri/Sat 9pm. (805) 595-2500. Located at 354 Front Street.

Joe Momma's Coffee/Juice Shop – coffee, juice, pastries, bagels, quiche, and smoothies. Open 6:30am-6pm. Winter 5pm; Fri/Sat 6pm. (805) 627-1500. Located at 310 Front Street.

HARFORD PIER

In the northern end of the harbor, on the busy Harford Pier, local fishermen unload their daily catches every morning. No fishing license is needed when fishing from the pier. Frolicking sea lions hang out at the end of the pier looking for fish that have escaped the fishermen's nets. Their loud barking can be heard for quite a distance. Use stairs on right side of pier, to see them up close, but keep your distance; they can bite. Brown pelicans stand by looking for tiny tidbits. Information on pelicans and sea lions under Morro Bay Appendix. Cars may be driven on the pier, but parking is limited. Wheelchair accessible. Leashed dogs okay (near this pier) on the beach.

Just prior to the Harford Pier:

Fat Cats Café – B,L,D – Menu includes inexpensive fish/chips, burgers, and salads. Dining indoors or outdoors on the patio. Daily 6am-10pm. (805) 595-2204.

Located on the Harford Pier:

Patriot Sportfishing – Book sport fishing trips from the pier, or make a reservation on the website. Summer hours from 4:30am all day, winter 8am-6pm. (805) 595-7200. (800) 714-FISH. www.patriotsportfishing.com.

Olde Port Fish Market – A market with freshly caught seafood sold daily. Many sea lions linger close to the market; they will bite if approached too closely. Mon-Fri 9am-4:30pm, Sat/Sun 8:30am-5:30pm. (805) 595-9456.

Olde Port Inn Restaurant – Dine indoors or on the outdoor patio with views of the sea while sitting in big comfy chairs. Seafood, steak, salad, and burgers are served. Summer 11:30am-8:30pm, Sat/Sun 9pm. Autumn/winter Mon-Fri (no lunch) 5-9pm, Sat/Sun 11:30am-9pm. (Kids' menu.) (805) 595-2515. www.oldeportinn.com.

BOB JONES BICYCLE/WALKING TRAIL

This popular trail can be entered from Avila Beach, as well as from other locations further north. (**Woodstone** is a nice patio restaurant found along the path. Details below.) Sycamore and ancient oak trees line the paved trail that zigzags along the San Luis Creek, where the croaking of red-legged frogs may be heard. A stroll down any of the short dirt paths to the creek will most likely reveal ducks, turtles, and steelhead trout swimming in the water. Leashed dogs are okay. (Details for bicycle rentals are under Avila Beach Information.) Trail: Easy 1.7 miles one way.

To find the trailhead when in Avila Beach, travel a couple of blocks up from the beach on Avila Beach Drive to reach San Miguel Street at a flashing yellow streetlight. Street parking is available on San Miguel Street. Cross over Avila Beach Drive at the flashing yellow light, and turn right to find the trailhead. From here, travel over the bridge and, follow the path across the golf course. Turn right onto the main trail. **Note:** There's access to the trail from the Avila Beach Resort Golf Course (details under the golf course) and from the Woodstone Market Place Restaurant (details under the restaurant). Both are wheelchair accessible.

To find the trailhead from the Avila Hot Springs Resort (details under Lodging), take Ontario Street alongside the resort, and cross a small bridge to the small parking area on the right side of road. Walk across the street, and follow the path along the Buddhist Temple driveway. Guests of the Sycamore Mineral Springs Resort may use the steel bridge crossing Avila Beach Drive; then follow the lane passing the resort cabins. At the intersection, turn left onto the main trail. (Details for the resort under Avila Beach Lodging.) **Note:** Bicycle rentals found at the Sycamore Mineral Springs Resort. The path from the Avila Hot Springs area and the Sycamore Mineral Springs Resort merge and hug the creek. Then the path curves along the golf course to a left turn, crossing a bridge, and ends at Avila Beach.

Woodstone Market Place – B,L,D – The tasty foods include, soups, salads, sandwiches, prime rib, chicken, fish, as well as wine, mixed soda drinks, and desserts. There is indoor seating and an outdoor patio with umbrellas. Mon 7am-8pm, Tues/Weds/Thurs 7am-7:30pm, Fri 7am-8pm, Sat 8am-7:30pm, Sun 8am-6pm. Access from the restaurant to the Bob Jones Bicycle/Walking Trail is wheelchair accessible. (805) 595-1018. www.woodstoneavila.com. The restaurant is located along the Bob Jones Trail, not far from the Avila Hot Springs Trail entrance, and just beyond the trail entrance from the Sycamore Mineral Springs Resort. To reach the restaurant without taking the trail, from the Sycamore Mineral Springs Resort, on Avila Beach Drive, drive toward the beach to the first stoplight; turn right crossing the bridge. Make the first left into tiny Avila Village.

INFORMATION

Information – www.visitavilabeach.com and www. avilabeachpier.com.

Joe Momma's – Coffee/Juice Shop with bicycle rentals. (805) 627-1500. Located at 310 Front Street.

Fish & Farmer's Market – Fresh fish, local produce, live music and dancing. April-Sept. Fridays 4-8pm. (Rain by 2pm cancels market.) $1 VIP parking. Downtown promenade.

Wheelchair Accessible Activities – (Details under Appendix.)

Mineral Springs:

Sycamore Mineral Resort – Soaking tubs for guests and non-guests. (Details under Lodging.)

Avila Hot Springs Resort – Day use 104 degree mineral pool. (Details under Lodging.)

LODGING

Avila Lighthouse Suites – These two-room suites with kitchenettes, deep-set tubs, Wi-Fi, and great harbor views, are just steps from the beach sand. Amenities include a heated outdoor pool, hot tub, fitness room, and extended continental breakfast. Spa treatments and beach weddings are available. (805) 627-1900. (800) 372-8452. www.avilalighthousesuites. com. Located at 550 Front Street.

Joe Momma's B/B and Coffee/Juice Shop – One-bedroom condos; some with ocean views. All condos are fully furnished and have Wi-Fi, a kitchen, and washer and dryer. (No children under ten.) Continental breakfast served in their coffee shop. Spa services and bike rentals are available. **Coffee/ Juice Shop** – pastries, bagels, smoothies. Open 6:30am-5pm, Fri/Sat 6pm. (805) 627-1500. www.joemommasbeachstay. com. 310 Front Street, corner Front and San Luis Streets.

Avila La Fonda Hotel – All of these nicely decorated rooms come with spa tubs for two, fireplaces, Wi-Fi, 42-inch TV, Bose CD player, bathrobes, and nightly wine and snacks. Morning OJ/coffee. (805) 595-1700. www.avilalafondahotel. com. 101 San Miguel Street, one block from the beach.

Avila Village Inn – Rooms have Wi-Fi, flat-screen TVs and DVD players; they include access to the **Avila Bay Health Club** (next door) with a Jaccuzi, two outdoor pools, tennis courts, and exercise classes. Continental breakfast. Dogs okay in some rooms. (805) 627-1810. (800) 454-0840. www.avilavillageinn.com. 6655 Bay Laurel Place, 1.5 miles from Avila Beach. (Close to the Woodstone Market Place Restaurant.)

Avila Hot Springs Resort – This resort offers cabins (with kitchens), RV park, and tent camping with a day use heated swimming pool (with water slides) and hot mineral soaking pool. Dogs okay in RV camp. Wi-Fi in lobby. (805) 595-2359. www.avilahotsprings.com. 250 Avila Beach Drive.

Sycamore Mineral Springs Resort/Spa – The resort is amid a lovely hillside garden, with impressive rooms and either sulfur or fresh water spas. All rooms include Wi-Fi. Yoga and Pilate classes, as well as the soothing soaking tubs, are open to everyone including non-guests. Bike rentals available at gift shop. **Gardens of Avila Restaurant** – Fine dining at the resort. Open 8:30am-2pm, 5-9pm, Fri/Sat 10pm. Bar opens at 4pm. Weddings. (805) 595-7302. (800) 234-5831. www.sycamoresprings.com. 1215 Avila Beach Drive.

DIRECTIONS – Avila

From Hwy 101, exit at Avila Beach Drive, (1 mile north of Pismo Beach and 5.5 miles south of San Luis Obispo). Travel beyond the Avila Hot Springs Resort, Avila Valley Barn, and Sycamore Mineral Springs Resort, and continue toward the beach.

From Pismo Beach, travel north on Price Street (becomes Shell Beach Road) continue to the end, and turn left (near Hwy 101 entrance) on Avila Beach Drive. After passing Avila Hot Springs Resort, Avila Valley Barn, and Sycamore Mineral Springs Resort, continue to Avila Beach and the Avila Beach Golf Course.

LAGUNA LAKE

The lake, trail, and children's play area, provide a quiet respite and picnic area for visitors traveling north from the Pismo Beach and Avila Beach areas (toward San Luis Obispo). A loop trail, that begins from the end-of-the road parking area, has physical fitness equipment strewn along it for hikers use. Here, amid the brush, birds are heard calling to each other. To find the children's play area and picnic tables, make a left turn just before the end of the park's main road. Ducks and geese wander up to the children's area from the nearby lake shore. From the play area, the road continues along the lake for a short distance, and then lends access to the lower end of the loop trail. **Note:** To avoid contact with rattlesnakes, do not walk in tall grass, stay on designated wide paths. Dogs okay. Park Rangers (805) 781-7302. Trail: Easy 1.5 mile loop. The lake is located in the southern end of San Luis Obispo, 10 miles north of Pismo Beach. Exit Hwy 101 on Madonna Road. Travel past the Madonna Inn, and turn right at the stoplight onto Dalidio Drive.

SAN LUIS OBISPO

SLO, as it is known, is a pretty town with an old-fashioned flair and a large bubbling creek flowing through the center. It features alfresco dining and music from restaurant patios. While the restaurants' back patios open to the creek, the fronts face lovely Higuera Street bordered by trees, flowers, boutiques, gift shops, galleries, bakeries, and ice cream shops. Ride the trolleys for 50 cents along Higuera Street, Monterey Street, and Marsh Street. 5-9pm: Thur all year; June thru Aug Thur/Fri; April thru Oct Thur/Sat. Just flag one down.

PATH OF HISTORY

The path begins at Mission Plaza (corner Chorro & Monterey Streets) and follows San Luis Creek, crossing it on small footbridges, and meandering past many restored historic buildings and restaurants. Path of History Information & maps – SLO Chamber of Commerce (805) 781-2777. (Details under Information and San Luis Obispo Directions.)

A few sites along the walk:

Mission San Luis Obispo de Tolosa – The mission was built in 1772 by Chumash Indians, and is now a Catholic Church. The sound of the mission bell spills over the town daily at every mass. Visiting hours 9am-5:45pm. Winter 4pm. No visiting during weddings and daily mass. Daily mass Mon-Fri 7am and noon, Sat 7am and 5:30pm, Sun 7am, 9am, 11am, 6pm. Spanish Sun 12:30 and 7:30pm. No visiting hours on Thanksgiving, Christmas, New Years Day, and Easter. Gift shop – (805) 543-6850. Wheelchair access is at side entrance. Donations welcome. **Note:** History of mission found on website. Mission (805) 781-8220. www.missionsanluisobispo.org. Located at 751 Palm Street, Mission Plaza.

History Center of SLO County – Museum open 10am-4pm. No entrance fee. Wheelchair access from side entrance. (805) 543-0638. Located at 696 Monterey Street, across from the mission.

Jack House – This restored 1880s Victorian home has lovely gardens. The gardens are wheelchair accessible. Docent Tours Sunday 1-4pm. (last tour 3:30pm) $2, under two free. (805) 781-7308. Located at 536 Marsh Street.

Dallidet Adobe & Gardens – The adobe was built in 1853. Free tours Sunday 1-4pm, March thru Thanksgiving.

CALIFORNIA VACATION PATHS

The garden is open Friday 10am-4pm all year except holidays that fall on Friday. Garden is wheelchair accessible. (805) 544-2303. Located at 1185 Pacific Street.

SAN LUIS OBISPO CHILDREN'S MUSEUM

The focus of this museum is on exciting games and exhibits for children. Experiences include, being surrounded by giant soap bubbles, playing an earth organ, and reassembling the bones of a big cat. Entrance Fee $8, seniors $5, under two free. No food in museum; outdoor picnic tables are available. Open Mon (except Labor Day thru spring), Tues, Wed 10am-3pm and Thurs, Fri, Sat 10am-5pm, Sun 1-5pm. Call or check the website for special holiday hours. Wheelchair accessible. No strollers. (805) 544-KIDS. www.slocm.org. 1010 Nipomo Street, corner Nipomo and Monterey Streets.

FARMER'S MARKET

The famous SLO Farmer's Market with street performers, arts, crafts, barbeques, fresh produce, and flowers, is held every Thursday night from 6-9pm, except Thanksgiving and when raining. The market is found on tree-shaded Higuera Street between Osos and Nipomo Streets. (805) 541-0286. www.downtownslo.com. (Directions for the market is under the San Luis Obispo directions.)

F. McLintocks – To participate in the Farmer's Market festivities, the restaurant serves barbeque dinners in front of their restaurant on Thursday nights from 6pm. (Restaurant details under Eateries.) (805) 541-0686. Located at 686 Higuera Street.

INFORMATION
SLO Chamber of Commerce & Visitor Center –

Open 10am-5pm, Thurs/Fri/Sat 10am-7pm. (805) 781-2777. www.visitslo.com. 895 Monterey Street.

Festival Mozaic – Chamber and orchestra music; musicians come from all over the country. Festivals held at various locations. Spring, summer, fall, winter festivals. (805) 781-3008. www.festivalmozaic.com.

Summer Concerts – Mission Plaza, in front of Mission San Luis Obispo de Tolosa on summer Fridays thru Labor Day. 5:30-7:30pm. (805) 781-2777. Corner of Chorro and Monterey Streets.

Wally's Bicycle Works – Bicycle rentals, sales, and repairs. 10am-6pm, winter 10am-5:30pm, Saturday 10am-5pm. (Closed Sun.) (805) 544-4116. www.wallysbikes.com. 306 Higuera Street.

Wheelchair Accessible Activities – (Details under Appendix.)

SLO County Airport – From Los Angeles and San Francisco, this airport is served by United Airlines/Sky West (800) 241-6522, and U.S. Airways (800) 428-4322. (Details and directions under Transportation in Appendix.) Airport Information – Mon-Fri 8am-5pm. (805) 781-5205.

Amtrak Train Station – (Details and directions under Transportation in Appendix.) (800) USARAIL. www.amtrak.com.

Parks & Recreation Dept – (805) 781-7300.

Music: Call for current information – Madonna Inn – (805) 543-3000. MoTav – (805) 541-8733. Creeky Tiki Bar & Grill – (805) 544-2200. Creekside Brewing Co. – (805) 542-9804. SLO Brewing Co. – (805) 543-1843. (Restaurant/music details under Eateries.) Summer concerts. (Details above.)

EATERIES

Madonna Inn – Gold Rush Steak House – The sparkling pink dining room has live music & dancing Wed-Sat 7-11pm; DJs, Sun/Mon from 7-11pm. Dinner 5-10pm. Reservations (805) 543-3000. (Directions under Lodging.)

Madonna Inn – Copper Café & Pastry Shop – B,L,D – They serve light meals and divine desserts. (Kids' menu.) 7am-10pm. (805) 784-2430. (Directions under Lodging.)

Applebee's – Lunch and dinner with casual dining and bar. Menu includes burgers, pasta, salads, steaks, and ribs. (Kids' menu.) 11am-midnight, Fri/Sat 1am, Sun 10am-midnight. (805) 782-9088. Located at 305 Madonna Road, .25 mile beyond the Madonna Inn.

F. McLintocks Saloon & Dining – There's creek side dining with wonderful steaks and seafood. B,L,D – 7am-9pm, Fri/Sat until 9:30pm. (805) 541-0686. Located at 686 Higuera Street.

MoTav – This is an impressive bar serving burgers, tacos, and salads. Dining 11am-9pm, Fri/Sat 9:30pm, bar until 1:30am. Thurs/Fri/Sat DJs from 10pm. (805) 541-8733. www.motherstavern.com. 725 Higuera Street.

Creeky Tiki Bar & Grill – Pleasant creek side dining. They offer pizza, salads, sandwiches, burgers, tacos, and burritos. Open 11am-midnight. Live music; call for current information. (805) 544-2200. Located at 778 Higuera Street.

Creekside Brewing Co. – The Pub Grub includes sandwiches, salads, ribs, brisket, chicken, and steaks. Food 11am-9:30pm. Bar until midnight, Fri/Sat/Sun until 1:30am. Happy Hour Mon-Fri 4-6pm. Live music some Fri/Sat/Sun. Call ahead for current information. Jukebox music other nights. (805) 542-9804. Located at 1040 Broad Street, (overlooks the creek.) Exit Hwy 101 at Marsh Street, and turn left on Broad Street.

SLO Brewing Co. – They serve chicken, fish, ribs, steak, great salads, and sandwiches, as well as many kinds of beer. Mon 4pm-2am, Tues-Sun 11:30-2am. (Food until 9pm.) Happy Hour – Mon-Fri 3:30-6:30pm. DJs or live bands most nights. (Check the website for menu and information on concerts and DJs.) (805) 543-1843. www.slobrewingco.com. 1119 Garden Street.

Apple Farm Restaurant – This charming restaurant has a cider press, an ice cream maker, and a 14-foot water wheel that powers a gristmill. Come here for scrumptious home-style foods and apple dumplings. Box lunches are available. Open 7am-9pm. (805) 544-6100. Located adjacent to the Apple Farm Inn. (Directions under Lodging, Apple Farm Inn.)

LODGING

Madonna Inn – The inn embraces uniquely themed rooms; no two are alike. See some of them online. All rooms have Wi-Fi. Everything is superbly decorated from the rooms, café, bakery, boutique, and steak house to the restrooms. (Details for restaurants under Eateries.) Extensive grounds show off a heated pool, lagoon, and waterfall. There is a spa/fitness center and Wi-Fi in the lobby and at the pool. Weddings. (805) 543-3000. (800) 543-9666. www.madonnainn.com. 100 Madonna Road. Exit Hwy 101, in southern end of San Luis Obispo, at Madonna Road. (Hwy 227)

Best Western Plus Royal Oak – They offer a heated pool, Wi-Fi, and continental breakfast. Dogs okay. (805) 544-4410. (800) 545-4410. www.royaloakhotel.com. 214 Madonna

Road. Exit Hwy 101, in southern end of San Luis Obispo at Madonna Road. (Hwy 227)

Embassy Suites – Fine rooms with pay Wi-Fi are complimented by an indoor heated pool, and a hot tub, and come with a full breakfast. **Atrium Café** and the **Greenhouse Grill** in the hotel. Weddings. (805) 549-0800. (800) 864-6000. www.embassysuitesslo.com. 333 Madonna Road. Exit Hwy 101, in the southern end of San Luis Obispo on Madonna Road. (Hwy 227)

Courtyard by Marriott – Rooms have Wi-Fi and come with room service. Heated pool, hot tub, and a restaurant on the premises. (805) 786-4200. (800) Marriott. www.marriott.com. 1605 Calle Joaquin Road. Exit Hwy 101, in the southern end of San Luis Obispo, at Los Osos Valley Road.

Garden Street Inn B&B – This bed and breakfast is housed in a lovely 1887 vintage Victorian house in a quiet area and features nice rooms with Wi-Fi; some with fireplaces and Jacuzzis or clawfoot tubs. A full breakfast is served. (805) 545-9802. (800) 488-2045. www.gardenstreetinn.com. 1212 Garden Street, two blocks from the Mission San Luis Obispo. Exit Hwy 101 at Marsh Street.

Apple Farm Inn – This inn presents lovely Victorian country-style rooms with Wi-Fi, inviting grounds, spa services, a swimming pool, and hot tub. Apple Farm Restaurant lies adjacent to the inn. (Details under Eateries.) Weddings. (805) 544-2040. (800) 374-3705. www.applefarm.com. 2015 Monterey Street. Exit Hwy 101, at Monterey Street, in the northern end of San Luis Obispo.

San Luis Creek Lodge – Pleasantly furnished rooms with Wi-Fi, some have fireplaces and jet-tubs. Breakfast is provided for guests. (805) 541-1122. (800) 593-0333. www.

sanluiscreeklodge.com. 1941 Monterey Street. Exit Hwy 101 at Monterey Street in the northern end of San Luis Obispo.

Holiday Inn Express – The inn features a swimming pool, hot tub, fitness room, and Wi-Fi. Full buffet breakfast. (805) 544-8600. (800) 505-0650. www.hisanluisobispo.com. 1800 Monterey Street. Exit Hwy 101 at Monterey Street in the northern end of San Luis Obispo.

Quality Suites – All suites come with microwaves, refrigerators, and Wi-Fi. There is a swimming pool and a spa; guests are served a full breakfast. (805)541-5001. (800) 228-5151. www.qualitysuites.com. 1631 Monterey Street.

INEXPENSIVE LODGING

Motel 6 – There are two motels on the same street (close to restaurants), both providing affordable rooms, swimming pools, pay Wi-Fi; dogs stay free. First location: (805) 541-6992. (800) 4motel6. www.motel6.com. 1625 Calle Joaquin. Second location: (805) 549-9595. (800) 4motel6. www.motel6.com. 1433 Calle Joaquin. Exit Hwy 101, in the southern end of San Luis Obispo, at Los Osos Valley Road.

Days Inn – All rooms come with Wi-Fi, and two of the rooms have spa tubs. They have a swimming pool and a hot tub, and offer a continental breakfast. Dogs okay. (805) 549-9911. (800) 544-7250. www.daysinn.com. 2050 Garfield Street, exit Monterey Street.

DIRECTIONS – San Luis Obispo

From Pismo Beach/Shell Beach, travel north 10 miles on Hwy 101. (From Los Angeles, see Directions for Pismo Beach.) San Luis Obispo 10 miles north of Pismo Beach. San Luis Obispo 202 miles north of Los Angeles.

To reach the San Luis Obispo shopping area, Mission Plaza, Chamber of Commerce, Thursday night SLO Farmer's Market, and the Children's Museum, exit Hwy 101 on Marsh Street, in the southern end of San Luis Obispo, and turn left on Chorro Street. For the Children's Museum, turn left on Nipomo Street. **Note:** SLO Farmer's Market parking is on the corner of Marsh and Chorro Streets; to reach the market, walk one block north to Higuera Street.

See photos of the 6 areas listed in this book at: www. CaliforniaVacationPaths.com.

Attraction prices and times listed in this guide are subject to change; call ahead. Information missing or incorrect? Contact author: Pati.Anne@yahoo.com.

KID FAVES

PISMO BEACH

Note: Details for the following activities are found under main sections of Pismo Beach. (See Table of Contents for page numbers.)

PISMO BEACH

Kids like building sand castles on the beach, and visiting the nearby shops on Pomeroy Street where cotton candy, candied apples, ice cream, and gifts are plentiful.

MONARCH BUTTERFLY PARK

Butterflies - Thousands of delicate orange and black butterflies are active (Dec thru Feb) during sunny part of the day; and there is a path down to the beach.

BLUFFS COASTAL TRAIL

Cave Landing – From the Cave Landing parking area, it's a short walk up to a cave which overlooks the sea.

ARROYO GRANDE

Picnic Area - Kids love the colorful wild roosters which run around crowing loudly. From the picnic tables, stairs lead down to the creek where a bridge crosses it and leads to some historical buildings.

OCEANO

Sand Dunes – Ride a horse, dune buggy, ATV, or hike in the Dunes. (Rentals on the beach.) Cars are driven on the beach close to the ocean.

AVILA

Avila Valley Barn - Kids will enjoy the hayrides and the barnyard animals. Fruits, vegetables, homemade jams, and pies are sold here. In November, there is cider, apples, and pumpkins.

AVILA BEACH

Harford Pier - Sea lions hang around the Olde Port Fish Market on the pier. Use caution with kids as sea lions can bite.

SAN LUIS OPISPO

Children's Museum - Exciting games and exhibits for kids like playing an earth organ or reassembling the bones of a big cat.

APPENDIX

PISMO BEACH/SHELL BEACH

PELICANS

A good place to view the amazing brown pelicans is from the Pismo Beach Pier (details under Pismo Beach), and the Ventana Grill, adjacent to the Best Western Plus Shore Cliff Hotel. (Details under Eateries/Lodging on the Bluff.) Information on pelicans and other wildlife under Morro Bay Appendix.

TIDE POOLING

A path leads, from the front of the Spy Glass Inn, along the north side of the inn down to the ocean where, at low tide, great tide pooling is found. (Details for inn under Eateries/Lodging on the Bluff.)

LODGING

Prices for rooms soar in summer, but are cut dramatically in winter. (Details for inexpensive lodgings are listed under Pismo Beach Lodging.) Call hotels direct, and check prices against website offerings.

WEATHER

Summer mornings are thick with billowing fog that usually burns off by mid-day, and begins to roll back in by early evening. Fall has the best weather with warm days, clear skies, and little fog. Winter brings rainy cooler days with little fog. Springtime, with showers and warm days, has some foggy mornings.

Pismo Beach Current Weather – www.classiccalifornia.com/
weather.htm.

TRANSPORTATION
San Luis Obispo County Regional Airport (SBP)
They serve Pismo Beach, Morro Bay, as well as San Luis Obispo.

Information – Mon-Fri 8am-5pm (805) 781-5205. To reach
the airport from Higuera Street in downtown San Luis Obispo,
follow Higuera Street south; turn left on Broad Street. (Hwy
227) Continue about 3 miles to the airport.

There are non-stop flights from the Los Angeles and San
Francisco International Airports served by United Airlines/
SkyWest (800) 241-6522 (press 0 to speak to an agent). U.S.
Airways offers flights from Los Angeles and San Francisco (thru
Phoenix, AZ) (800) 428-4322 (press 0 to speak to an agent).

Car Rentals at San Luis Obispo Airport: Avis (805) 544-
0630 or (800) 230-4898. Budget (805) 541-2722 or (800) 527-
0700. Hertz (805) 781-3380 or (800) 654-3131. Enterprise
– Mon-Fri 8am-6pm, Sat 9m-midnight. (Closed Sun.) (805)
595-5455 or (800) 261-7331.

Amtrak

Daily train service to San Luis Obispo is via the Coast
Starlight coming from Seattle and San Francisco, and the
Pacific Surfliner from San Diego and Los Angeles. (800) 872-
7245. www.amtrak.com. To reach the Amtrak Station, from
Higuera Street in downtown San Luis Obispo, follow Santa
Rosa Street southeast to the end.

Car Rentals at SLO Amtrak Station: Avis (805) 595-1464.
Enterprise – Mon-Fri 8am-6pm, Sat 9am-midnight. (Closed
Sun.) (805) 546-6270.

Note: In Grover Beach, daily Amtrak Train service is provided from San Diego, Los Angeles, and San Francisco. The station is at Grand Avenue and Hwy 1, two miles south of Pismo Beach.

WHEELCHAIR ACCESSIBLE ACTIVITIES

Note: See Table of Contents for page numbers of activities.

PISMO BEACH

Monarch Butterfly Grove – Follow path among the eucalyptus trees.

Dinosaur Caves Park – Art/Crafts Fair, 1st Sun of month.

Margo Dodd Park – View sea birds atop offshore rocks.

Spyglass Park – Children's play area.

Bluffs Coastal Trail – One-mile paved trail runs along bluff.

GROVER BEACH

Grover Beach – Cars may be driven on the beach, and beach wheelchairs available at entrance.

Grover Beach Boardwalk – Paved path thru sand dunes.

OCEANO

Oceano Beach – Cars may be driven on the beach; beach wheelchairs available at entrance.

Guiton Trail – Part of the trail and fishing area are paved.

OSO FLACO LAKE STATE PARK

Willow-lined Path and Beach Boardwalk – Lake fishing (license required), and a large lookout point over the sea.

AVILA

Avila Valley Barn – Barnyard animals, fruits, vegetables, homemade ice cream, jams, and pies.

Avila Pier – Fishing from the pier, no license required.

Harford Pier – Barking sea lions hang out near end of the pier.

Bob Jones Bicycle/Walking Trail – Trail accessible from the Avila Beach Resort Golf Course Clubhouse and Woodstone Market Place.

Avila Fish & Farmer's Market – Fridays 4-8pm. April-Sept.

SAN LUIS OBISPO

San Luis Children's Museum – Games and exhibits for children.

Farmer's Market – Thurs nights – street performers, barbeques, fresh produce, and flowers.

Path of History – paved path leads to the following:

> **Mission San Luis Obispo de Tolosa** – Wheelchairs use side entrance.
>
> **Summer Concerts** – Mission Plaza, in front of the mission. Summer Fridays (5:30-7:30pm) thru Labor Day.

County Historical Museum – Wheelchairs use side entrance.

Jack House & Dallidet Adobe – Beautiful gardens are accessible.

RESOURCES/INFORMATION

PISMO BEACH

www.classiccalifornia.com
www.pismobeachtourism.org/
www.slostateparks.com
www.gotopismo.com
www.parks.ca.gov/

OCEANO

Information – www.beachcalifornia.com/oceano.html

GROVER BEACH

Information – www.beachcalifornia.com/grover.html

Twilight to Dawn

At the edge of twilight, colors grow dim
and shadows grow deep.
As if a veil has fallen, objects appear
fuzzy and awry.
The setting sun shoots off hues of raspberry and
marmalade coloring clouds and sky.
Before the night curtain falls, mountains and lakes
turn fiery gold, then into the night all colors seep.
Colors and harmony are not illusions.

Pati Anne

Book SIX

Morro Bay

Morro means a "rounded hill" in Spanish. This fishing port village, with a slow, quiet pace, faces the bay and famous gigantic Morro Rock. The Embarcadero (waterfront) is bustling with activity, especially colorful and busy in summertime, is embraced by the peaceful bay where moored sailboats cast their reflections upon the water. To feel the heart and soul of Morro Bay, walk close to the water's edge day or night. Hear the creak of the moored boats, the cry of the seagulls, and the rippling of the waves; the call of the sea lions can be heard above all. See the starfish clinging to the rocky shore, and the playful sea lions sunning on boat docks and rocks along the edge of the bay. Early in the day, watch fishermen bringing in their catches. At sunset, Morro Rock's reflection shimmers in an illuminated bay. (Details for Morro Rock below and in Appendix.)

6.1 MORRO BAY
What To Do & See

MORRO ROCK

This tremendous volcanic rock is nearly surrounded by the bay. *The Rock*, as locals refer to it, rises up almost 600 feet out of the sea. Peregrine falcons nest upon the top, and fishermen's boats run close to the 50 acre base. When the morning mist slips silently away and the sun caresses the bay, Morro Rock casts its reflection onto the water in a stunning display. Along the right side of the road, running out to *The Rock*, is a long sandy beach a favorite of surfers. On the left side is a boardwalk (wheelchair accessible) and a bicycle path close to the bay. Here in the sea jellyfish and sea otters are frequently spotted. At the end of the road, a short walk leads to a tiny sandy beach near a rocky sea breaker where, when the surf is up, tremendous waves crash up and over it. It's very dangerous; no walking on the breaker is allowed. **Note:** The trolley runs here from the center of the Embarcadero. (Details under Information.)

SAND SPIT

The spit looms like an island out in the bay, but connects to land in Montana de Oro State Park south of Morro Bay. (Details for the sand spit, park, and trails are listed under Day Trips South of Morro Bay.) Rent a kayak or canoe to explore the bay or for paddling to the sand spit. (Details for tide tables under Information.) Boat rentals are available from Kayak Horizons on the Embarcadero (details under the Embarcadero) and the Morro Bay State Park Marina.

THE EMBARCADERO

Running along the water's edge, the Embarcadero is teeming with fresh seafood restaurants, fish markets, specialty shops, and art galleries; there's also an aquarium and wine tasting. (Details under Wine Tasting.) Morro Bay trolleys carry passengers from the Embarcadero along the waterfront out to Morro Rock. (Details under Information.)

The following are found along the waterfront:

Kayak Horizons – Explore the fabulous estuary or cross the bay to the sand spit in a kayak or canoe. Rentals. See tide tables on website. Open 9am-5pm. (805) 772-6444. www. kayakhorizons.com. 551 Embarcadero.

Morro Bay Aquarium – Watch and feed the intriguing sea lions as they bark and clap for food; then enter the tiny, but special aquarium. Wheelchair accessible. Summer 9:30am-5:30pm, winter until 5pm. Entrance fee: 12yrs. and older $2, 5-11yrs. $1, under 4 free. (805) 772-7647. Located at 595 Embarcadero.

Sub Sea Tours – Take the boat with glass windows, which offers above-water views of harbor seals, sea lions, sea otters, and underwater views of the fish. Weekends on the hour beginning usually at 11am. (Depends upon weather.) Call for tour times and tide information. There are also kayak and canoe rentals and whale watching. 9am (weather permitting). (805) 772-9463. www.subseatours.com. 699 Embarcadero, at Pacific Street.

Bay Cruises – Rent a canvas-top electric boat (seats up to 8 adults) or a kayak. Take a 45 minute guided tour around the harbor or a 1 hour sunset cruise. Summer daily. Tours from 11am on the hour; rentals from 9am. (Winter closed Tues/Wed.) (805) 771-9337. www.baycruises.com. 845 Embarcadero, across from the visitor center.

Chablis Cruises – There are Sat night murder mystery dinners and weddings/receptions. Saturday champagne brunch at 11am. Check website for times and parking instructions. (805) 772-2128. Tickets (800) 979-3370. www.chabliscruises. com. Located at 1185 Embarcadero. Boarding is near the Great American Fish Co.

Virg's Landing – They offer deep-sea fishing. Whale watching tours in winter thru March/April. Office 5am-5pm. (805) 772-1222. (800) 762-5263. www.virgs.com. 1215 Embarcadero, on the waterfront, across from the huge power plant.

TIDELANDS PARK

The park is a fun area for kids to play while watching sailboats out on the bay. 7am-sunset. Located at the south end of the Embarcadero.

MORRO BAY STATE PARK

The state park offers views of the estuary, a marina, museum, hiking trails, and camping. Many species of birds migrate here including the Brant goose and the rare white pelican. Visitors may be able to observe both of these birds from the Museum of Natural History. (Details under the Museum of Natural History.) Morro Bay State Park Information – (805) 772-7434. (#7 for Ranger.) www.parks.ca.gov. Information available at the campground entrance, on State Park Road, beyond the golf course. (Details for Campground under Inexpensive Lodging.) To reach the state park from Morro Bay, take Main Street south, until it becomes State Park Road.

The park includes the following:

MORRO BAY STATE PARK GOLF COURSE

A marvelous 18-hole regulation course overlooks the bay. Lower rates apply after 12:30pm; twilight rates apply after 4pm. **19th Hole** - B,L – Open 7am-3pm, sandwiches until 5pm. Restaurant (805) 772-1922. Golf course (805) 772-1923. www.centralcoastgolf.com. 201 State Park Rd, across from the Inn at Morro Bay.

BLACK HILL TRAIL

This short trail begins at the end of the road that runs through the golf course. From the small hikers' parking area, take the trail uphill to the left. The dirt path widens and curves around the hillside under tall pine trees. From the top of the hill, there's an outstanding 360 degree view of the entire Morro Bay area. Bring a camera. Trail: Moderate 15 minute uphill walk one way. From Morro Bay, take Main Street south until it becomes State Park Road in Morro Bay State Park. Turn left into Morro Bay State Park Golf Course, and continue past the clubhouse. At the fork in the road, keep left (uphill) and continue to the end of the road and the hikers' parking area.

HERON ROOKERY

Many species of birds like herons, white egrets, and cormorants nest and roost among the eucalyptus trees. The fascinating blue herons mate and have their young here; males share in the feeding of the babies. Observe the birds from the deck of the Museum of Natural History, from the fence along the Inn at Morro Bay, or from a kayak upon the bay. (No kayak landing at the rookery.) It's located in Morro Bay State Park, across the road from the golf course, next door to the Inn at Morro Bay.

MUSEUM OF NATURAL HISTORY

The museum's focus is on the natural world with interactive exhibits and information about tidal forces, geology and human impact on the land. There are stunning displays of many species of birds and touch screens for children. Visitors can even build a sand dune. View the birds in the nearby Heron Rookery and the rare white pelicans in the bay using the telescopes on the museum's outdoor deck. Observe the Brant geese, November to April. For a fantastic view of the estuary and Morro Rock, climb up the short rocky trail above the museum or stroll down to the waterfront of Windy Cove to watch the shorebirds. Guided walks in Morro Bay State Park begin at the museum. There is a small gift shop inside the museum open during the museum hours 10am-5pm. (Closed Thanksgiving, Christmas, and New Year's Day.) Admittance $3, under 16 free. **Note:** Information on pelicans, geese, sea otters, sea lions, and seals under Appendix. (805) 772-2694. www.morrobaymuseum.org. From Morro Bay, follow Main Street south until it becomes State Park Road inside Morro Bay State Park. The museum is found beyond the golf course, Inn at Morro Bay, and the Heron Rookery on the right side of the road.

MORRO BAY STATE PARK MARINA

They provide boat launches and kayak and canoe rentals. Paddle the immense shallow marsh and the bay to experience up-close views of wildlife including the snowy egrets, hawks, and brown pelicans always on the lookout for food, skimming the water and making swift dives when they suddenly spot fish. (Information on the white and brown pelicans under Morro Bay in the Appendix.) 9am-4pm. Winter, weekends only. (805) 772-8796. It's located just south of the Museum of Natural History in Morro Bay State Park.

Bayside Cafe – Fresh local seafood, soups, salads, burgers, sandwiches, pasta, fish/chips, & desserts. Local wines. Lunch Mon-Wed 11am-3pm. Dinner Thurs-Sun 11am-8:30/9pm. (805) 772-1465. Located in the Morrow Bay State Park Marina.

INFORMATION

Morro Bay Visitor Center – Information on the over-the-bay 4th of July fireworks with a kid's carnival, BBQ, and live music. www.morrobay4th.org. Information on April's Kite Festival (parade and arts/crafts) and other activities. Daily 9am-5pm. (805) 225-1633. (800) 231-0592. www.morrobay. org. 255 Morro Bay Boulevard, two blocks from waterfront.

Morro Bay Chamber of Commerce – Mon-Fri 10am-4pm. See website for special events. 695 Harbor Street. (805) 772-4467. www.morrobay.org.

Morro Bay National Estuary Program – Nature Center – Information, displays, and wonderful bay views. 10am-6pm. (805) 772-3834. www.mbnep.org. Upstairs in the building at corner of Marina and 601 Embarcadero.

Tide Predictor – Check out the tides for Morro Bay at: http://tbone.biol.sc.edu/tide and click on U.S. West Coast, then click on California (near bottom of list) and on Morro Bay.

Farmer's Kites & Surreys – Bicycle rentals. Kites for sale. 9:30am-6pm. Winter 10am-5pm. (Closes in bad weather.) (805) 772-0113. 1108 Front Street, north end of Embarcadero.

Kayak /Canoe Rentals – At the Helm and Kayak Horizons. (Details under the Embarcadero and under Morro Bay State Park Marina.)

Morro Bay State Park – Information – (805) 772-7434. www.morrobaystatepark.org.

Camping Reservations – (800) 444-7275. www.reserveamerica.com.

Morro Bay Farmer's Market – Summer Sat 3-6pm. Fall/Winter until 5:30pm. (805) 772-4467. Located at 800 block of Main Street.

Transportation – (Details for airport and Amtrak under Morro Bay Transportation in the Appendix.)

Morro Bay Trolley – Links the Embarcadero with Morro Rock, the campgrounds, and Morro Bay State Park. Open Memorial weekend thru 1ˢᵗ weekend of Oct. Runs 4 days a week: Mon, Fri, Sat and Sun. (After Labor Day, Sat and Sun only.) Hours: Mon 11am-5pm, Fri/Sat 11am-7pm, Sun & holidays 11am-6pm except on July 4ᵗʰ runs from 11am until an hour after the fireworks. Fares: All day pass $3, age 5 and older $1, under 5 free. Wheelchair accessible. (805) 772-2744. See routes online. www.morro-bay.ca.us/trolley.

Wheelchair Accessible Activities – (Details under Appendix.)

Beach Wheelchairs – Available at the shed in the Morro Rock parking lot. Call ahead for reservations. (805) 772-6254.

Music: Call for current information – **Inn of Morro Bay** (805) 772-5651, **Otter Rock Café** (805) 772-1420, **Tognazzini's/Dockside Patio** (805) 772-8100. (Details under Eateries.)

WINE TASTING

Note: The wine tasting tours are fascinating during the grape harvests in September and October.

Elegant Image Wine Tours – Free lunch deli plate set up at winery includes Champagne and water. (805) 772-5390. www.elegantimagelimos.com.

Stax Wine Bar – Five tastes for $10. Cheese/meat plates, salads & desserts. Mon-Thur, and Sun noon-8pm; Fri/Sat 10pm. 1099 Embarcadero. (805) 772-5055. www.staxwine.com.

Morro Bay Wine Seller – Wine tasting with view of the bay. Beer, cheeses, etc. Thur/Fri/Sat 11am-8pm; Sun-Wed 11am-6pm. 601 Embarcadero, #5. (805) 772-8388. www.morrobaywineseller.com.

EATERIES

Harada – Japanese Restaurant & Sushi Bar –
Overlooks the town. Lunch 11:30am-2pm. Dinner 5-10pm. (805) 772-1410. Located at 630 Embarcadero.

Windows on the Water – Perched above the shops with views of the bay; they serve gourmet dinners. Dinner 5-9pm, Fri/Sat until 9:30pm. Winter, closes earlier. (805) 772-0677. Located at 699 Embarcadero, upstairs over gift shops.

Blue Skye Coastal Café – Breakfast served all day. Lunch: Sandwiches and soup. Dinner: Pasta, clams, fish, and steak offered indoors or alfresco along the bay with outstanding views of Morro Rock. Open 8am-8pm. Winter 8am-6pm, Fri/Sat until 7pm. (805) 772-8988. Located at 699 Embarcadero, behind the gift shops.

Dutchman's – Affords wonderful bay views with steaks and seafood; nice fish/chips. Open 11am-9pm. (805) 772-2269. Located at 701 Embarcadero.

Dorn's Café – Sits up above the Embarcadero with distant bay views. – B,L,D – Dinner includes, pasta, chicken, salads, seafood and homemade desserts. 7am-9pm. (805) 772-4415. Located at 801 Market Street, at Morro Bay Boulevard. (From the middle of the Embarcadero, visitors may climb the wooden stairs that go up to the restaurant.)

The Galley Seafood Grill & Bar – Restaurant offers steak, chicken, and seafood from lobster tails to fish/chips. Kids menu. Lunch is from 11am-2:30pm. Dinner from 5pm. (805) 772-7777. Located at 899 Embarcadero, adjacent to the Anderson Inn.

Inn at Morro Bay – The Orchid – Breakfast Mon-Sat. 7-11am, Sun to noon. Fine dining from 4-9pm. Live music

Fri/Sat 6 to 9pm. (See Bay Club Lounge for more options.) (805) 772-5651. Inn at Morro Bay, on State Park Road, across from the Morro Bay Golf Course.

Inn at Morro Bay – Bay Club Lounge – The lounge is presented in an enclosed veranda with casual atmosphere overlooking the ocean. Serves light menu. Happy hour, every day 3:30 to 6:30pm. (805) 772-5651. Inn at Morro Bay, on State Park Road, across from the Morro Bay Golf Course.

INEXPENSIVE EATERIES

Otter Rock Café – B,L,D – Fresh seafood and burgers. Kids' menu. Open Mon 10am-9:30pm. Weds/Thur 10am-10:30pm. Fri/Sat 8am-1am. Sun 8am-9:30pm. Bar - midnight. (Closed Tues.) Winter closes at 10pm. Karaoke summer Wed 8pm-11pm. Live music and dancing 8pm to midnight most nights; Sun 5-9pm. (805) 772-1420. www.otterrockcafe.com. Located at 885 Embarcadero Street.

Hofbrau – This inexpensive bar and restaurant has fantastic bay views and great French dip sandwiches, soups, and seafood. 11am-9pm, winter 8pm. (805) 772-2411. Located at 901 Embarcadero Street.

Tognazzini's and Dockside Restaurant – Fresh local fish served 11am-9pm. **Dockside Patio & Fish Market** (behind main restaurant) – Dogs may dine with owners on outdoor patio that offers up close views of the bay, the sailboats and *The Rock*. Open 10am-6:30-7pm, Fri/Sat 8pm. (Closes early in cold or rainy weather and in winter.) Live music most days on the patio, weather permitting. Music 11am-3pm; different musicians 3pm to 6:30-7pm. (805) 772-8100. Located at 1245 Embarcadero Street. (The patio and fish market are located behind the main restaurant and the taffy shop.)

LODGING

In summer, hotel rates soar, and there is a two-night minimum for Friday and Saturday stays. Rates are cut drastically in winter.

Embarcadero Inn – Rooms and suites with Wi-Fi lend views of Morro Rock and the bay. There is a Jacuzzi and a continental breakfast. (805) 772-2700. (800) 292-7625. www.embarcaderoinn.com. 456 Embarcadero.

Estero Inn – Views of the bay. Rooms come with granite vanities, fireplaces, and continental breakfast. Wi-Fi. 501 Embarcadero. (805) 772-1500. www.esteroinn.com.

Grays Inn – The inn's three plain rooms overlook the bay and come with Wi-Fi and kitchens. They all have tremendous close-up views of Morro Rock. Reservations 11am-5pm. (805) 772-3911. www.graysinnandgallery.com. 561 Embarcadero.

Anderson Inn – View Morro Rock from the elegant harbor-view rooms with Wi-Fi and some have fireplaces and deep-jetted tubs. Massages are available. (805) 772-3434. (866) 950-3434. www.andersoninnmorrobay.com. 897 Embarcadero.

Blue Sail Inn – This inn on the bluff boasts lovely furnished rooms, and several have fireplaces and balconies with a view of the bay. All rooms come with Wi-Fi, microwaves, refrigerators, and weekend continental breakfast. (805) 772-7132. (888) 337-0707. www.bluesailinn.com. 851 Market Street.

El Morro Masterpiece Motel – Framed art is displayed in the hallways and rooms. Many rooms have patios and fireplaces; all rooms contain microwaves, refrigerators, and Wi-Fi. There is a continental breakfast and evening wine with snacks. Their large indoor spa is amazing. (805) 772-5633. (800) 527-6782. www.masterpiecemotels.com. 1206 Main Street, three minutes from the waterfront.

Ascot Suites – Most of the charming rooms are arranged with spa tubs and fireplaces; all rooms have Wi-Fi. Guests can share in the evening wine reception, the hot breakfast, and the relaxing roof-top sun deck. (805) 772-4437. (800) 887-6454. www.ascotinn.com. 260 Morro Bay Boulevard, two blocks uphill from waterfront.

Comfort Inn – Some rooms have balconies and views of bay and Morro Rock. Hot breakfast buffet. Microwaves & refrigerators. Fitness center. Wi-Fi. 590 Morro Avenue. (805) 772-4483. (800) 424-6423. www.comfortinn.com/morrobay.

Inn at Morro Bay – This inn, sprawled along the waterfront, offers simply gorgeous bay views from the outdoor patio and lounge. Many rooms have bay views and come with fireplaces and hot tubs. Massages and an outdoor pool are available. All rooms have Wi-Fi. Dogs okay, some rooms. Pleasant well-groomed grounds accommodate weddings. **The Orchid Restaurant** and the **Bay Club Lounge** are on the premises. (Details under Eateries.) (805) 772-5651. (800) 321-9566. www.innatmorrobay.com. 60 State Park Road, across from the Morro Bay Golf Course.

INEXPENSIVE LODGING & CAMPING

Morro Bay State Park Campground – Fully accessible sites. Information (805)772-7434. Reservations – (800) 444-7275. www.reserveamerica.com. Campground entrance on State Park Road, in the state park. Driving from Morro Bay, campground is beyond the golf course. (Directions to state park under Morro Bay State Park.)

Pleasant Inn Motel – Some rooms have kitchenettes. Wi-Fi. Dogs okay. (805) 772-8521. 235 Harbor Street, 1 1/2 blocks from waterfront.

Days Inn – Harbor House – Some rooms offer bay views, all rooms have microwaves, refrigerators, and Wi-Fi. Continental breakfast. Dogs okay. (805) 772-2711. (800) 247-5076. www.daysinn.com. 1095 Main Street.

Motel 6 – Affordable rooms with an outdoor swimming pool, laundry room, and pay Wi-Fi. Dogs stay free. (805) 772-5641. (800) 4motel6. www.motel6.com. 298 Atascadero Road, 2 miles from Morro Bay.

Sundown Inn – Uniquely decorated rooms. Microwaves and refrigerators. (805) 772-7381. Located at 640 Main Street, 5-minute walk to waterfront. www.sundowninn.com.

DIRECTIONS – Morro Bay

From Los Angeles, take Hwy 101 north (toward Ventura) to Santa Barbara. Two miles north of Santa Barbara, take the scenic route and exit on Hwy 154 (signed *Lake Cachuma/State Street*). Follow Hwy 154 (San Marcos Pass) as it meanders past the 18-hole **San Marcos Golf Course** (805) 683-6334, horse ranches, vineyards, and **Lake Cachuma**. (Boat rentals, fishing, camping, wildlife cruises.) Lake Information – (805) 686-5054. www.cachuma.com. Beyond the lake (11.5 miles), is the quaint town of **Los Olivos**. (From Hwy 154, turn left on Grand Avenue.) The town, surrounded by flowers and trees, is a peaceful place with gift shops, wine-tasting rooms, and restaurants in historic buildings. (Details for Los Olivos' restaurants under Directions to Pismo Beach/Shell Beach.) Information – www.losolivosca.com. Three miles from Los Olivos, Hwy 154 re-joins Hwy 101. Continue north 54 miles (passing Pismo Beach) to San Luis Obispo.

Note: Scenic Hwy 154 is subject to flooding in the (winter-spring) rainy season and visitors should then continue on Hwy

101 from Santa Barbara to Gaviota State Park. From here Hwy 101 veers inland (north), and in 10 to 12 miles reaches a turn-off for **Nojoqui (no-Ho-wee) Falls County Park.** This is a great picnic/rest area. (Details under Pismo Beach Directions.) Return to Hwy 101, and continue north (passing Pismo Beach) to San Luis Obispo.

From San Luis Obispo take the exit for Hwy 1 (signed *MorroBay/Hearst Castle*). Follow the signs for Hwy 1 north, 13 miles, and exit from Hwy 1 at Morro Bay Boulevard or Main Street.

To bypass San Luis Obispo and take the longer scenic route to Morro Bay, exit from Hwy 101 on Los Osos Valley Road. (This is the first of ten exits in the southern end of San Luis Obispo.) Continue west, (toward Baywood Park) and, after passing spring/summer fields of flowers and grazing cattle (10 miles) the town of **Los Osos** (Details under Los Osos & Baywood Park.) comes into view. From here, either travel 2.5 miles ahead to explore the wonderful **Montana de Oro State Park** (details below) or turn right on South Bay Boulevard, and in 6 miles turn left on State Park Road. This road meanders through **Morro Bay State Park** and eventually becomes Main Street in Morro Bay. Morro Bay is 205 miles north of Los Angeles and 219 miles south of San Francisco.

To reach Yosemite National Park or Sequoia & Kings Canyon National Parks from Hwy 1, just north of Morro Bay turn right onto Hwy 41 (Atascadero Road). A nice stopping-off place is the **Charles Paddock Zoo.** Located off Hwy 41 at 9100 Morro Road, Atascadero. Information – (805) 461-5080. Travel 135 miles northeast to Fresno. (Details to reach the parks from Fresno under Directions for each of the parks.)

6.2 DAY TRIPS SOUTH OF MORRO BAY
What To Do & See

MONTANA de ORO STATE PARK

Park was named "Mountain of Gold" for the hundreds of gold poppies that bloom there in late spring and summer. This peaceful natural wonder is amazing in all types of weather. Fog, rain, and sunshine cast different shades of color upon the sea crashing on offshore rocks and the weather-beaten shoreline.

SAND SPIT TRAIL

Near the park's entrance, a 3.5-mile, straw-colored sandbar juts out like a long finger pointing north into the bay toward Morro Rock. The sandbar shields the bay from the ocean's powerful surf. Take the short gravel path that descends from the parking area to the beach on the ocean side of the sandbar. From here, to the left (south) is an easy mile walk for exploring the beach and climbing the dunes. The shoreline to the right heads toward Morro Rock; and, it's an easy 3.5-mile walk to the end of the sand spit. Watch for jellyfish that have been washed up on the shore. But to enter the dunes in this area (most of the dunes are roped-off to protect nesting birds) or to walk on the bay side of the spit (strenuous walk), visitors must take the **Rim Trail**. To find the trail, look for an opening in the roped-off area. It's about 200 yards north of the path coming from the parking area. (Signed *Rim Trail*.) Open 6am-sunset. Boat rentals to the spit (at proper tide) available at the Morro Bay State Park Marina and the Embarcadero in Morro Bay. Trail: Easy on the ocean side, strenuous on the bay side; 3 miles one way. To find the trail, follow the road from the park's entrance. Just beyond the first grove of eucalyptus trees that border the road, turn right. (Signed *Sand Spit.*) Take the paved road to the end for parking, restrooms, and the trailhead.

DUNE TRAIL

The trail heads down to the sand dunes. Horses are allowed on this trail, but no dogs. Maps and information available at the park's visitor center. Trail: Moderate 1.5 miles one way. Trailhead is found beyond the Sand Spit Trail turnoff, just prior to Spooner's Cove and the visitor center.

SPOONER'S COVE

This stunning cove has a sandy beach for sunbathers, and tall rock outcroppings offshore for the adventurous to climb. Breathe in slowly and absorb every moment here as everything changes quickly. While cool ocean breezes sweep across the park year round, thick fog may appear, especially in summer, with only a moment's notice. To fully enjoy the spectacular scenery, follow Bluff Trail described below. Spooner's Cove is across the road from the visitor center.

BLUFF TRAIL

From the parking area, follow the trail as it crosses a tiny bridge and rambles along the bluff top lending a view of Spooner's Cove. Soon a small sign is reached that displays pictures of sea life. This marks the short pathway down to Corallina Cove. In the cove are polished beach stones; at low tide, rocky tide pools come alive with sea anemones, starfish and crabs. After leaving the cove, the path crosses a wooden bridge and turns right unfolding along the bluff edge where nature unites land and sea. Here, visitors find a dramatic contrast of colors: sapphire-blue sky, luminous-white clouds, aquamarine sea, glossy-white spindrifts, and tall dark-brown rock formations dotted with sea birds. The scene is breathtaking! Powerful images seem to come to life before one's eyes. The sea's perpetual pounding has sculptured the craggy shoreline, creating arches that ocean waves splash through, and crevices where tiny sea life hide.

The sea also molded the offshore rock outcroppings where birds huddle in their nests and waves crash upon them shooting spectacular spindrifts up into the air. Follow the trail to the end, and return on the same trail. Maps found at the park's visitor center. **Note:** A wheelchair accessible path (along the Bluff Trail) is scheduled to be completed soon. Trail: Easy 1.7 miles one way. Trailhead is just past the visitor center at end of the small parking pullout on right side of the road.

VALENCIA PEAK TRAIL

This trail ascends more than 1,300 feet displaying a view of Morro Rock, the sea, and migrating gray whales from November through January. In late spring and summer, the hillside is overwhelmed by yellow wildflowers revealing the color that gave the park its name *Mountain of Gold*. Bring Water. Maps found at the park's visitor center. **Note:** Part of the trail is being leveled out and a vista point created, which will be wheelchair accessible. Trail: Moderate 2 miles one way. The trailhead is across the road from the Bluff Trailhead, just beyond the visitor center.

COON CREEK TRAIL

This trail was named for the numerous raccoons in the area; now they are found mainly in and around the campgrounds. A dirt path travels through the brush down to a fork, where gravel stairs (to the right) head down toward the sea. Continue (left) on the path where the brush gets higher and, in half a mile, it crosses a wooden bridge over a murmuring creek. Soon the path becomes shaded with tall brush and trees; and in .25 mile, it crosses another wooden bridge, then narrows and meanders along the creek. Continue past the sign for *Rattlesnake Trail*, where the path becomes mostly un-shaded to the end. Stay on the trail, as lots of poison oak is found here especially along the creek. Maps at the park's visitor center. Trail: Moderate 2.5 miles one way. The trailhead is near the small parking area at the end of the park's paved road.

POINT BUCHON TRAIL

This trail is located on PG & E's private property. From their check-in station, a gravel trail descends .4 mile to a short side path (to the right) leading down to Coon Creek Beach. Continuing beyond the short beach path is a fenced sinkhole where part of the cliff caved in. Here, the sea can be seen rushing into the depths below. The path continues along a fenced-in area of goats, and it loops around to meet the main path coming directly from the check-in station. When the two paths meet, it zigzags along the ragged coastline. Visitors can rest at the benches provided and watch as the sea crashes around the offshore rock outcroppings sending foamy spindrifts up many feet into the air. Open 8am-5pm Thurs thru Mon. (Closed Tue/Wed.) Nov-March 8am-4pm. (Closed Thanksgiving, Christmas, and New Years Day.) Call for current information (805) 305-8304 or (805) 528-8758. No dogs allowed. Trail: Easy 3.4 miles one way. This trail is reached by traveling to the end of the state park's road to the parking area shared with Coon Creek Trail. From the parking area, walk around the locked gate and down .3 mile (strenuous uphill walk on return) to PG & E's check-in station where everyone is required to sign in.

INFORMATION

Spooner Ranch House – Visitor Center – A few picnic tables are available in front of the visitor center. No park entrance fee. Summer daily; winter Thurs/Fri/Sat/Sun, 11am-3pm. No telephone service. Information (805) 772-7434. Park is open sunrise to sunset. To avoid contact with rattlesnakes, stay on designated trails. No dogs on any trails. The visitor center is housed in the Spooner Ranch House 2.6 miles from the park's entrance, across the road from Spooner's Cove.

Park Information – www.slostateparks.com and www.parks.ca.gov.

State Park Rangers – (805) 772-7630, press #7.

Montana de Oro State Park Camping – 50 regular sites, horse sites, and hike-in environmental sites. (800) 444-7275. www.reserveamerica.com.

Horses – There are day-use horse trails in the park for those with their own horses; horse trails are clearly marked.

Dogs – Not permitted on any trails.

Wildlife in Park – Raccoons, coyotes, fox, deer, rabbits, and opossum.

Summer High Temperatures – 65-75 degrees.

Foggiest Months – July, August, September.

DIRECTIONS – Montana de Oro State Park

From Morro Bay, follow South Main Street through Morro Bay State Park. Turn right on South Bay Boulevard, and travel to the end (6 miles). Turn right on Los Osos Valley Road (becomes Pecho Valley Road) and, in 2.5 miles, it curves left into the park.

From San Luis Obispo, exit Hwy 1 on Los Osos Valley Road (first of ten exits in southern end of San Luis Obispo). Follow sign for *Baywood Park*. (Details under Directions for Morro Bay.)

LOS OSOS & BAYWOOD PARK
Towns outside Montana de Oro State Park

SWEET SPRINGS NATURE PRESERVE

Enjoy turtles, waterfowl, and graceful white herons from wooden bridges that reflect into the fresh water ponds, or walk the paths (wheelchair/stroller accessible) through the saltwater marsh. In mid-day, red-legged frogs come out to sun themselves. Open dawn to dusk. Free. Trail: Easy .5 mile one way. Follow directions to Montana de Oro State Park except from Los Osos Valley Road, traveling toward the bay, turn right (from Montana de Oro State Park, turn left) on 9th Street and left on Ramona Avenue; continue .5 mile to the preserve.

LOS OSOS OAK STATE RESERVE

Gnarled, twisted old oak trees guard the entrance to the shady trails. The path leads across a small wooden bridge to trail signs indicating a left turn for Creek Trail, right turn for Chumash Loop Trail, and straight ahead for the Oak View Trail. This trail eventually connects to Chumash Loop and the Creek Trail. Take the Oak View Trail amid large oak trees and small trees covered in lichens, and continue under the old oaks with unusual twisted limbs. In less than .5 mile, signs indicate a right turn to Chumash Loop and a left turn to the Creek Trail; both lead back to the parking area. Stay on trails, lots of poison oak. Information – (805) 528-4884. Trail: Easy .75 mile loop trail. From Montana de Oro State Park traveling on Los

Osos Valley Road, continue beyond the Los Osos Chamber of Commerce (.75 mile) to *State Reserve* sign on the right side of the road and a small parking area.

From Morro Bay, follow South Main Street through the Morro Bay State Park and turn right on South Bay Boulevard to the end. (6 miles) Turn left on Los Osos Valley Road, continue .75 mile beyond the Los Osos Chamber of Commerce to *State Reserve* sign on right side of the road and a small parking area.

ELFIN FOREST

A boardwalk (wheelchair/stroller accessible), above the bay, passes hundreds of plants and unique pygmy trees while showing off views of Morro Rock, sailboats out on the bay, and many varieties of birds. Parking, trailhead, and wheelchair ramp are located at the end of 16th Street. Leashed dogs okay. Trail: Easy .8 mile loop. (Directions under Los Osos/Baywood Park Directions.)

BAYWOOD PIER

This tiny pier is perfect for relaxing, studying clouds, and viewing sunsets. At low tide, the pier is surrounded by mud flats, at high tide, bay water laps around the pier pilings.

Good Tides Organic Bistro – at the pier. B,L,D – 6am-8pm. (Closed Thurs.) Winter closed Weds/Thurs. (805) 528-6000. www.goodtides.com. Located across from the Bay Back Inn. (Directions under Lodging, Bay Back Inn.)

INFORMATION

Los Osos/Baywood Park Chamber of Commerce – Mon-Fri 10am-4pm. (805) 528-4884. www.lobpchamber.org. 781 Los Osos Valley Road.

EATERIES/LODGING

Note: Summer two-night minimum on Fri/Sat. (Lower room rates October to Easter.)

Celia's Garden Café – Breakfast and lunch is served surrounded by flowers and greenery with indoor/outdoor seating. (Roast turkey sandwiches are popular.) 7:45am-2:30pm. (805) 528-5711. Located at 1188 Los Osos Valley Rd, Los Osos.

Back Bay Inn – Most rooms in this country inn, which is set along the water's edge, have telescopes to view wildlife on the bay, fireplaces, kitchens, and balconies. All rooms have Wi-Fi. Breakfast in the **Back Bay Café** and wine/snacks in the evening are included. Front desk has binoculars for guests to use. (805) 528-1233. (877) 330-2225. www.backbayinn. com. 1391 2nd Street, Baywood Park. From Morro Bay, follow South Main Street through Morro Bay State Park, turn right on South Bay Blvd, turn right (at stoplight) onto Santa Ysabel Avenue. Head toward the bay (18 blocks), and turn left on 2nd Street.

Baywood Inn B/B – Most of the uniquely-themed rooms and suites have bay views. All rooms have fireplaces, kitchenettes, and Wi-Fi. A complimentary breakfast is served in the adjacent restaurant or in the coffee shop. (805) 528-8888. www.baywoodinn.com. 1370 2nd Street, Baywood Park. Follow the directions for Back Bay Inn.

La Palapa – Mexican cuisine – Tues-Fri – L,D – 11:30am-9pm. Sat/Sun – B,L,D – 8:30am-9pm. (Closed Mon.) (805) 534-1040. (Adjacent to the Inn.)

Sea Pines Golf Resort – The lodge, tucked among the pines, and the 9-hole golf course, overlook the sea. Rooms have Wi-Fi and dogs are okay in some rooms; there is an outdoor Jacuzzi. Ask about their hot tub/golf packages. (805) 528-5252. (888) 732-7463. www.seapinesgolfresort.com. 1945 Solano Street, Los Osos. From Los Osos Valley Road, heading toward the sea, turn right at the end of the road onto Pecho Road. (Left turn leads into Montana de Oro State Park.)

Club House Sports Bar and Grille – B,L,D – Sun-Thurs 7am-8:30pm; Fri/Sat 9pm. Bar 10pm. Call the resort phone number and press 4 to reach the bar and grill. (Adjacent to the resort.)

DIRECTIONS – Los Osos/Baywood Park

To reach Baywood Park, from Morro Bay take Main Street south and it becomes State Park Road, which meanders through Morro Bay State Park. At the end of the park, turn right on South Bay Boulevard and continue to a right turn (at stoplight) onto Santa Ysabel. From here, to reach the Elfin Forest, turn right on 16th Street or to reach Back Bay Inn, Baywood Inn, and the tiny Baywood Pier, continue to a left turn on 2nd Street. To reach Montana de Oro State Park, Sea Pines Golf Resort, Sweet Springs Nature Preserve, and J & J Riding Stable (in Los Osos) stay on South Bay Boulevard (past Santa Ysabel Street) to the end, and turn right on Los Osos Valley Road, or turn left to reach the Los Osos Oak State Reserve. (Further directions under Montana de Oro State Park, Sea Pines Golf Resort, Sweet Springs, and J & J Riding Stable.)

6.3 DAY TRIPS NORTH OF MORRO BAY
What To Do & See

CAYUCOS

A tiny, quiet village is sprawled along the beach. It harbors the old Cayucos Wharf (built in 1875), which offers fishing (no license required), an up-close look at surfers, and a distant view of Morro Rock. The wharf is lit for night fishing.

INFORMATION

Cayucos State Beach Information – www.slostateparks.com.

Cayucos Visitor Center and Chamber of Commerce – Fri-Mon 11am-4pm. 41 S. Ocean Avenue. (805) 995-1200. (800) 563-1878. www.cayucoschamber.com. www.cayucosbythesea.com. www.cayucosbythesea.com/history.html.

Good Clean Fun – Kayak rentals. Beach clothing, surfboards, boogie boards, wet suits, sunscreen, sandals, beach chairs, and umbrellas. Surfing lessons. Summer daily 9am-6pm. Winter 10am-5pm. Sat-Sun 9am-6pm. (805) 995-1993. www.goodcleanfunusa.com. Located at 136 N. Ocean Avenue.

Cayucos Surf Co. – Surfboard rentals/lessons. Summer 9am-6pm, Fall 10am-6pm, after Nov 1st 10am-5pm. (805) 995-1000. Located at 95 Cayucos Drive, near the pier.

WINE TASTING

Note: The wine tasting tours are fascinating during the grape harvests in September and October.

Cayucos Cellars – Wine tasting (includes Zins/Cabs) and gifts. 11am-5:30pm. (Winter, closed Tues.) (805) 995-3036. Located at 131 N. Ocean Avenue.

Full Moon Wine Bar & Bistro – Wine tasting with soups, salads, cheeses, olives, and handmade dips and sauces. Thurs/Fri/Sat 4-10pm; Sun/Mon 2-7pm. (805) 995-0095. www. fullmoontastingroom.com.

EATERIES & FUN

Schooners Wharf Restaurant – From the restaurant is a view of the Cayucos Wharf, the surfers, and the sea. Bar (open until 1am) is upstairs where lunch is served; dinner (steaks, seafood) is served on the main floor. Open 11am-10pm, (bar menu 3-5pm). Dinner 5-9pm, Fri/Sat 9am-10pm. Closes an hour earlier in winter. (805) 995-3883. Located at 171 N. Ocean Avenue.

Old Cayucos Tavern – There's pool and live music. 10am-2am. Dancing on Friday and Saturday from 9pm. (No food.) (805) 995-3209. Located at 130 N. Ocean Avenue.

Café della Via Restaurant & Wine Bar – Italian fare – Open 5pm-8:30pm. Fri/Sat 9pm. (Closed Mon-Tues.) (805) 995-1610 Located at 155 N. Ocean Avenue. www. cafedellavia.com.

LODGING

On the Beach B/B – Some rooms show off ocean views, and all rooms come with fireplaces, Jacuzzi tubs, terry robes and Wi-Fi. Private balconies. Guests can partake of a full breakfast and evening wine/snacks. A roof-top hot tub is also available. (805) 995-3200. (877) 995-0800. www.californiaonthebeach. com. 181 N. Ocean Avenue, near the Cayucos Wharf.

Shoreline Inn – On The Beach – All rooms have either full or partial ocean views, and some rooms and suites have fireplaces. Ground floor rooms open to the grassy area next to the beach. Wi-Fi. Continental breakfast. (805) 995-3681. (800) 549-2244. www.cayucosshorelineinn.com. 1 N. Ocean Avenue.

Cayucos Sunset B/B – Lovely rooms, some with ocean views; all rooms have jacuzzi tubs and Wi-Fi. Breakfast and evening wine/cheese. (805) 995-2500. (877) 805-1076. www.cayucossunsetinn.com. 95 S. Ocean Avenue.

DIRECTIONS – Cayucos

From Morro Bay, take Hwy 1, 5 miles north; exit at the signed *Cayucos* exit. Travel under the overpass, turn right on South Ocean Avenue (Hwy 1) and continue into the tiny village.

See photos of the 6 areas listed in this book at: www. CaliforniaVacationPaths.com.

Attraction prices and times listed in this guide are subject to change; call ahead. Information missing or incorrect? Contact author: Pati.Anne@yahoo.com.

KID FAVES

MORRO BAY

Note: Details for the following activities are found under main sections of Morrow Bay. (See Table of Contents for page numbers.)

Morro Bay

Walk along Water's Edge – Kids will be amazed at colorful starfish clinging to the rocky shore (especially early mornings) and sea lions sunning on boat docks.

Morro Bay Aquarium

Kids can watch and feed the intriguing sea lions as they bark and clap for food just before entering the tiny, but special, aquarium.

Museum of Natural History

The focus is on the natural world with interactive exhibits. There are stunning displays of many species of birds and touch screens for kids. A climb up the short rocky trail above the museum affords fantastic views.

Sub Sea Tours

Kids love to look through the windows of the sub at the many fish lured here because tour guides feed them. There are close-up views of harbor seals, sea otters, and sea lions.

Tidelands Park

Kids play while watching sailboats out on the bay.

APPENDIX

MORRO BAY

MORRO ROCK

In the past, *The Rock* was not connected to the mainland. It was cut away to build various breakwaters, and cut again to build a causeway to connect it to the shore. Today it's a protected bird sanctuary, with no climbing allowed.

It can be reached by a road where, in summer, a trolley runs out to the base from the Embarcadero in town. A boardwalk (wheelchair accessible) and a bicycle path run along the roadway.

Resources

www.pelicannetwork.net/morrobay.htm
www.slostateparks.com

Pelicans

Pelicans, an endangered species, are easily spotted with their huge bodies and tremendous bills and pouches. Brown pelicans (grayish-brown) have wing spans of six to seven feet and are seen scanning the water gracefully, then dive-bombing to catch a fish. Rare white pelicans have wingspans of eight to ten feet and tend to stay together in groups. When fishing, a few of them will form a circle around clusters of fish, and swoop up gallons of water along with fish; as they are swallowing, the water drains from their bills. To view the rare white pelicans,

371

visit the Museum of Natural History in Morro Bay State Park. A group of them live nearby year round and, from the museum's observation deck, they sometimes are seen up close.

Resources

Museum of Natural History docents (Morrow Bay State Park).
www.pelicanlife.org
www.fws.gov/arcata/es/birds/brnpelican/b_pelican.html
www.whozoo.org/Intro98/stewwarr/stewwarr1.htm

Brant Geese

Brant geese migrate from Alaska, (sometimes Russia) where their goslings are hatched and learn to fly in about a week; but in October or November, they arrive in Morro Bay and stay until April. These small geese, weighing about three pounds, wear a necklace of white feathers around their black necks to match the white feathers under their dark brown tails. To view the geese, visit the Museum of Natural History's observation deck (located in Morro Bay State Park) or the Morro Bay Estuary.

Resources

Museum of Natural History docents (Morro Bay State Park).
www.wabrant.org/about-brant/

Sea Otters

Simply adorable, sea otters float on their backs in the bay, with females holding babies on their chests. They like to cluster together to rest. Late in the day, they usually begin to play together. One will dive and surface a few feet away, and the others soon follow. Then one will dive farther away, pop up and float on its back. Soon another will join him until they all are diving and catching up to each other across the water. When feeding, they usually dive between two to four minutes at a time. In Morro Bay, they are frequently spotted in the bay, on the left side of the road leading out to Morro Rock.

Sea otters are light to dark brown with small external ears; their fore limbs, with short padded paws, are used to hold rocks for cracking open clams; the hind limbs are webbed. Females weigh 35 to 60 pounds, while males usually weigh 65 to 90 pounds; females reach approximately four and a half feet in length and males are slightly longer.

Per the U.S. Geological Service's 2009 springtime count of sea otters, from Half Moon Bay to Santa Barbara, a total of 2,654 sea otters were present. The highest number of sea otters, along the California coastline, was found in the Monterey area, and the second highest number, between San Simeon and Cayucos.

Resources

Museum of Natural History docents (Morrow Bay State Park). www.nationalgeographic.com/animals/mammals/sea-otter www.defenders.org/wildlife_and_habitat/wildlife/sea_otter.php

Sea Lions

Stay your distance, the curious and playful sea lions will bite. Shiny silken coats glisten in the sunshine. Brown coats turn almost black when wet. Long whiskers and huge round eyes adorn cute faces. Their distinct bark is heard day and night, especially when grouped together on rocks or boat docks. They love frolicking in the bay and they love the boat docks close to shore, where fishermen, bringing in their catches, might miss a fish or two. Many of them are spotted along the shore most every day quietly sunning or barking and flapping their fins around.

They are distinguished from harbor seals by their small external ears. Harbor seals have small holes for ears. Female sea lions weigh about 200 pounds, and reach about five to six feet long. Males usually weigh about 800 pounds, and reach between seven to eight feet in length.

Resources

Museum of Natural History docents (Morrow Bay State Park). www.marinemammalcenter.org/education/marine-mammal-information/pinnipeds/california-sea-lion/

Harbor Seals

These seals are harder to find as they shy away from humans. They come in a range of colors from light gray or tan to dark brown. Those with spots, are leopard seals. In Morro Bay, they haul out in secluded areas, or swim into the estuary, and lie out on the mudflats.

Harbor seals differ from sea lions, not only because they have no external ears, but the males are much smaller than male sea lions. Males weigh between 150 to 200 pounds, (occasionally larger) and reach five to six feet in length. Females are just slightly smaller, making it hard to tell males from females.

Resources

Museum of Natural History docents (Morrow Bay State Park). www.marinemammalcenter.org/education
www.wildlife.ca.gov/ (Search: harbor seals California.)

Morro Bay History/Information

www.morrobay.com
www.morrobay.org
www.slostateparks.com

LODGING

Prices for rooms soar in summer, but are cut dramatically in winter. (Details for inexpensive lodgings are listed under Morro Bay Lodging.) Call hotels direct, and check prices against website offerings.

WEATHER

Summer mornings are thick with billowing fog that usually burns off by mid-day, but begins to roll back in by early evening. Fall has the best weather with warm days, clear skies, and little fog. Winter brings rainy cooler days with little fog. Springtime, with showers and warm days, has some foggy mornings.

Morro Bay Current Weather – www.findlocalweather.com/forecast/ca/morro+bay.html.

TRANSPORTATION

San Luis Obispo County Regional Airport (SBP)
They serve Pismo Beach and Morro Bay, as well as San Luis Obispo.

Information - Mon-Fri 8am-5pm (805) 781-5205. To reach the airport from Higuera Street in downtown San Luis Obispo, follow Higuera Street south, turn left on Broad Street. (Hwy 227) Continue about 3 miles to the airport.

There are non-stop flights from Los Angeles and San Francisco International Airports served by United Airlines/SkyWest (800) 241-6522 (press 0 to speak to an agent). U.S. Airways offers flights from Los Angeles and San Francisco (thru Phoenix, AZ) (800) 428-4322 (press 0 to speak to an agent).

Car Rentals at San Luis Obispo Airport: Avis – (805) 544-0630 or (800) 230-4898. **Budget** – (805) 541-2722 or (800) 527-0700. **Hertz** – (805) 781-3380 or (800) 654-3131. **Enterprise** – Mon-Fri 8am-6pm, Sat 9am-12pm. (805) 595-5455 or (800) 261-7331.

Amtrak

Daily train service to San Luis Obispo is via the Coast Starlight coming from Seattle and San Francisco, and the Pacific Surfliner from San Diego and Los Angeles. To reach the Amtrak Train Station, from Higuera Street in downtown San Luis Obispo, follow Santa Rosa Street southeast to the end.

Amtrak – (800) 872-7245. www.amtrak.com.

Car Rentals at Amtrak: Avis – (805) 595-1464. **Enterprise** – Mon-Fri 8am-6pm, Sat 9am-12pm. (805) 546-6270.

WHEELCHAIR ACCESSIBLE ACTIVITIES

Note: See Table of Contents for page numbers of activities.

MORRO BAY

Morro Rock – Nice boardwalk along edge of bay leads to Morro Rock.

Morro Rock Beach – Beach wheelchair. Call ahead for reservations. (805) 772-6254.

Embarcadero – Paved sidewalk meanders to shops and restaurants with fantastic view of the bay.

Morro Bay Trolley – Links the Embarcadero with Morro Rock, campgrounds, and Morro Bay State Park.

Morro Bay Aquarium – Intriguing small aquarium.

Museum of Natural History – Outstanding interactive displays and view of bay where rare white pelicans may be seen.

Morro Bay State Park Campground – Fully accessible sites.

Montano de Oro State Park - A wheelchair accessible path along the Bluff Trail is scheduled to be completed soon. Also plans have been made to build a wheelchair accessible pathway, with a vista point, along part of the Valencia Peak trail.

LOS OSOS & BAYWOOD PARK – (South of Morro Bay)

Sweet Springs Nature Preserve – Enjoy turtles, ducks, and white herons from wooden bridges.

Elfin Forest – Boardwalk with great views of the bay passes unique pygmy trees.

Baywood Pier – Nice sunsets from tiny pier and nearby coffee shop.

CAYUCOS – (North of Morro Bay)

Cayucos Wharf – Fishing (no license required) and distant views of Morro Rock.

Acclaim for CALIFORNIA VACATION PATHS

"Pati you have realllly done a nice job with this guide. What detail and what interesting and thorough information. I especially like the way you have described some of the areas— very nicely done. It is just music and poetry."

PATRICIA FRY, FREELANCE WRITER, AUTHOR AND EDITORIAL CONSULTANT

"Pati's affection for the natural areas of the Golden State is obvious, and she's worked diligently to share that enthusiasm with readers."

JOAN TAPPER, AUTHOR OF *The Most Beautiful Villages and Towns of California*

"This book provides information for people with mobility issues to enable them to vacation with their able-bodied friends and families. The Mammoth Lakes area has a wealth of natural beauty and athletic opportunities and much of it is accessible to all! This is a great resource for visitors and locals alike."

LAUREL MARTIN, SUMMER PROGRAM MANAGER/GUEST SERVICES MANAGER, MAMMOTH LAKES

"All in all, this looks like a great guide. Hope it's a best seller!!!"

TAWNI THOMSON, EXECUTIVE DIRECTOR, BISHOP CHAMBER OF COMMERCE & VISITORS BUREAU

"Pati your book is a great reference guide for the Central Coast, it offers ideas on the best of the best to see and do when visiting San Luis Obispo."

LINDSEY MILLER, DIRECTOR OF MARKETING, SAN LUIS OBISPO CHAMBER OF COMMERCE

"The chapter on Yosemite National Park provides an in-depth overview of the park and everything it has to offer. The information in these pages provides invaluable information, insight, and tips that future visitors will find useful. (Pati Anne) created a manual for exploring Yosemite in a way that is easy to follow and understand."

KARI COBB, PUBLIC AFFAIRS OFFICER, OFFICE OF THE SUPERINTENDENT, YOSEMITE NATIONAL PARK

"Your accuracy for trail travel navigation and how to get to the trailhead…is right on. I enjoyed descriptions of each trail as well."

KERRY KELLOGG, WILDERNESS AND TRAILS MANAGER, SANTA BARBARA RANGER DISTRICT, LOS PADRES NATIONAL FOREST, SANTA BARBARA

"If you want to visit Pismo Beach and surrounding areas of California I recommend that you use this fabulous book as your guide."

SUZEN BRASILE, EXECUTIVE DIRECTOR, PISMO BEACH CONFERENCE & VISITORS BUREAU

"Morro Bay truly is the undiscovered natural "treasure-trove" of California! With our intimate bay, estuary, miles of beautiful beaches, local family-owned hotels, restaurants and shops, we are a wonderful vacation destination. When visitors happen to stumble upon us, their first question is, "What is there to do here?" Pati has managed to answer this question in spades. Thank you Pati for putting Morro Bay on the map!"

MORRO BAY CHAMBER OF COMMERCE & VISITOR CENTER

See photos of the 6 areas described in this book at:
www.CaliforniaVacationPaths.com

1. Regions of Hwy 395 – Death Valley, Mono Lake…
2. Yosemite National Park
3. Sequoia and Kings Canyon National Parks
4. Santa Barbara
5. Pismo Beach
6. Morro Bay

Made in the USA
Las Vegas, NV
26 December 2024

15362395R00233